D0465160

WHEN TIGERS RULED THE SKY

WHEN TIGERS RULED THE SKY

The Flying Tigers:
American Outlaw Pilots over China
in World War II

BILL YENNE

BERKLEY CALIBER, NEW YORK

BERKLEY
CALIBER

An imprint of Penguin Random House LLC
375 Hudson Street, New York, New York 10014

This book is an original publication of the Berkley Publishing Group.

Copyright © 2016 by American Graphic Systems, Inc.
Penguin supports copyright. Copyright fuels creativity, encourages diverse voices, promotes free speech, and creates a vibrant culture. Thank you for buying an authorized edition of this book and for complying with copyright laws by not reproducing, scanning, or distributing any part of it in any form without permission. You are supporting writers and allowing Penguin to continue to publish books for every reader.

BERKLEY CALIBER and its colophon are trademarks of Penguin Random House LLC.
For more information, visit penguin.com.

Library of Congress Cataloging-in-Publication Data

Names: Yenne, Bill, date—author.
Title: When tigers ruled the sky : the Flying Tigers : American outlaw pilots
over China in World War II / Bill Yenne.
Description: First edition. I New York : Berkley Caliber, 2016. I Includes
bibliographical references and index.
Identifiers: LCCN 2016007734 (print) I LCCN 2016007986 (ebook) I ISBN
9780425274194 (alk. paper) I ISBN 9780698155022 ()
Subjects: LCSH: Flying Tigers (AVG), Inc. I Sino-Japanese War,
1937–1945—Aerial operations. I Sino-Japanese War,
1937–1945—Participation, American. I World War, 1939–1945—Aerial
operations, American. I United States. Army Air Forces. Air Force, 14th. I
China. Kong jun. American Volunteer Group.
Classification: LCC DS777.533.A35 Y46 2016 (print) I LCC DS777.533.A35
(ebook) I DDC 951.04/2—dc23
LC record available at http://lccn.loc.gov/2016007734

First edition: July 2016

PRINTED IN THE UNITED STATES OF AMERICA

10 9 8 7 6 5 4 3 2 1

Jacket design by Colleen Reinhart
Jacket photos: plane courtesy of author; men by Clare Boothe Luce;
clouds © Vadym Zaitsev/Shutterstock Images.
Title page art © Peshkova/Shutterstock.
Book design by Laura K. Corless.

While the author has made every effort to provide accurate telephone numbers and Internet addresses at the time of publication, neither the author nor the publisher is responsible for errors, or for changes that occur after publication. Further, the publisher does not have any control over and does not assume any responsibility for author or third-party websites or their content.

Penguin
Random
House

CONTENTS

PINYIN NAMES AND PLACES

For reasons of consistency, this book uses the pinyin system of translating Chinese proper names into the Roman alphabet, a convention that was adopted in China in the 1950s and that has been in standard use in the West since the 1980s. However, during World War II and throughout the first half of the twentieth century, when the events described herein were occurring, Westerners datelined these events from places known by names transliterated under the nineteenth-century Wade-Giles system. Some important place names, such as Hong Kong and Shanghai—the latter being China's largest city then, as now—remained unchanged. Likewise, Kunming, the first home of the Flying Tigers in China during World War II, is still known by that name.

Other city names, such as Nanking and Chungking, which became Nanjing and Chongqing, changed recognizably. However, others changed significantly. China's great southern metropolis, previously known as Canton, is now Guangzhou. Loi-Wing (or Loiwing) on the border with Burma, which was the location of an aircraft assembly and repair facility established by Curtiss-Wright and a base used by the Flying Tigers, is now Lei Yun.

One of the more complicated examples of a name change is that of China's ancient and modern capital, which is known under the pinyin system as Beijing. From the fifteenth century, the time of the Ming Dynasty, it was known in the West as Peking, meaning "Northern Kingdom." When Chiang Kai-shek's Nationalist government moved the capital to Nanjing (then Nanking) in 1927, Peking was renamed as Peiping, meaning "Northern Peace." Ironically, the years during which it was known by this name were among the least peaceful in its history. As datelined in the West, it became Peking again after World War II.

Meanwhile, when it comes to the country to which the Flying Tigers were first deployed before going into China, there is still an ongoing discussion over the use of the term "Burma," by which it was known internationally until the 1980s, versus "Myanmar," the name adopted officially late in the twentieth century, but still not used universally, even within the country. We have chosen to stay with "Burma," the name in use at the time in which this narrative takes place. Likewise, we use the term "Rangoon" for its capital, a city now known as Yangon.

INTRODUCTION

Who *Are* These Flying Tigers?

The victories of these Americans over the rice paddies of Burma are comparable in character, if not in scope, with those won by the RAF over the hop fields of Kent in the Battle of Britain. —WINSTON CHURCHILL

They seemed to materialize out of nowhere at a time when the American people, stunned by the horrible defeat at Pearl Harbor, yearned in vain for news that Americans *somewhere* in the world were striking back against the Axis. In December 1941, the headlines were filled with grim reports of the backbone of the American fleet at the bottom of Pearl Harbor and an American air force destroyed on the ground in the Philippines. Suddenly, there were reports of American fighter pilots sweeping Japanese bombers from the skies over China. Few in America had heard of them, and the question was asked, Who *are* these Flying Tigers?

As with the fighter pilots of the Royal Air Force who had saved the United Kingdom during the Battle of Britain to whom Churchill compared them, the Flying Tigers would become a heroic symbol at a historically dark moment.

Today, the Flying Tigers endure as probably the best-known American fighter aircraft group in history. Their name still resonates in the historical memory of World War II, just as the image of their shark-faced P-40s is an essential icon of American airpower in that conflict.

Their well-justified fame is entirely out of proportion to their numbers. Churchill compared them to the heroes of the RAF about whom he had said "never was so much owed by so many to so few." The Flying Tigers were also a "few"—indeed, a much, much fewer "few," a few so few that today it is incomprehensible that an outfit that could put fewer than a dozen warplanes into the sky on a good day could have been so effective. Over China, the Japanese estimated that they were opposed by about three hundred Flying Tigers, but the tenacious Americans rarely had more than a tenth of that number of aircraft in flyable condition, and many fewer in action in any given battle.

Like Alexander the Great and a mere handful of heroes and heroic units throughout military history, the Flying Tigers were never defeated in combat. They fought about fifty major aerial battles against hugely lopsided odds and never lost one. They were usually outnumbered by more than four to one, and yet they routinely emerged from combat without a loss. They are confirmed to have shot down well over two hundred enemy aircraft, but they probably downed close to twice that number, never mind those they destroyed on the ground. Meanwhile, only ten Flying Tigers were lost in combat, and only three were captured.

Because they so long ago achieved such lasting fame, it is hard to imagine that they were in action for only seven months, and so *early* in the war. Their amazing exploits had already been headlines for four months when Jimmy Doolittle bombed Tokyo. Because of their place in the pantheon of great American military organizations, it is hard to imagine that they did not wear the uniform of any American service. They were not so much soldiers as soldiers of fortune.

To call them outlaws would come close to being the truth, as their very existence teetered on the edge of noncompliance with existing neutrality laws. They came into existence because President Franklin Delano Roosevelt anxiously wanted to help save China from the Japanese war machine that had captured most of China's major cities, had killed millions of innocent people, and had ravaged China's capital in the infamous "Rape of Nanking."

The Flying Tigers came into being because a chain-smoking former US Army pilot with a face that seemed to have been cut from worn leather with a dull knife convinced Roosevelt that he had a plan. Claire Lee Chennault, the man with the plan, had been serving as a consultant to the Chinese Air Force for four years and had the ear of Chiang Kai-shek. He had a crazy idea of a "foreign legion" of American fighter pilots in China skies, and the president liked it.

The idea was crazy because this was in the early days of 1941, and the United States was not a declared combatant in World War II, nor yet at war with the Japanese. The United States was still neutral and bound by neutrality laws that technically still prohibited American citizens from donning the uniform of a foreign country.

In a scenario cut from an improbable conspiracy theory, Roosevelt, Chennault, and those around them cooked up a scheme involving a series of interlocking Chinese shell companies and joint ventures to buy airplanes and hire pilots. They could not, of course, hire just any pilots. They needed American military pilots trained for combat. Therein lay a conundrum. How could they purloin pilots from the United States armed forces? Roosevelt, who was used to laying waste to red tape to get things done, issued an order allowing pilots to resign their commissions and join Chennault without penalty. The chiefs of staff of the US Army and US Navy did not like the idea, but Roosevelt was the commander in chief. Contrary to what is often supposed, there was no executive order. Within the numbered, consecutive list of 381 executive orders issued by the president in 1941, the scheme is never mentioned. The order was more of a wink and a nod. One can almost see Roosevelt's wry grin, and hear him chuckle, as the plan came together.

To call them bounty hunters would be accurate. The men who would become the Flying Tigers—when someone, nobody knows exactly *who*, finally coined that phrase late in 1941—were literally hired away from the US Navy, Marine Corps, and Air Corps as *bounty hunters*. They would be paid a salary by the Chinese government, but they were also promised—and were ultimately *paid*—a "bonus" for each and every Japanese warplane that they destroyed. There were 296 bonuses paid, with several pilots collecting bonuses in the double digits.

It was for more than the money that they went overseas. Under the laws of natural selection, Chennault's plan attracted pilots anxious for adventure, excited to escape the routine, and eager for combat. They were the ideal archetype of the kind who would succeed at the job for which they had been hired.

When they sailed beneath the Golden Gate Bridge in the final unsettled months before the United States went to war, they did so having cut all ties with the American military establishment as an imposer of discipline *or* as a source of supplies. They were on their own. They sailed westward wrapped in a cloak of secrecy, with passports that identified them not as pilots, and certainly not as outlaws or bounty hunters, but as students, bank clerks, and members of the clergy. In fact, they were a band of daredevils and idealists, some of them noble and others scoundrels, but all of them adventurers of the highest order.

Though knowledge of their existence had slipped out and was mentioned briefly in the media—from *Time* magazine to Radio Tokyo—few Americans were aware of them, nor would they be aware of them until the end of the year. By then, the world would know the answer to the question, Who *are* these Flying Tigers?

They sailed into the unknown and into the blank pages of a history they were about to write. This book is the story of that complex and uncertain world into which they sailed, and the story that they would leave for posterity, a story written in .50-caliber lead and with the blood of a unique and incomparable cadre of young Americans.

ONE

The Warlord and the Japanese

As the 1930s gave way to the 1940s, and as the stage was being set for the entrance of the Flying Tigers, China was a once-powerful empire that had collapsed into a morass of warlord fiefdoms and was now losing a war with Japan. Within that morass, there was a Chinese warlord who had found his time and place. His name was Chiang Kai-shek.

"Difficulty at the beginning works supreme success," reads the judgment of the Hexagram Zhun in the *I Ching*, or *Book of Changes*, which is probably the most ancient, and perhaps the most respected of the Chinese philosophical classics. The image of that hexagram, clouds and thunder, is an easy metaphor for China in the 1930s and 1940s. The *I Ching* continues by saying that at the difficult beginning, amid those clouds and thunder, "the superior man brings order out of confusion." Chiang found himself with a unique opportunity to become that superior man.

Beginning in the long ago of China's Zhou Dynasty period, when the misty mythical past had barely given way to the historical past, and when the *I Ching* was new, China had been known as Zhongguo, which is roughly translated from the Mandarin as meaning "Central Kingdom." The historian Barbara Tuchman, who worked as a journalist in China before World War II, points out that "throughout her history China had believed herself the center of civilization, surrounded by barbarians. She was the Middle Kingdom, the center of the universe, whose Emperor was the Son of Heaven, ruling by the Mandate of Heaven."

Back then, and for many centuries thereafter, China was sufficiently powerful militarily and economically to warrant the belief that it *was* the center of the world. That China had more in common with the China of the twenty-first century than the China of the nineteenth or twentieth.

"From Marco Polo to the eighteenth century, visiting Westerners, amazed and admiring, were inclined to take China at her own valuation," Tuchman writes, speaking to China's center of the world theory. "Her bronzes were as old as the pyramids, her classical age was contemporary with that of Greece, her Confucian canon of ethics predated the New Testament if not the Old. She was the inventor of paper, porcelain, silk, gunpowder, the clock and movable type, the builder of the Great Wall, one of the wonders of the world, the creator of fabrics and ceramics of exquisite beauty and of an art of painting that was sophisticated and expressive when Europe's was still primitive and flat."

For centuries, mysterious and distant China continued to amaze outsiders, not only with its fireworks and printing presses, but also with its export goods. Silk, once available only from China, gave its name to the Silk Road, one of the most important trading routes of the ancient world, and became a metaphor for Chinese cultural sophistication.

By the nineteenth century, though, China was in decline, eclipsed in trade and technology by Europe. Symptomatic of China's decay were the concessions made to foreign powers by the increasingly impotent potentates of the fading Qing Dynasty. Europeans gradually took control of Chinese foreign trade. Dozens of treaty ports and outright colonial possessions were ceded. Hong Kong is just one example, one of many. In Shanghai, China's largest city and its financial capital, an eighteen-hundred-acre International Settlement fronting the Huangpu (then Whangpoo) River was established in the 1850s, expanding to fifty-six-hundred acres by the end of the century.

No longer the central kingdom of the world, China was not even the central kingdom of Asia. Across the East China Sea was another insular kingdom where they thought of *their* emperor as the son of heaven. As every story needs an antagonist to its protagonist, China now had Japan, and vice versa.

While China receded, Japan was on the rise. When Emperor Meiji ascended to his throne in 1867, Japan was ruled in name by an emperor, but in fact by regional warlords called shoguns. Meiji not only asserted himself as emperor in fact, but he enforced the rapid transformation of a feudal, preindustrial society into an analog—indeed, a purpose-built imitation—of the West's great industrial powers. While China's Qing Dynasty eschewed the trappings of the industrial revolution, which they considered irrelevant, Meiji was eagerly building steel mills, railroads, and modern warships.

In the last half of the nineteenth century, while the once-fragmented Japan was coalescing around Emperor Meiji, China was going the other way, splintering from a central kingdom into a patchwork of fragments ruled by quarreling warlords. When the two countries came to blows in the Sino-Japanese War of 1894–1895, Qing China was no match for Meiji's modern war machine. The Qing Dynasty finally imploded at the end of 1911, dying with less a "bang" than a "whimper," albeit an angry and contentious whimper. Four millennia of China as a monarchy came to a close.

Despite its decline and international impotence, China was hard for the world to ignore. As it is today, China was the most populous nation on earth throughout the nineteenth and twentieth centuries. Yet it was one of the most dreadfully underdeveloped. Barbara Tuchman wrote that at the time the empire was imploding, China's 40 million "were a people 70 to 80 percent illiterate, who on the average had no milk and virtually no other animal products in their diet, who had no sanitation, no running water, no privacy, no electricity, no vote, whose industry was still 90 percent handiwork and whose transportation was still largely conducted by human muscle, was not considered, if considered at all, incompatible with democracy."

Despite early international optimism, democracy would not take root in the new entity that called itself the Republic of China. Shepherded by Hawaii-educated Sun Yat-sen, a medical doctor turned gentleman revolutionary, the republic was formally declared on the first day of 1912, but just as China had been an empire in name only for decades before that day, China after 1912 was a republic in name only. The regional warlords of China, like the regional shoguns of medieval Japan, continued to wield the real authority. The country was a jigsaw puzzle of autonomous domains whose warlords granted lip service but never their allegiance to the concept of a central government, where the reins of power resided in the hands of whichever warlord had the biggest army in the capital—then called Peking and now called Beijing—at the moment.

As nature abhors a vacuum, within that simmering cauldron of competing factions there was the inevitability that one force would eventually emerge as dominant. Though the Communists were growing in influence by the late 1920s, the force that came to dominate China in the second quarter of the twentieth century and through World War II was the Kuomintang, or Chinese National People's Party.

Within the Kuomintang, the dominant personality was Chiang

Kai-shek. He was an ambitious military officer and Sun Yat-sen protégé, who emerged from among those of the party's founding members jockeying for power within the Kuomintang after Sun died in 1925. A year later, Chiang became the commander of the National Revolutionary Army—China's nominal national army—and led it in several successful campaigns against other warlords, especially in northern China, to consolidate the power of the central government.

By 1928, thanks to Chiang's subduing those northern warlords on its behalf, the Republic of China's Kuomintang-dominated Nationalist government now controlled enough of China to gain for itself a measure of international legitimacy. As China's most powerful warlord, Chiang became China's generalissimo and the chairman of the Nationalist government, as the Republic of China's presidency was now known. Though he relinquished the chairmanship to a reclusive figurehead named Lin Sen in 1931, the generalissimo would remain in full control of the Kuomintang, and of the Nationalist government and armed forces, for nearly half a century. Throughout World War II, he was *the* face of China as seen by the outside world.

John Gunther, a journalist who toured Asia extensively before World War II and got to know Chiang, wrote in his 1939 book *Inside Asia* of the "inconspicuous son of a village merchant [who] was the strongest man China has produced for generations, and a terrific disciplinarian; but the enemies he has forgiven—and given jobs to—are many. His dominating mission is to unite China, consolidate it, and indeed he has united it—more than any man in centuries of history—but he spent ten dreary years fighting civil wars against his own people."

However, the most pressing problem casting a shadow across Chiang's aspirations came from the outside in the form of the territorial ambitions of Imperial Japan.

After they soundly defeated the Qing Dynasty in 1895, the Japanese had humiliated the great Russian Empire a decade later in the Russo-

Japanese War. A decisive defeat of the Russian Army in March 1905, followed by an equally conclusive defeat of the Russian Navy at the Tsushima Strait between mainland Japan and Korea two months later, defined Japan as a twentieth-century world power and as Asia's super-power.

It was Manchuria, that great swath of Chinese territory north of Korea three times the size of Japan that was to be the theater of the Kuomintang's first face-off against the Japanese with Chiang in his role as China's ruler. Coveted by Japan for its vast expanses of farmland and potential farmland, Manchuria was also eyed by both the Japanese and the Russians for its great coal reserves.

In September 1931, near the Manchurian city of Mukden, Japanese troops set off an explosion on a section of the Japanese-owned South Manchuria Railway and blamed the Chinese. The so-called Mukden Incident provided a provocation for a Japanese invasion, during which they quickly defeated the army of Chiang's surrogate warlord, Zhang Xueliang, and occupied Manchuria before Chiang could react. This set off a round of international condemnations, but there was little that could be done. When the League of Nations took up the matter in 1933, Japan's delegation dramatically marched out of the League chamber in Geneva. This was the beginning of the collapse of the League into irrelevance, and a step toward Japan's embracing Fascist Italy and Nazi Germany within the Rome-Berlin-Tokyo Tripartite Axis in 1940.

As the concessions that would be made to Hitler in the name of peace in Europe in 1938–1939 only served to whet his appetite for more, the Japanese were emboldened by the lack of serious opposition to their Manchuria annexation. In 1937, Japan would make its move, with a full-blown invasion of China and its occupation of China's major population centers.

Within China, Japanese actions were seen as a major blow to Chiang Kai-shek's prestige. However, this disaster had the counterintuitive effect of strengthening his hand by uniting various factions under a common antagonism toward the Japanese. The generalissimo had not only the recognition and the empathy of the international community, but also a de facto recognition within China that he was the country's rallying point. In a marriage of convenience, Chiang had even patched up his differences with the Communists. From the outside, Chiang's army received a great deal of support in both weaponry and training from the Soviet Union, Japan's perpetual antagonist, and even from Hitler's Germany, Japan's future ally.

"It furthers one to remain persevering," continues the commentary on the Hexagram Zhun of the *I Ching*. "It furthers one to appoint helpers."

Over the coming years, as Chiang endeavored to bring order out of confusion by enlisting aid from the outside world, perhaps no group of helpers would be more important for its diminutive size and considerable effectiveness than a band of American soldiers of fortune led by a no-nonsense man named Claire Lee Chennault.

TWO

The Formative Years
of a Visionary Loner

Commerce, Texas, sixty miles northeast of Dallas in the black-land prairie country, is a very long way from China. On September 6, 1893, when Chiang Kai-shek was five years old, Claire Lee Chennault was born there, although he insisted throughout his life—and wrote in his memoirs—that he was born in 1890. Either way, the United States was still at least half a decade shy of the Spanish-American War, that short moment of a war that ended with an abrupt turn toward the Far East that was to define the United States through the twentieth century.

He was the first son of John Stonewall Jackson Chennault and Jessie Beatrice Lee Chennault, who had been married in December 1892 when John was thirty and Jessie was sixteen. She died when Claire was still a preschooler, but he lived into his eighties. As the names suggest, the family's heritage was deeply rooted in the region's Confederate military history. There are even stories of a distant relationship of the family to Robert E. Lee.

The family descended from Huguenots, persecuted French Protestants who had come to the United States from France and the Netherlands early in the eighteenth century. The Chenault (one *n*) Family National Association notes that the first member of the family to cross the Atlantic was Estienne Cheneau (later called Stephen Chenault), who arrived with his first wife in Yorktown, Virginia, aboard the sailing ship *Nassau* in March 1700 or March 1701, depending upon whether one uses the Old English calendar. His second wife, whom he married in Virginia, was from an English family named Howlett. The association also notes that Stephen's descendants use about fifty alternate spellings, ranging from "Shinault" and "Shinall" to the "Chennault" used by John and Jessie and their family.

Though Claire Lee Chennault was born in Texas, his parents had both been born, were married, and had roots in northeastern Louisiana. They returned there soon after Claire was born, and divided their time between two small towns near the Mississippi River—Gilbert in Franklin Parish and larger Waterproof in neighboring Tensas Parish. The latter was thusly named to boast that it was protected from flooding by a levee. When Claire was growing up there, Waterproof had fewer than four hundred residents, and it has only about six hundred today. Both of his siblings were born in Franklin Parish. John Leslie Chennault was born in 1895, but died just short of eighteen months, and William Stephen Chennault was born in 1897.

"He gave me a free hand in wandering, and many times I stayed out for a week at a time—with a piece of bacon to fry freshly caught fish and a sack of corn meal to make bread," Claire Chennault wrote of growing up in the wilds of Louisiana. "Always I returned with a bag of game for the family table. I learned to hunt with the unique zest of a man who hunts to eat his kill. It is a passion that has never left me. I shot my first gun, a Winchester rifle, when I was eight, and hunted before then with a pack of terrier dogs chasing rats, possums, and skunks. . . . Life in the woods and on the bayous and lakes of northeast Louisiana taught me self-confidence and self-reliance and forced me to make my own decisions. After reaching the age of twelve, I preferred to hunt and fish alone. I was too young for adult companionship and knew too much of woodcraft to desire companionship of boys of my own age. I made my own camp, found and cooked my food, and felt most at ease when buried deep in the woods."

Apparently, Claire Lee Chennault the loner was also the smartest kid in his class, and he graduated from high school three years early. According to Robert Hessen, who curated his papers at the Hoover Institution Archives, he and his father may have concocted the story about his being born in 1890 for him to apply for college in 1909 when he was only sixteen.

When Chennault did apply, he aimed high—or at least he aimed for schools at which there would be no tuition.

"I applied for admission to both West Point and the Naval Academy," he recalled in his memoirs. "In 1909 I went to Annapolis to take entrance examinations. Sight of the grim gray walls on the Severn chilled my enthusiasm to become an admiral. After two days of sweating through examinations, some kind soul informed me that midshipmen were confined to Academy grounds for their first two years. Thought of two solid years behind stone walls was too much for a lad used to wandering the Louisiana wilderness all summer long. I turned in a blank final examination paper, telegraphed my father I had failed, and caught the next train back to Louisiana."

He spent a year at Louisiana State University in Baton Rouge before transferring to the Louisiana State Normal School (now Northwestern State University of Louisiana), the state teachers' college, in Natchitoches. His career as a schoolteacher was short. As he explained, "my first post was in the one-room Athens, Louisiana, country school where the annual crop of oversize farm boys made the life of a teacher miserable."

Along the way, his dreams of a life of adventure turned his gaze toward that great new technology that was capturing the imagination of the era of his youth.

"A rickety old Curtiss pusher biplane, wobbling through the air at the Louisiana State Fair in 1910, first turned my ambitions upward," he reflected. "Like most young men, I was looking for bright new worlds to conquer and, as is the habit of youth, regretted that I had been born so late when all the most glamorous frontiers had disappeared. There was no new land to open in the West—no more Indians to fight—and the future seemed very dull indeed. That primitive flying machine bumping through the thermals of a hot, sticky summer day in Shreveport gave me my first glimpse of a new frontier and sowed the seed of my desire to fly."

Like his mother, Claire Lee Chennault married young, wedding Nell Thompson in Winnsboro, Louisiana, on Christmas Eve in 1911 when they were both just eighteen. John Stephen Chennault and Max Thompson Chennault were born in 1913 and 1914, respectively.

As he later wrote, "marriage and the first two children of an eventual octet made economic problems more acute and I drifted through the South in a succession of teaching jobs, looking for better pay—English instructor in a Biloxi, Mississippi, business college; assistant physical-training director of a YMCA in Louisville—and finally wound up in 1916 in an Akron, Ohio, war plant making automobile tire tubes for the Allies. When the United States declared war in April 1917, I immediately applied for flight training. The answer was the first of many firm 'no's.' I was then 26 [actually 24] and the father of three children, a superannuated old dodo by modern airmen's standards."

Nevertheless, the US Army accepted him in an officer training program in Indiana in August 1917, and he emerged in November, a "ninety-day wonder with silver bars and a commission as a first lieutenant of infantry."

His first assignment was with the 90th Infantry Division at Fort Travis, across San Antonio from the newly constructed Kelly Field, destined to become the center of US Army flight training for a generation. Chennault would find himself at Kelly, not as the aviation cadet whom he aspired to be, but as an infantry drill instructor for the "hordes of green aviation cadets pouring off the trains in San Antonio."

As he recalled, "I stayed at Kelly almost a year, and while the Signal Corps was rejecting me for flight training three more times, I learned to fly. Taking advantage of the general confusion around Kelly, I found a few genial instructors who were willing to explain the fundamentals of flying from the rear cockpit of a [Curtiss JN-4] Jenny."

By the time he earned his wings as a fighter pilot—then called a "pursuit" pilot—there was no longer a need for his skills over the battlefront of World War I, and not having gotten into battle was a source of great frustration for him. Also upsetting was the downsizing and retrenchment that gripped the Air Service after the war. Thousands of pilots were mustered out, with 95 percent of the 1918 Air Service personnel strength gone by 1920. Flight time for those who remained was slashed because of budget cuts, and it was a disappointing life for those planning on a career.

By now, Claire and Nell had five children: Charles Lee, Peggy Sue, and Claire Patterson Chennault were born between 1918 and 1920. Three more came by the end of the decade: David Wallace was born in 1923; Robert Kenneth in 1925; and the youngest, Rosemary Louise Chennault, joined the family in 1928.

In 1922, Chennault was assigned to the 1st Pursuit Group, which was relocating from Ellington Field, near Houston, to Selfridge Field, near Detroit. At the time, the group commander was Major Carl "Tooey" Spaatz, who would later achieve lasting fame as a commander of a succession of strategic air forces over Europe during World War II and as the first chief of staff of the US Air Force after that war.

A year later, Chennault was transferred to the 5th Composite Group at Luke Field (not to be confused with the later Luke Field in Arizona) on Ford Island in the middle of Pearl Harbor in Hawaii. In the mid-1920s, the Hawaiian Islands were a good place for a fighter pilot. With excellent flying weather and unlimited airspace, the Air Service (US Army Air Corps after 1926) assigned two fighter squadrons to the 5th Composite Group—the 6th and 19th Pursuit Squadrons—along with bomber and observation units.

The air defense necessity of having pursuit squadrons based on Oahu went in and out of fashion on the priority lists, but it *was* on the minds of many, including Chennault. Its importance would, of course, be dramatically underscored in December 1941.

"In 1925 we experienced one of the Japanese attack scares that periodically swept the islands," he recalled in his memoirs. "It proved to be a baseless rumor. However, for three weeks I had the 19th [Pursuit] Squadron warming up their planes in the dark of early morning. We took off before the first streaks of dawn to rendezvous over Oahu at 10,000 feet where it was already day. We patrolled the approaches to Pearl Harbor until long after sunrise hit the ground. There were no orders from my superiors to stand this alert, and our squadron took a lot of ribbing for the performance. I knew, as does every Regular Army officer, that the first responsibility of a unit commander—whether he heads an infantry platoon or an air force—is to take measures to ensure his own unit against tactical surprise by the enemy."

Filed and forgotten?

———

After returning Stateside, Chennault helped form the "Three Musketeers," an Air Corps aerobatic team that made public appearances across the United States. In the 1920s, the air arms of both the

US Navy and the US Army were very active in promoting themselves through participation in civilian air shows and competitions. Indeed, both services operated aircraft explicitly as race planes, which had no practical function other than to fly against civilian planes in the numerous national and international air races that studded the aviation calendar during the Roaring Twenties. In 1925, the Schneider Cup race was won by another US Army pilot, named Jimmy Doolittle.

Chennault's career path next took him to Maxwell Field in Alabama to attend the Air Corps Tactical School (ACTS). Here his important theories about the future of combat aviation began to take shape. By this time, just as the Air Corps itself was relegated to the sidelines by traditionalists within the US Army who focused on land warfare, so too was fighter aviation marginalized within the service by those, including his old boss Tooey Spaatz, who believed that the true calling of the service should be offensive bombardment.

As Robert Lee Scott wrote in his biography of Chennault, "most of the senior military aviators were already relegating pursuit aviation to a smaller and smaller role. Everybody appeared to be sold on the growing belief that bombardment planes were invincible and that fighter aircraft were obsolete. This was the beginning of an argument that was to go on and on for years to come. . . . Chennault did not advocate the replacement of bombardment aviation with pursuit or fighter techniques. He knew very well that the next war was going to be one of aerial invasion and that the bomber plane was going to carry the burden of the offense. But he also saw what few of the military planners saw, that there would be a very critical need for defensive fighter planes, both for interception and for escort for the strategic bombers as they flew deeper and deeper into the territory of the enemy."

Scott went on to say that a "great drawback in those days when fighter aviation was losing its battle to survive was the impossibility of accurate, timely interception. Chennault contended that this could be improved. He did not merely say it could be done; he explained in detail how such interception could be accomplished. . . . He divided the problem into the same three phases which during World War II, nearly twenty years later in China, proved so very, very effective: *detection, interception, destruction*. . . . This was a most radical stand in the face of those who dared speak out positively for any form of military aviation at all. Most of these were older military men without much actual experience in what could have constituted strategic bombardment and without any experience in what could have been called modern fighter techniques."

It was in 1931 at the Air Corps Tactical School that Chennault first crossed paths with Clayton Lawrence Bissell, a World War I fighter ace who was now an instructor. Chennault complained that Bissell was "still teaching the fighter tactics of 1918 . . . he seriously recommended that fighters drop a ball-and-chain affair from above in the hope of fouling a bomber's propellers."

Often noted in military histories are friendships forged between junior officers that would become important to later careers when the men reconnected as senior officers. In the case of Chennault and Bissell, it was an *animosity* formed in 1931 that would cast a dark shadow across their dealings when they met again in China during World War II.

After Chennault graduated from the ACTS, he returned to serve as an instructor in pursuit aviation and later as head of the ACTS Pursuit Section, while he finished his manifesto on airpower, *The Role of Defensive Pursuit*, a book that was published in 1935.

"Pursuit interception," Chennault explained, "can be reduced to a mathematical formula of air speed, altitude, rate of climb. With properly trained personnel manning observation posts and supplying necessary information to a filter center, the problem can be broken down rapidly enough for the alerted fighter planes to intercept."

He also served on the Pursuit Development Board, and led a crusade against "the trend toward multiseater fighters [specifically the cumbersome Bell XFM-1 Airacuda] that provided interesting engineering problems but were useless for combat. . . . The young engineering officers had no ideas on its tactical employment but were fascinated with the intricacies of its construction." But it was an era—not unlike the last quarter of the twentieth century—of multirole combat aircraft, which were favored by the establishment "because it would be cheaper if one plane could perform all the functions of military aviation."

It was also during his time at Maxwell that Chennault revived his interest in aerobatics, forming a successor to the Three Musketeers that was called Three Men on the Flying Trapeze. Rounding out the threesome were Sergeant John "Luke" Williamson and Lieutenant Haywood "Possum" Hansell, who later went on to serve as an important strategic air planner during World War II. When Hansell left the team, Chennault replaced him with another noncommissioned pilot, Sergeant William "Billy" MacDonald. As with today's US Air Force Thunderbirds, Chennault's team served to promote the Air Corps to the general public, but he also was keen to use the Musketeers to promote the advancement of fighter aviation *within* the Air Corps.

THREE

Young Tigers

M iss Viola, may I fly my glider off the top of your house?"
Robert Lee Scott Jr. asked respectfully. Viola Napier, age
seventy-five, looked at the young neighbor boy, whom she
had known for most of his twelve years, and tried to imagine what his
youthful imagination had gotten him into on this auspicious summer
day in 1920. "I promise to be careful of the flowers."

As though that would make all the difference, she nodded her
consent.

The large Macon, Georgia, colonial house, in Scott's recollection,
was sixty feet high, so it took him and two friends a long while, with a
rope and pulley, to get the fragile machine—constructed by Scott himself after studying the designs of the Wright brothers—up to the roof.
This done, the three boys grabbed the glider and ran down the sloping
copper roof as fast as they could to give it some reasonable forward
momentum. While the others let go, Scott remained inside his winged
apparatus.

He felt himself soaring, held aloft only by air and aerodynamics. He experienced the thrill and satisfaction of flying over a magnolia tree before he heard the cracking of wooden spars and felt the absence of aerodynamics that comes with the crumbling of a failing aircraft. He watched helplessly as the ground, covered at this location by Miss Viola's precious flowers, rushed up at him.

Thoughts of Eugene Ely leapt into the boy's mind. The first man ever to take off from the deck of a ship, Ely had been one of aviation's first generation of pioneer airmen. He had been killed in Macon two days shy of his twenty-fifth birthday. His last flight and his fatal crash had been the first time that Robert Lee Scott had ever seen an airplane.

Scott was born in Waynesboro, Georgia, on April 12, 1908, and was barely five years old when he watched Ely's demise, but he remembered it well—more with fascination than with any sense of horror. As Scott later recalled, "my horrified mother dragged me from the scene. It most certainly should have been an ill omen for my flying future. However, I know that it whetted my appetite to fly. I liked anything that flew and freed one from the earth, but most of all I prayed that destiny would make me a pilot of the fast, little single-seaters—a fighter pilot."

Scott's father reacted angrily when he learned what had happened in Mrs. Napier's roses.

A furious Robert Lee Scott Sr. demanded that his son take the broken glider and break it again and again, and break it until it could never again be used as a flying machine.

It was the end of gliders, but not the end of flying machines for the boy. The oldest of three, the younger Robert Scott was a precocious lad. A high-achieving Boy Scout, he already could drive a car, and he was not one to be kept down by a father whom he considered irrationally overprotective.

In 1921, a year after the glider crash, the thirteen-year-old Robert

Scott fired up his Model T Ford and drove eighty miles to an aircraft auction in Americus, intent on buying a powered airplane.

The early 1920s were a wide-open time in the evolution of aviation. It was an era, to embrace an inescapable metaphor, when the sky was no limit for boys—and girls as well—who had expansive imaginations and dreams of flying. The Wright brothers had made it possible, the daring fighter pilots of World War I made it seem exciting, and the barnstormers, the freelance aerobats who had started crisscrossing the country doing exhibitions at county fairs made it seem accessible. It was an era when a thirteen-year-old could buy himself an airplane—without his parents' knowledge—and have a reasonable expectation of learning to fly it.

"As the auctioneer's hammer hit the block for the first time that morning I opened with my maximum bid—seventy-five dollars! The auctioneer did look my way, but the look was merely a frown. Far in the back of the hangar a heavy voice called, 'Six hundred dollars.' And to this fat man the Jennys went, one by one."

That afternoon, he kept bidding, and as he said "seventy-five dollars" for what he calculated as the hundredth time, he heard no counter. He turned to look at the man who had been overbidding him.

"Now listen, son," the man said. "I'm going to let you have this one for your seventy-five dollars. Get it and get the hell out of here, because I'm buying all the rest for an airline."

The boy was now the proud owner of a war surplus Curtiss JN-4 Jenny, which he took home on a truck and hid in another boy's barn so his parents wouldn't find out. The problem was that it was disassembled and crated, and he had little more than a guess at how to put it together.

This dilemma was resolved when Scott crossed paths with a streetcar conductor who had been a pilot in the Army Air Service and who had dreamed of being a barnstormer. The two struck a deal under which he would help the boy assemble his Jenny in exchange for Scott's loaning it out on the weekends. The man offered to throw in flying lessons. How could he refuse?

For several months, the arrangement was everything Scott and his benefactor had hoped. Then one night, the barnstormer experienced a landing mishap, and everything, including the first phase of Scott's aviation career, ended in a ball of fire.

———

Across the country in the Idaho panhandle, the first impressions that young Gregory Hallenbeck had of aviation were less dramatic but equally memorable. Born in Coeur d'Alene on December 4, 1912, he was only six when a barnstormer passed through Benewah County giving airplane rides—and one of those rides was the one that changed Greg's life. The man was Clyde Pangborn, a fellow Idahoan and a former US Army flier whose name was destined to become a household word in the world of aerobatics and long-distance flying during the coming years.

"I had always loved the idea of flying," Greg later told Colin Heaton of *Aviation History* magazine. "I used to read all of the books about the World War I fighter aces, and I built model planes, gliders and things."

Greg was the only son of Charles Boyington and Grace Gregory, but he never knew his father, and used the surname of his mother's second husband, Ellsworth Hallenbeck, for more than two decades. He grew up in St. Maries, the seat of Benewah County, and even after the family moved west to Tacoma, he worked summers—all the way through college—in the silver mines in Idaho's Shoshone County, and in the national forests that account for most of northern Idaho's land area.

Having graduated from Lincoln High School in Tacoma, he went on to the University of Washington in Seattle, where he earned the

Pacific Northwest intercollegiate middleweight wrestling title, and majored in aeronautical engineering. He also enrolled in ROTC. A job as an army officer—even a reserve officer—after graduation was better than the uncertainty that faced most college graduates during the depths of the Great Depression. When he earned his diploma in June 1934, newly minted Second Lieutenant Gregory Hallenbeck found a place with the US Army's Coast Artillery Reserve, and a short active duty tour at Fort Worden at the mouth of Puget Sound.

Among the roster of men who would join the ranks of the Flying Tigers in the skies over China, James Howell Howard later conceded that he had *not* grown up dreaming of being a pilot—although, coincidentally, he *had* grown up in China. Three years before he was born on April 13, 1913, Howard's father had accepted a post as a professor of ophthalmology at Canton Christian College. As Canton is now known as Guangzhou, the school is now Lingnan University. At the time that Howard's father arrived, it had recently incorporated Hackett Medical College for Women, the first medical college for women in China.

In 1927, when Jim Howard was fourteen, his parents moved the family back to St. Louis, Missouri, where they had lived before going to China. Though he had never lived in the United States, he was anxious to fit in. Being a teenager is an awkward time under the best of circumstances, but it was especially disconcerting for Howard, who was promptly uprooted a second time and sent away from the family to a Quaker boarding school in Haverford, on the "Main Line," the well-heeled northwestern suburbs of Philadelphia. It was an alien world and a difficult adjustment, made worse by hazing from both students and teachers.

"One day my third-form master accused me sarcastically of being Chinese since I had been born in Canton," he recalled in his memoirs. "From then on my nickname was China. I was devastated at the time, because I desperately wanted to be an American like my classmates. Father later explained to me that since my parents were both American, I was automatically an American according to the Constitution."

He later transferred to John Burroughs School in Ladue, near St. Louis, and was accepted at Pomona College in Claremont, California. Like Greg Hallenbeck, Howard graduated from high school in the darkest days of the Great Depression, but unlike him, Howard had been insulated in private school, the son of a father equally isolated by his comfortable place as a professor of ophthalmology at Washington University Medical School in St. Louis. It was not until he made his way west that Howard became aware of the hardships and the suffering.

"Even though America was in the midst of a deep depression, the student body was oblivious to the hordes of destitute Okies who crossed the California border and passed within six blocks of our campus," he wrote. "The misery that streamed by on Highway 66 was part of a different world, a world we didn't understand. In contrast, my primary concern was to get my degree and get on with the business of life. . . . The results of the Depression could be seen everywhere. Driving old jalopies loaded with mattresses, beds, kitchen utensils, and kids, refugees from the Midwestern dust bowl were being harassed at the Arizona-California border by Los Angeles police."

Charles Rankin Bond Jr. was born in Dallas, Texas, on April 22, 1915, the fourth of the six children of Charles Sr. and Magnolia Turner Bond. As with most people, the Great Depression hit the family hard, and young Charles grew up helping his father in the family painting and wallpapering business.

A hardworking student, Bond was in the National Honor Society as well as ROTC in high school. He wanted to go on to Texas A&M, but the family had no money to send him to college, so he decided to try for West Point. He enlisted in the US Army in 1935 on the promise that he would be sent to the US Military Academy prep school at Camp Bullis near San Antonio.

Like Jim Howard, David Lee Hill was born in Asia, the son of one of the many American missionaries who went to the Far East in the early days of the twentieth century. Dr. Pierre Bernard Hill and his wife, Ella, had moved to Korea with their three small children—Martha, the youngest, was just a baby—in 1912, just two years after the Japanese Empire had annexed the former kingdom. David was born in Kwangju (now Guangju), near the southwestern tip of the Korean Peninsula, on July 13, 1915.

In 1916, David was a year old when the family resettled on a farm in Amelia County, Virginia, accompanied by Hung Nim, a Korean man who had worked for them while they were in Kwangju. When the United States entered World War I a year later, Dr. Hill turned down a commission as a US Army chaplain, but instead patriotically asked to serve as an artilleryman. However, his history of bacteremia led to his being turned down altogether, and he began casting about within the Presbyterian community for a church that needed a pastor. After a short stint in Roanoke, he accepted a longer-term position in Louisville. He was still planning to return to Korea eventually, but the Presbyterian Committee on Foreign Missions cautioned him about a relapse of the bacteremia, and he took his family instead to the First Presbyterian

Church in San Antonio in 1921. He later took on parallel careers as a radio minister on WOAI and as the chaplain of the Texas Rangers.

David Lee Hill, who is known to aviation history by the nickname "Tex," did not first set foot in the Lone Star State until he was ready to start elementary school, but he thereafter embraced it as his home state. He grew up fishing in the Guadalupe River and deer hunting in the nearby hill country with his brothers, becoming skilled at both. He also developed a great interest in the paper kites that Hung Nim liked to make. This, and the fact that San Antonio was becoming the center of flight training for the US Army Air Service, were the beginning milestones in Tex Hill's infatuation with aviation.

The next milestone came one Sunday, when he and a friend sneaked out of church with the coins that had been intended for the collection plate that day and headed to a nearby airstrip where a barnstormer was appearing. They traded all their money to Marion "Dick" Hair for a short ride in his Travel Air 4000.

In 1928, as had been the case with Jim Howard two years earlier, Tex Hill's parents sent him out of state for high school. In his case it was the McCallie School in Chattanooga, Tennessee, then a military prep school that happened to be on the site of the Civil War Battle of Missionary Ridge.

Hill got through the hazing reasonably intact, but wanderlust became his undoing when this led to him and a friend riding a freight train south to Mississippi for something to do. Stranded in Arkansas on the return trip, Hill was convinced by a local minister to phone home. Dr. Hill generously wired train fare back to Chattanooga for the two boys, and charitably did not reprimand his son for the incident. The school was not so kind when the errant lads returned, but at least they were not expelled. The following year, Tex Hill returned to Texas for high school.

The fork in Hill's life that followed high school drew him toward enlisting it the US Navy, but his father steered him toward academics. He enrolled at Texas A&M, then a military school where membership in the Corps of Cadets remained mandatory until the 1960s, and joined the Corps' Cavalry Troop A. When a chemical warfare troop was formed, Tex was transferred to it because of his major in chemical engineering. This didn't meet with his liking, so he impulsively dropped out of school. When Dr. Hill finally talked his son into going back to school, it was to the much more modest Austin College.

Robert Tharp Smith grew up in Red Cloud, Nebraska, one of those typical midwestern farm towns with its two-block main street, where it is beastly hot in the summer, and where the snow drifts deep during the biting cold of winter. The son of the school superintendent, he grew up hunting, fishing, and spending long summer days at the swimming holes along the Republican River. In memoirs, he recalled that as a boy, he yearned for nothing more elaborate than a bicycle— until he discovered airplanes. As with Scott, Hallenbeck, and Hill, he made his first flight with a barnstormer before he reached his teens— and *not* with his parents' permission.

"Not surprisingly, perhaps, I didn't half-appreciate those Huckleberry Finn–like years, and assumed that every other kid in the country was growing up under much the same conditions and circumstances," Smith reminisced. "It was only in later years, after being exposed to the real, outside world, that I was to learn differently. Only one thing remained constant throughout that period, and that was my determination to become a pilot."

Though Earl and Ulden Smith punished their ten-year-old son

severely—he used the word "deservedly" in his memoirs—for going behind their back for his first ride, they acquiesced to his second when the Inman Brothers Flying Circus passed through a few years later.

"I read everything I could lay hands on pertaining to airplanes and aviation in general, and of course built model planes with whatever crude materials I could find," he remembered. "The walls of my bedroom were covered with pictures of planes and famous pilots of the time culled from old magazines and newspapers. Eddie Rickenbacker, Clarence Chamberlin, Richard E. Bird, Wiley Post, Jimmy Doolittle and many others were familiar faces, not to mention the most famous of all, Charles A. Lindbergh. In my adolescent eyes they were all heroes of the highest order."

FOUR

Chiang Kai-shek
and the Americans

Before Claire Chennault had even imagined that his career would ultimately take him to China, the man who would one day be his American antagonist in that country had been coming and going to and from the Central Kingdom, and living there for extended periods, for nearly two decades.

History recalls Joseph Warren Stilwell equally for his effective military leadership and for his irritable, curmudgeonly personality. Like Chennault, he was strong-willed in the extreme, but while Chennault was a prophet of the potential of military aviation, Stilwell had an infantry officer's disdain for the usefulness of aviation that predestined the two men for rivalry. The two also diverged dramatically in their opinion of Chiang Kai-shek, a man with whom the climactic moments of their two careers would be closely entwined. Like bookends bracketing Chiang Kai-shek, Chennault, on one side, respected him greatly, while Stilwell detested and belittled him.

Born in Palatka, Florida, in 1883, a decade before Chennault came into the world, Stilwell grew up in New York and earned a reputation as a youthful troublemaker before his well-connected doctor father called in all his favors and managed to get his wild-child son a presidential appointment to the US Military Academy at West Point. Stilwell, who had always done well athletically and academically, suppressed his inclination to misconduct and graduated in the top third of the Class of 1904. He was even tapped to return as an instructor. In 1911, he had made his first trip to China. While posted to the Philippines, he had the misfortune—or fortune—to go on leave to Shanghai just as the Qing Dynasty was in the midst of its tumultuous moment of collapse.

His aptitude for languages brought Stilwell back to West Point as an instructor a second time, which was where he was assigned when World War I began in 1914. When the United States entered the fight in 1917, he went overseas and headed the G-2 Staff for IV Corps during the offensive at St. Mihiel.

Returning to Washington in the summer of 1919, Stilwell growled to an old friend in the Personnel Division that he'd like to be posted as far from the capital as possible. In 1920, after finishing a language course at the University of California, he found himself headed seven thousand miles away from Washington for a three-year tour of duty in Beijing as the first ever Chinese-speaking military attaché in the US Army.

Now a major, he arrived at a time when the wars of the warlords were ongoing as they had been for some time, and as they would be for as long as Stilwell was acquainted with China. At the time, Wu Peifu, the "Jade Marshal," was the warlord in charge in the capital, while Zhang Zuolin, known as "Marshal Chang," the master of Manchuria, cast his shadow across the rest of China. The American attaché managed to get out into the country, visiting remote areas, observing the skirmishes, visiting the rival warlords, getting a feel for the stark poverty of the country, and developing a fondness for the Chinese people.

He also started to get a feel for the Japanese. He visited Manchuria, where the Japanese Kwantung Army was in de facto control, and was disturbed by Japanese arrogance and their bigotry toward the Chinese. Stilwell would serve two further tours in China. The first came in 1926, as a battalion commander within the 15th Infantry Regiment, which had taken over the former German compound at the treaty port of Tientsin (now Tianjin) after World War I. It was here that he met George Catlett Marshall, destined to rise to the post of chief of staff of the US Army on the eve of World War II. Getting to know Marshall would be a milestone in Stilwell's career. Marshall used phrases such as "a genius for instruction," "farsighted," and "qualified for any command 'in peace and war'" when writing evaluations of Stilwell, and he would be important in Stilwell's being assigned to China in World War II.

Politically, the China of the late 1920s was still a rolling boil of warring factions, with the principal difference now being the growing influence of Chiang Kai-shek as the increasingly dominant warlord. As he had earlier been plunged into the chaos of revolution in 1911, Joe Stilwell now stepped into the turmoil of Chiang's northern offensive, a major initiative by the Nationalist Army, supported by Communist-instigated strikes aimed at securing Kuomintang control of China's major population centers from squabbling warlords. They seized Hankou and Hangzhow, and early in 1927, they swept into Nanking (now Nanjing), where Chiang would maintain his Nationalist capital for the next decade.

L ate in March, the Nationalist Army reached China's largest city, the international financial center of Shanghai, where Chiang swept aside its squabbling bosses to seize control of the Chinese part of the city. Because expedience had drawn Chiang into a tacit alliance with the Communists during the consolidation of his power, the foreigners who still ran the treaty ports as colonies, and Shanghai's International Settlement as a de facto European country, were understandably nervous to find him in control.

They need not have worried.

Almost immediately upon reaching Shanghai, Chiang abruptly reinvented himself and embraced Shanghai's bankers, industrialists, and financiers—its ruling elite. Meanwhile, he carefully did not violate the "sovereignty" of the International Settlement. Once distrusted by Westerners and Chinese business leaders for his perceived coziness with the Communists, Chiang had now been reborn as what the apprehensive foreigners would come to call a "moderate."

He divorced his past, just as he divorced the Communists, to climb into bed—literally—with China's capitalist elite. He next divorced his wives and concubines to marry into the powerful Soong family.

It is hard to overestimate the importance of the Soongs in the second quarter of the twentieth century, and no telling of the story of China in those years is complete without mention of the "Soong Sisters," three of the most influential women in twentieth-century Chinese history, whose father was Charles Jones "Charlie" Soong, an American-educated former Methodist minister who had become a wealthy banking and publishing magnate, and China's most powerful businessman.

Soong May-ling, the youngest of the sisters, became Chiang Kai-shek's "Madame Chiang." An astute politician in her own right, she studied at Wesleyan College, graduated from Wellesley, learned to speak fluent English with an engaging Georgia accent, and is generally considered to have been the "brains" behind Chiang's many decades of power. He also trusted her as his English translator. Though he understood the language, Chiang allowed his wife to translate for him, and importantly, to intuit subtleties that he feared he might be missing in important conversations.

Each of May-ling's sisters also married well. Soong Ai-ling, the eldest, was married to Kung Hsiang-hsi (who Westernized himself as H. H. Kung), a banker and politician who was considered to be the richest man in China. Soong Ching-ling, the middle sister, was one of the wives (she was twenty-seven years his junior) of Sun Yat-sen. According to Barbara Tuchman, Chiang had originally tried to woo her after Sun died in 1925, but she rebuffed his advances.

Of the Soong family, John Gunther wrote in the 1930s that "it represents what is beyond doubt one of the most striking agglutinations of personal power in the world. . . . The three Soong girls make the Chinese republic what might almost be called a matriarchy or a sorority. They accomplished the complex and unprecedented miracle of marrying a continent. Nothing like this has been known in history before, and probably nothing like it will ever happen again, though participation by women in politics is an old Chinese tradition."

Meanwhile, one of the sisters' three brothers was Harvard-educated Soong Tzu-wen (known as T. V. Soong), who became the most important *man* in Chiang Kai-shek's power circle and second only to Chiang in the Kuomintang government. He was also Chiang's second most influential adviser—after Madame Chiang. The ambitious Soong, who held many posts, official and unofficial, became Chiang's foreign minister in December 1941. He imagined himself better suited to have Chiang's job and expected to be his successor.

By the time he reached Shanghai, Chiang had also sufficiently consolidated his power to the extent that he could now concentrate on his quest for international legitimacy for his Nationalist government. As noted in the first chapter, by their very act of stealing Manchuria, the

Japanese ironically underscored Chiang's legitimacy by adding international empathy to international affirmation for him and his Kuomintang regime.

Maintaining the regime and its international legitimacy also involved financing it, and this is where T. V. Soong and H. H. Kung came in. In 1933, Chiang Kai-shek tapped Kung to serve simultaneously as both minister of finance and governor of the Central Bank of China, posts he would hold for more than a decade. Soong, meanwhile, established the China Development Finance Corporation, designed to bring foreign capital investment, mainly American, into China in the 1930s.

It was a symbiotic relationship. Kung and Soong provided the financing that allowed the Nationalist government to remain standing, and Chiang provided the political stability that allowed his brothers-in-law and their circle of investors to become wealthy—or *wealthier*. Meanwhile, the influx of foreign investment capital also helped to finance a variety of projects intended to develop China's backward infrastructure.

A generation earlier, foreign investors had financed Chinese railroads. Now the focus was on airlines. The Germans, who were investing heavily in airlines from Iran to South America during the 1920s and 1930s, entered into a joint venture with Chiang Kai-shek's government to start Eurasia Aviation, filling Chinese skies with trimotor Junkers Ju-52 airliners.

Another joint venture was China Airways (later China National Aviation Corporation or CNAC), formed in 1929 by the Chinese government, which held a 55 percent share, and the American firm Curtiss-Wright Aeronautical of Buffalo, New York. The latter was a conglomerate that had been formed in 1929 through a merger of various companies, especially the Curtiss Aeroplane and Motor Company and Wright Aeronautical. Though the names were familiar, and the firms traced their roots to the companies started by the Wright brothers and Glenn Curtiss, neither Orville Wright (Wilbur died in 1912) nor Glenn Curtiss had been involved in their namesake companies for many years at the time of the merger. Primarily a manufacturer of aircraft under the Curtiss brand name and of engines under the Wright name, Curtiss-Wright was expanding rapidly and globally, and was getting into airlines as an extension of its core business. Though the company sold its interest in CNAC in 1933 to Juan Trippe's Pan American Airways (later Pan American World Airways), Curtiss-Wright would remain active in China, and an important part of the story of Claire Chennault and his Flying Tigers.

J oe Stilwell returned to China for his third tour in 1935, this time as the military attaché at the US embassy. In this post, he spent his time observing the border skirmishing between Chiang's army and the Japanese in Manchuria. Stilwell was appalled. He had developed a great fondness for China and its people, and he was disgusted with the stewardship being afforded them by their leader. He was beginning to form an impression of and an immense dislike for Chiang Kai-shek.

"No evidence of planned defense against further Japanese encroachment," he wrote in a 1936 report to the Military Intelligence Division, which was forwarded to Secretary of State Cordell Hull. "No troop increase or even thought of it. No drilling or maneuvering. [Chiang had either] concealed [his preparations to defend China] more skillfully than any other military power has yet learned to do or they have made none at all."

To his credit, Chiang Kai-shek did recognize the inadequacies of his armed forces and had been casting about for foreign military advisers to help him. Back in the late nineteenth century, when Emperor Meiji had consolidated his power and was ready to bring Japan into line with the great European powers, and to do so quickly, he had imported Europe's best—Prussian officers to mentor his new army, and the British to help him build a world-class navy.

Now, more than half a century later, Chiang also turned to Europe. He allowed himself to be wooed by the Italians and the Soviets, and especially by the Germans, all of whom generously supplied matériel and advisers. Indeed, distinctive German Stahlhelm helmets are conspicuous in pictures of Chinese soldiers published in the 1930s.

H. H. Kung toured Europe in 1937 and was favorably impressed during his meetings with both Adolf Hitler and Benito Mussolini. Kung was successful in wooing German and Italian commercial investment in China, and for a time in keeping them distrustful of Japanese expansionist intentions in the Far East.

Thanks to the financing arranged by Kung and T. V. Soong, China had become a significant arms market. Manufacturers from many countries, including those in the United States, were eager to market their products, especially aircraft, to the Nationalist government.

One man in the right place at the right time was William Douglas Pawley, the Curtiss-Wright sales rep for China, who had earlier served as president of CNAC. Born in South Carolina, Pawley was the international businessman son of an international businessman, Edward Pawley, who had extensive interests in Cuba. Bill Pawley was among that class of daring entrepreneurs who spearheaded the international investment in China upon which T. V. Soong's business model and Chiang Kai-shek's government depended.

Curtiss-Wright had long been a leading producer of high-performance American combat aircraft, and Pawley saw an opportunity to set up a joint venture with Chinese interests to build Curtiss warplanes inside China. The Central Aircraft Manufacturing Company (CAMCO) was established in Hangzhou (then Hangchow), a port city about 150 miles southeast of Nanjing, to assemble crated aircraft shipped in from the United States. CAMCO began operations in the spring of 1933, assembling the first of 50 Curtiss Model 34 Hawk II biplane fighters similar to the aircraft serving the US Army Air Corps under the designation P-6, as well as Model 68 Hawk III biplane fighter-bombers comparable to the US Navy's BF2C Goshawk.

Of course, Chiang Kai-shek was also being courted by Benito Mussolini, who matched the Curtiss-Wright initiative with a similar production facility at Luoyang to build Savoia-Marchetti bombers and Fiat fighters, also shipped to China in kits for reassembly. Like the Americans, the Italians set up a flying school to teach Chinese pilots to fly the new aircraft, but they trumped Curtiss-Wright by sending in the flamboyant General Tenente Silvio Scaroni to run the facility. The second-highest-scoring Italian ace during World War I, Scaroni had gone on to serve as the Italian air attaché to the United States in the 1920s and had raced in the Schneider Trophy Air Race in 1926.

Pawley perhaps did not consciously set out to recruit an American of a stature analogous to Scaroni, but two years later in Miami, he found himself talking to such a man—Claire Lee Chennault.

At the time, Pawley was touring the United States with General Mao Pang-tsu of the Nationalist Chinese Air Force. Also known as Mao Pang-chu or the anglicized "P. T. Mao" (or "P. T. Mow"), the general hailed from Fenghua, Chiang Kai-shek's hometown, and had become Chiang's favorite military air adviser. Mao also later established his own credibility as a fighter pilot for having shot down four Japanese aircraft during the Japanese invasion in 1937.

Mao had held various posts in the Nationalist air arm, but spent much of his later career in the United States. During his early visits, he often accompanied Pawley on aircraft-buying excursions. During their trip in late 1935 and early 1936, they watched the Three Men on the Flying Trapeze perform in Miami, and were duly impressed. It was one of those auspicious moments that greatly affected the futures of all concerned.

Shortly after the Three Men team broke up at the end of the tour, Chennault got a telegram from Roy Holbrook, a former Air Corps pilot whom he had known in Texas. Holbrook was now working as a flight instructor in China, and Mao had asked him to contact Chennault to recommend additional American pilots and aircraft mechanics. Among those whom Chennault suggested were Sergeants Luke Williamson and Billy MacDonald, the other two of the Three Men on the Flying Trapeze.

Meanwhile, as the outgoing head of the Pursuit Section of the Air Corps Tactical School at Maxwell Field in Alabama, where he had served from 1931 to 1935, Chennault participated in the evaluation of the candidate aircraft for the Air Corps' next generation of pursuit aircraft. Of the several types that were flown, Chennault preferred the Seversky P-35, though the Air Corps chose to favor the Curtiss P-36 with a much larger order. Though a Curtiss product had been the airman's *second* choice. Chennault still had the eye of Bill Pawley.

Early in 1936, Chennault was back in northern Louisiana as the executive officer of the 20th Pursuit Group at Barksdale Field, near Shreveport, and a few months short of turning forty-three. Chennault was long in years in the young man's game of fighter aviation, and staring at the end of his career. Still a captain, his options on the organizational ladder were limited, and if that was not enough, recommendations of Army doctors underscored the handwriting on the wall. His decades as a three-pack-a-day cigarette devotee had left him with chronic bronchitis. His time around thundering aircraft engines had degraded his hearing, and this was also in his medical record.

With his Air Corps career at an end, he and Nell bought a farm, and with their four children under eighteen, they decided to retire to Tensas Parish, Louisiana. Before he could retire, though, the bronchitis caught up with him, and he spent that summer lying on a hospital bed at the Army Navy Hospital—now the State of Arkansas Department of Rehabilitation—in Hot Springs, Arkansas, contemplating his future.

"Ever since my boyhood in Louisiana I have watched the eddies of the muddy Southern rivers as they boiled to life in the spring," he reflected in his memoirs. "Particularly on the Mississippi, where I have seen them smash a steamboat into kindling wood and drag a full-grown cypress down into their whirling vortex, these eddies have been symbolic. . . . Several times I have felt myself swirling in one of life's eddies and struck out desperately for open water and the main current of my ambitions. This time I knew that I would have to find something that would give me a chance to keep flying, to fight, and to prove my theories on tactics. When the Army suggested retirement I accepted the offer. Several aircraft manufacturing firms made flattering overtures, but I had no urge to fly a desk."

However, as he lay there, he was also receiving "letters with Chinese postage stamps, bringing news of Billy MacDonald, Luke Williamson, and Roy Holbrook, [which] interested me more [than retirement]."

Finally, by way of Holbrook, there came an amazing offer of a job as the chief consultant to Chiang Kai-shek's air force. After his years on an Air Corps salary, their offer of a three-month contract at $16,000 a month (in today's dollars), "plus expenses, a car, chauffeur, and interpreter, and the right to fly any plane in the Chinese Air Force" was too good to turn down. On the first day of May in 1937, one day after his retirement became effective, Claire Lee Chennault left for China. He went for three months, but stayed for eight years. It would be two and a half years before he even returned to Louisiana for a brief visit with his family.

Because he owned farmland in Louisiana, Chennault's passport identified him as a "farmer," though officially, he was an "adviser" to the Central Bank of China. He was never to be offered a rank of any level in the Chinese Air Force, though he was always referred to informally in China—and later by the American fliers who served under him—as "Colonel Chennault."

He stopped briefly in Japan, where he was met in Kobe by Billy MacDonald, who was traveling under a visa that listed him as the manager of an acrobatic troupe. The Japanese were naturally loath to allow advisers to the Chinese Air Force to travel between China and Japan. Acrobats, like farmers, attracted no red flags.

After a tour of strategically interesting Japanese industrial locations, they sailed for Shanghai, where Chennault was to report to Madame Chiang. The generalissimo had made her China's aviation tsar, placing her in charge of China's Aeronautical Affairs Commission, a role that she seems to have shared with General Chou Chih-jou, who went by the Westernized name C. J. Chow. Like P. T. Mao, he was a member of her husband's inner circle of aviation experts. Her position served to make Madame Chiang Chennault's boss in his new role. In turn, throughout World War II, she also served as the honorary leader, somewhat analogous to a royal patron, of the Chinese Air Force, a role that she took very seriously. Later, Claire Chennault named her also as the honorary commander of the American Volunteer Group, which she also took seriously.

"We were told she was out and ushered into a dim cool interior to wait," Chennault wrote of the day that Roy Holbrook took him to meet his new boss. "Suddenly a vivacious young girl clad in a modish Paris frock tripped into the room, bubbling with energy and enthusiasm. I assumed it was some young friend of Roy's and remained seated. Imagine my surprise when Roy poked me and said, 'Madame Chiang, may I present Colonel Chennault?' It was the Generalissimo's wife, looking twenty years younger than I had expected and speaking English in a rich Southern drawl. . . . Despite her tremendous feminine charm, on that sticky Shanghai day Madame was all business. She had recently shouldered heavy responsibilities and much official scorn in tackling the tangled affairs of the Chinese Air Force, but she was determined to see it through."

It was the beginning of a relationship that would last eight years, during which Chennault would become a household name in both China and the United States.

"Flying dragons in the heavens," reads the fifth line in the first hexagram of the *I Ching*. "It furthers one to see the great man." Both Claire Chennault and Chiang Kai-shek had each just met one, but not to be overshadowed, was the importance of a great *woman*.

———————

Joe Stilwell, who had learned the language, and who had been developing a deep understanding of China and its military affairs over nearly three decades, had yet to have had an audience with the Chiangs. Chennault, who would never learn the language, and who had been in China for less than a week, was now part of their court.

FIVE

Young Tigers Get Their Wings

I flunked out of two colleges," Robert Lee Scott Jr. admitted in his memoirs, though having "preemptively dropped out" would have been technically more accurate. "Then I did something few college failures do: returned to high school for the rudiments of learning I had missed. I had to have been learning a little even to have gone back for what I called my 'postgraduate courses,' and I think I was spurred on by the tears I saw in my dad's eyes. He was a Clemson graduate, class of 1905. It was a military school and he wanted me to attend it."

He goes on to say that they settled on his trying the Citadel, the Military College of South Carolina, which is known as the "West Point of the South." This lasted only a brief time, for he again dropped out and came home, announcing that he had "decided to attend the real West Point."

As competition for the service academies was fierce and most who entered did so through congressional appointments, this seemed an impossible fantasy, and a source of immense consternation for Robert Scott Sr., who thought his son a budding failure. However, the younger Scott was a young man with a plan. He had previously joined the Georgia National Guard, and knew that he could resign and transfer to the regular army, which would make him eligible for a West Point prep school that would give him a crack at a backdoor entrance. This scheme worked, and Robert Lee Scott found himself as a member of the Class of 1932 at the US Military Academy.

He spent the summer of his graduation year attempting to duplicate the entire route of Marco Polo on a Soyer motorcycle that he bought in Cherbourg, France. He made it across Europe and most of Turkey before halting his expedition near the Soviet border and turning back.

That autumn, Scott's long-imagined goal of becoming a US Army Air Corps flier began to take shape at Randolph Field, one of the flight training bases that fed into the advanced flight school at Kelly Field or Brooks Field on the other side of San Antonio, Texas.

It was also during that time that, like so many other Air Corps flying cadets passing through San Antonio, he met his future wife, Catharine Rix "Kitty" Green. Indeed, as he reminds us in his memoirs, San Antonio in those years had earned the reputation as the "mother-in-law of the Air Corps," because so many of its men met their wives there.

After earning his wings, but still a bachelor, Second Lieutenant Bob Scott reported to his first duty station, Mitchel Field, New York, in October 1933. Almost immediately, he incurred the wrath of his commander for racking up thirty-two hours of flying time during his first week when the maximum was supposed to be four hours a *month*. An aging former cavalry officer, he told the exasperated flier that the Great Depression was on, budgets were tight, and conserving fuel and time on airframes was more important that giving pilots the skill they needed to become *experienced* pilots.

While Scott made his way into the sky by way of the US Army's service academy, Greg Hallenbeck, Jim Howard, and Tex Hill were among the thousands of young men of their generation who became naval aviators, thanks to the Naval Aviation Cadet program. Authorized by Congress in April 1935, the program provided for flight training for civilian college graduates and a road to being commissioned in the US Navy or Marine Corps.

Having graduated from the University of Washington in 1934 in aeronautical engineering, Hallenbeck had settled down and married nineteen-year-old Helene Wickstrom, a girl from Coos Bay, Oregon. He took a job as an engineering draftsman at the Boeing Company, but soon realized that he wanted to be a lot closer to flying than sketching aircraft components on drafting vellum. His commission in the US Army Reserve was in the Coastal Artillery, and he was stymied in his efforts to transfer to the US Army Air Corps. The Naval Aviation Cadet program opened the door of opportunity for him.

One catch for Hallenbeck was that the program did not accept candidates who were married. In the meantime, however, he had applied for and received his birth certificate, and had realized—evidently for the first time—that he was *not* Gregory Hallenbeck, but Gregory Boyington. His birth name had never been legally changed. Because there was no record of a "Gregory Boyington" having been married, Gregory Boyington was able to transfer into the US Marine Corps Reserve and be eligible for Aviation Cadet training!

In February 1936, Boyington reported to Naval Air Station, Pensacola, in Florida for flight training, earned his wings in March 1937, was commissioned as an active duty Marine Corps second lieutenant four months later, and was assigned to fly Grumman F3F biplane fighters with Marine Fighting Squadron 2 (VMF-2).

In 1937, during his senior year at Pomona College, the Naval Aviation Cadet program came to the attention of James Howell Howard. In his memoirs, he wrote of a warm spring evening of daydreaming when his mind settled on "a talk that had been given [at the school one] evening by a recently graduated naval aviation cadet who was touring college campuses to recruit applicants for aviation training at Pensacola, Florida. . . . Some twenty of us crowded into the room, where we were met by a young man dressed in the dark blue uniform of the US Navy, with a single gold stripe on the cuff of each sleeve and gold wings on his left breast. . . . He told of a program in which, if we passed the exacting physical exam, personal interview, and scholarship requirements, we would be given thirty days of primary flight training and a month of ground school during the summer. Those who passed would be sent on to Pensacola for a full year of training. After graduation they would be designated naval aviators, commissioned officers in the Naval Reserve, and assigned to squadrons in the fleet—perhaps even to a carrier."

Howard explained that he and his classmates "were dedicated, almost servile, to their intended careers. At the time I planned to follow my father into medicine, which meant six years of medical school and internship—an exercise I didn't look forward to with much anticipation. . . . I felt I would not be happy following the road of tradition and respectability that the field of medicine offered. I needed to ask myself if my goal in life might not be different. . . . I made up my mind then and there that I wanted to do something exciting and challenging. The incident that forced me to rethink my career was, of course, that evening's talk by the young naval officer. I knew that the path to being a naval aviator had many treacherous and devious turns. If I could make it, I was sure I'd find romance and adventure of the highest order!"

He became a cadet immediately after graduation and began flight training at Pensacola in January 1938, surrounded mainly by graduates of the US Naval Academy at Annapolis. After running up 377 hours in trainers and operational aircraft from F3F and F4B fighters to TBD Devastator dive bombers, Howard earned his wings as a naval aviator in January 1939.

"The misfits and those lacking self-discipline were eliminated by giving them enough rope to hang themselves," he wrote of his year at Pensacola. "The weeding-out process took its toll, not only on the flight line but during off-duty hours. By the end of our tour at Pensacola, the cadet battalion had developed into a well-regulated group that reflected the Navy stamp of approval. From here, we went out into the active duty world alone and separated from the homogeneous atmosphere of cadet life. . . . New and intriguing associations were about to begin. I was now right where I wanted to be."

His first assignment was to Fighting Squadron 7 (VF-7) aboard the carrier USS *Wasp* (CV-7), but because the ship's delivery was running late, he was diverted to VF-2, assigned to the USS *Lexington* (CV-2) at Naval Air Station North Island in San Diego for carrier landing training. When the *Wasp* was further delayed, Howard was among those reassigned to VF-6 aboard the USS *Enterprise* (CV-6), which was destined to be the most decorated American warship of World War II. His introduction to the "Big E" came as he landed his F3F on her flight deck as the ship was under way at sea between San Diego and Pearl Harbor.

Over the ensuing weeks, the men of the "Fighting Six" were engaged in continuous combat training missions—bombing and gunnery— alone and in conjunction with the bomber (VB-6), torpedo (VT-6), and scouting (VS-6) squadrons aboard the *Enterprise*. It was not all work and no play while the ship was operating out of Pearl Harbor, though. There were dances at the "pink palace," the Royal Hawaiian

Hotel, on Waikiki Beach—replete with smiling hula girls—and in his recollections, Howard writes effusively of the spectacular scenery over which he and his fellow pilots flew on training flights over the outer islands. Redeployed to Pearl a second time after a stint at North Island, Howard even took up surfing.

W hile the US Navy initiated its Aviation Cadet program in 1935, the US Army had a similar program that dated back to 1907. The Flying Cadet Pilot Training Program, which had reached its peak during World War I but had declined in scope in the 1920s, was like the program of the sister service, seeking unmarried men with at least two years of college or three years' experience in a technical field that would be useful to aviation. The Navy program, meanwhile, required a college *diploma*.

That Charles Rankin Bond had no college degree was not for want of his having tried. In 1935, he had enlisted in the US Army to go to the US Military Academy prep school at Camp Bullis near San Antonio. However, West Point took only a handful of graduates of the USMA prep schools, and Bond was not in that handful, so he decided to try for a slot as a flying cadet.

This time his efforts were met with success. In March 1938 he was accepted, and a month later he had soloed in a Stearman PT-13. He moved on to P-12 fighters, which he greatly enjoyed, but in January 1939, after being commissioned as a second lieutenant, he was assigned to the bomber side of the Air Corps and ordered to report to the 2nd Bombardment Group at Langley Field in Virginia, the only unit equipped with the new B-17 Flying Fortresses.

Given that the Air Corps cadet program was headquartered at Randolph Field in San Antonio, Tex Hill's hometown, it was only natural that this was his first stop when he decided to become a pilot courtesy of the US armed forces. Indeed, he had already met a number of cadets who had visited his home while courting his sister Martha.

Hill's biographer Reagan Schaupp writes that in the spring of 1938, "the Army's aviation program included a battery of written tests, medical exams, and interviews by Army psychiatrists. Tex waded through them all, then returned to await the results. A few weeks later they arrived: he had failed to qualify. No reason was given, and Tex never learned it."

The fact that he had almost completed his degree at Austin College, got him to first base when he decided to visit the Navy recruiter on his rebound from disappointment. As Schaupp notes, the Navy exams "were essentially identical to the Army's as far as Tex could tell, and once again, he played the waiting game back at Austin College. This time, however, the news was good."

As with Boyington and Howard before him, Hill passed through the Naval Flight Training at NAS Pensacola. Like nearly every pilot who earned his wings as a naval aviator at Pensacola in 1939, Hill had dreams of being a fighter pilot, but instead, he found himself assigned to fly TBD Devastator torpedo bombers with Torpedo Squadron 3 (VT-3) aboard the USS *Saratoga* (CV-3), the sister ship of the USS *Lexington*, aboard which Jim Howard had served briefly.

Like the *Enterprise*, where Howard made his home, the *Saratoga* was assigned to the Pacific Fleet, so operational training was divided between being ported at North Island and at Pearl Harbor. While operating out of Pearl Harbor, Hill and VT-3 participated in the exercise known as Fleet Problem XXI. Between 1923 and 1940, the Navy's annual large-scale combat exercises were known as "Fleet Problems," as in arithmetic problems. Reagan Schaupp reminds readers of the irony

WHEN TIGERS RULED THE SKY

that Fleet Problem XXI, conducted in the spring of 1940, involved a scenario in which a foreign naval force would attack Pearl Harbor. It was no secret that the only naval force capable of such a thing was the Imperial Japanese Navy.

After Fleet Problem XXI, Tex Hill was reassigned—from torpedo bombers to dive bombers, and from the Pacific to the Atlantic Fleet. Assigned to Scouting Squadron 41 (VS-41), he transitioned to Vought SB2U Vindicators and shipped out aboard the USS *Ranger* (CV-4). After being a part of mere exercises in the Pacific, Hill now found himself at war in the Atlantic. The North Atlantic was alive with "wolf packs" of German U-boats, and although the United States was not yet a declared combatant, the US Navy's Atlantic Fleet was tasked with escorting the supply convoys crossing the Eastern Seaboard to the embattled United Kingdom. For Hill and his fellow airmen, it was a reconnaissance mission. Royal Navy warships, also part of the escort detail, did the shooting.

Spotting and shadowing U-boats was part of a tedious routine punctuated by brief moments of excitement, but as when the men were operating out of Pearl Harbor, it was not all work and no play. The diversions available during tropical port calls in Bermuda matched those of Waikiki.

After he had graduated from Red Cloud High School in 1935, Robert Tharp Smith had gone on to the University of Nebraska in Lincoln, which is where he was when he decided to take to the sky. Because the US Army Air Corps Flying Cadet Pilot Training Program did not require a college degree for admission, Smith might have simply dropped out, but after he took the tests—and passed—the Air Corps allowed him to finish his last few months at Lincoln before reporting for duty. His first assignment was to primary flight training at Santa Maria on California's central coast, where, coincidentally, Bob Scott was one of his flight instructors.

It is still common for men to earn lifetime nicknames in the early days of their military careers, and it was at Santa Maria that he earned his service nickname.

"While I had always been called Bob by my family and friends, it was not long after my flying training began that my classmates began calling me 'R. T.,'" he recalled in his memoirs. "There was a very simple reason for this; there were three Smiths in my class, and the cloth name-tapes sewed on the left breast of our uniform shirts read, 'Smith, B. P.,' 'Smith, F. M.,' and 'Smith, R. T.' That's the way they were called out whenever we had to respond to a roll call, which was several times a day, and since our initials were constantly on display while our first names were not, our classmates adopted the easy way out. As time went on Bernard P. was often called 'Beep,' and Frederick M. was occasionally called 'Fum.' By the same logic it would appear inevitable that I would become 'Art,' or 'Artie,' but strangely enough that never happened; it was always just 'R. T.'"

As had been the case for Scott, Boyington, Howard, and Hill, R. T. Smith later recalled the joy of flying, writing that his first solo flight in a Stearman PT-13 was "easily the greatest thrill I'd ever experienced, difficult to describe, but a feeling which all pilots know and remember."

However, as he progressed toward advanced training, a disappointment loomed in the form of a regulation decreeing that pilots taller than five feet, ten inches, could not fly in the cramped cockpits of fighter aircraft—which was the dream of every kid who had grown up devouring pulp fiction about World War I fighter aces. It was, he recalled, "as if the musicians union had told Tommy Dorsey he couldn't play trombone because his arms were too long."

A second roadblock of frustration confronted him as he finally graduated from advanced training and awaited his duty assignment. Smith was a victim of his own skill as a pilot. The saying goes that "those who can, do, while those who can't, teach." In the Air Corps, it was exactly the opposite. Those who were the most skilled of pilots were retained as flight instructors. Instead of going off to an operational unit, R. T. Smith was ordered *back* to Randolph Field to teach.

SIX

A Bridge to War

In the summer of 1932, if he had ridden his Soyer motorcycle far enough during his effort to match the epic journey of Marco Polo, Robert Lee Scott would have ridden across the bridge of the same name spanning the Yongding River about a dozen miles southwest of the center of Beijing. Five years later, Marco Polo Bridge became one of the crossroads of the twentieth century.

On the sultry, sticky evening of July 7, 1937, Japanese troops based at a compound near the bridge had just wrapped up nighttime maneuvers when a soldier was found to be missing. The Japanese blamed the Chinese, and the Chinese claimed they had done nothing. Officers on both sides at the Marco Polo Bridge intervened to calm things down, and the missing man was found, having not been kidnapped. However, just as this seemed to have worked, there were more shots, and a rapid escalation of gunfire on both sides. An episode that should have been allowed to deescalate into a continued uneasy cease-fire quickly mushroomed out of control.

As with the Mukden Incident in September 1931, it was a minor provocation that caused little damage and could and should have been sorted out within hours, but instead it tipped the dominoes of disaster. Again, an accidental event flew out of control and became the driving force of Japanese foreign policy.

Since the heady days of the swift and easy victories in the First Sino-Japanese War and the Russo-Japanese War, Japan's leaders had thought of their nation as possessing an almost divine responsibility to dominate the Far East politically as well as economically. Now, suddenly, Japan was faced with an unexpected opportunity to put its military might where its rhetoric had been. It was a golden opportunity wrapped in unseen danger.

In numerous previous incidents, starting with the 1931 Mukden Incident, the politicians in Tokyo had gone head-to-head with the generals to restore calm, but times had changed. Fumimaro Konoe, who became Japan's prime minister only a month and three days before that night at the Marco Polo Bridge, fully embraced the ancient doctrine of *Hakko ichiu*, under which the legendary emperor Jimmu had imagined, more than four thousand years earlier, "the eight corners of the world under one roof." Konoe had suggested that China should lie submissively beneath Japan's roof.

Chiang Kai-shek, meanwhile, was not in a submissive mood, having been emboldened by the support that he had been receiving from the outside world. Though his armed forces were still in pitiful condition to go head-to-head with the most powerful war machine in the Far East, Chiang could not dare to lose face by not reacting.

Cannons and machine guns were brought to bear by both sides, and the situation erupted into the Second Sino-Japanese War, which later became a theater of World War II, and Claire Chennault's career-defining campaign.

Chennault was at the Italian aircraft production facility at Luoyang, calling on General Tenente Silvio Scaroni, when he received word of the Marco Polo Bridge Incident. The Italians were still three years away from their alliance with Japan that would become the Rome-Berlin-Tokyo Axis, so Scaroni and Chennault, as advisers to Chiang Kai-shek, were on the same side that day.

By the time that the airmen at Luoyang learned of the incident, the Japanese had already captured the Marco Polo Bridge and a parallel railroad bridge. With open warfare now sanctioned by Emperor Hirohito, the highest authority in Japan, the Japanese troops began a full-fledged effort to capture Beijing.

Chennault quickly wired Nanjing for instructions and was ordered to take over "final combat training" for the Chinese Air Force. Ironically, on the same day as the Bridge Incident, Chennault was learning exactly how unimaginably dreadful Chinese flight training had become.

"Despite the tremendous flurry of aviation activity under the Italians, nothing was done that really strengthened the Chinese Air Force," Chennault recalled in his memoirs, suggesting that the Italians were engaged in deliberate sabotage. "The Italian Flying school at Luoyang was unique. It graduated every Chinese cadet who survived the training course as a full-fledged pilot regardless of his ability. This was in sharp contrast to the American policy of weeding out incompetents in early training and then only graduating the best students. However, the Generalissimo was pleased with the Italian method. Chinese aviation cadets were carefully selected from the top social strata, and when they were washed out at the American-style Hangzhou school, protests from their influential families caused the Generalissimo acute embarrassment. The Italian method solved this social problem and all but wrecked the air force."

Meanwhile, a scattering of foreign pilots who had hired on as mercenaries with Chiang's air arm were little better. Bob Scott recalled them, echoing Chennault's opinion at the time, as a "conglomeration of international adventurers and hired leeches, ready to suck the blood of China."

Not only Chiang's air force, but also his army, were incapable of stopping the Japanese, or even of effectively resisting them. He sent his best German-trained divisions to defend Shanghai, but chose not to mount a major defense of Beijing because of its proximity to Japanese sources of supply in Manchuria. The old imperial capital fell to the invaders inside of a month, and Shanghai was attacked in August, creating tidal waves of refugees streaming across China. The bloody, house-to-house fighting in China's largest city, which lasted until November, was described by John Gunther as "the biggest battle in the world since Verdun; Chinese casualties alone are calculated at not less than 450,000." The Chinese government now calculates military casualties alone at 283,000. The International Settlement, however, remained largely inviolate—the Japanese made sure not to attack—and its international residents were mere witnesses to the carnage that was ongoing only a few blocks away.

Joe Stilwell, the American military attaché, decried the Japanese pilots who buzzed the American embassy in Beijing, calling them "arrogant little bastards," but learned to accept the new order in the Japanese-occupied city. He had choice words for Chiang Kai-shek and the Chinese leadership as well, calling them "oily politicians . . . treacherous quitters, selfish, conscienceless, unprincipled crooks."

Stilwell, in his role as attaché, began scrupulously to monitor Japanese troop movements. However, when the War Department, eager to avoid an incident with the Japanese, ordered him to stop, he referred to his bosses within the Military Intelligence Division as "the pack of fools in Washington." The State Department, meanwhile, ordered civilians to leave Beijing, though Stilwell's wife and daughters stayed on.

Claire Chennault, in the employ of the Chinese government, was not only in a position to take more overt action, but also he was *commanded* to do so. At first, he had been tasked with overseeing training for the Chinese Air Force, but when he reported to Chiang Kai-shek in Nanjing, Chennault was told to work with General P. T. Mao to take offensive action. As Bob Scott wrote in his biography of Chennault, the former Air Corps captain was now "chief of staff for air to Chiang Kai-shek."

The Imperial Japanese Navy sent warships, notably the turn-of-the-century armored cruiser *Izumo*, up the Huangpu River to bombard Shanghai at point-blank range. These were a particular embarrassment to Chiang and an obvious target for Chennault.

On August 14, the second day of the Battle of Shanghai, Chennault mustered the Curtiss Model 68 Hawk III biplanes, fitted them with bombs, and ordered them to sink the Japanese cruiser. At least two waves of bombers bore down on the warship, but none of the bombs found their mark. Some of them even drifted into the International Settlement, which was dangerously near. They impacted on the street, their explosions shattering the windows of the Cathay Hotel and the Palace Hotel, where foreign newspaper reporters had been watching the action out on the river. One Chinese Hawk, damaged by Japanese antiaircraft fire, attempted an emergency landing at the racetrack inside the French Concession, and jettisoned its bombs into the Great World Amusement Building, which was then being used to house refugees. More than a thousand died.

The *Izumo* remained in the vicinity of Shanghai for the next four years but was never sunk. It was an inauspicious beginning for Chennault's air war over China.

His activities now turned to the air defense of Nanjing, Chiang Kai-shek's capital city, which was under routine air attack by Japanese bombers. It was a futile effort, as the aging Curtiss biplanes and a squadron of Boeing P-26 Peashooters were no match for the Japanese.

As Chennault recalled, "I noted in my diary, 'The Chinese Air Force is not ready for war.' It was a vast understatement."

Around this time, Chennault and P. T. Mao were summoned to give Chiang Kai-shek a report on the Chinese Air Force.

"How many first-line planes are ready to fight?" Chiang asked Mao.

"Ninety-one, Your Excellency," Mao replied.

Chennault recalled that he thought Chiang "was going to explode. He strode up and down the terrace, loosing long strings of sibilant Chinese that seemed to hiss, coil, and strike like a snake."

"The Generalissimo has threatened to execute him," Madame Chiang whispered to Chennault. "The Aero Commission records show we should have five hundred first-line planes ready to fight."

"What does your survey show?" Chiang asked the American as Madame Chiang translated.

"General Mao's figures are correct," Chennault replied.

"Go on," Madame Chiang said. "Tell him all of the truth."

As Chennault later reflected, this exchange "laid the foundation of a reputation for absolute frankness" that was to define his relationship with the generalissimo for the remainder of a long war.

"Lack of honest, technically competent, loyal subordinates was his worst problem," Chennault said of Chiang. "He managed by playing off one against the other, getting what he could from them, and every now and then lopping off a few heads as a warning that there was a limit to his patience."

Sometime later, when Chennault asked Madame Chiang why her husband did not clean house and rid himself of all the incompetents in his command structure, she explained that he was well aware of the problem, but he had told her—with an absolute frankness of his own—that they were "the only people he has to work with, and if we get rid of all those people who are at fault, who will there be left?"

SEVEN

Warplanes for a Generalissimo on the Run

Through Bill Pawley and CAMCO, Claire Chennault was able to get his hands on a few Curtiss Model 75 monoplane fighters, an export variant of the P-36, which the US Army Air Corps was operating.

As CAMCO was delivering these, Chiang Kai-shek was also able to conclude a deal with the Soviets for delivery of maneuverable Polikarpov I-15 biplane fighters and fast Polikarpov I-16 monoplanes. The biplanes were so similar to the Curtiss Model 34 Hawk II biplanes that they had earned the nickname "Curtiss" while in action during the Spanish Civil War. With the Soviet aircraft, there came a flood of Soviet pilots—indeed, there were whole intact squadrons of Red Air Force planes and pilots, whose presence undercut Chennault's authority with Chiang.

"The Russians sent four fighter and two bomber squadrons completely staffed and equipped to fight the Japs in China," Chennault explained in his memoirs. "The Russians didn't pause to play partisan politics or trip over ideological folderol when their national interests were at stake in China. All of the Soviets' aid went to the Central Government of the Generalissimo. The Russians had had no love for the Generalissimo since the 1927 split when he drove the Russian-supported Chinese Communists from the Kuomintang and slaughtered them by the thousands. . . . The Russians sent their aid to the Generalissimo solely because he represented the strongest and most effective force opposing Japan and they supported him exclusively, ignoring the Chinese Communist armies, which badly needed external support. Japan had been preparing an attack on Russia for 20 years, and unnumbered shooting rehearsals had been held along the Siberian border. The Russians were willing to help anybody who was fighting and weakening Japan."

The bombers that the Soviets supplied to Chiang were the fast and reasonably sophisticated Tupolev Ant-40 type, nicknamed "Skorostnoi Bombardirovschik," or "high-speed bomber." The 122 "SB" bombers delivered in 1937–1938 were crewed mainly by Soviet "volunteers" who flew missions deep into Japanese-held territory as far afield as Taiwan.

As with Chiang Kai-shek's parallel air forces, the Japanese also operated separate air forces in China and throughout Asia and the Pacific during World War II. The Imperial Japanese Army (IJA), and the Imperial Japanese Navy (IJN) each had an air force, complete with a separate command and control network, but with dissimilar aircraft types. Army-Navy rivalries existed within the armed forces of most countries, and still do. However, in Imperial Japan, they operated with an antagonism that verged on hostility. Each side jealously guarded its own turf, considering cooperation to be a sign of weakness. Nevertheless, in the air as on the ground, the Japanese maintained an organization and discipline within their parallel services that was superior to that of the Chinese, where rival advisers, residual warlord rivalries, and autonomous fiefdoms ruined the vital coordination necessary for effective operations.

Meanwhile, even as the Soviets and Americans were now present within the Chinese command structure, German and Italian advisers were also still around. This was despite their being cosignatories with Japan of the 1936 Anti-Comintern Pact, which opposed the Communist International movement and Soviet expansion.

"Germany is Japan's ally in the Anti-Comintern Pact, and Japan is engaged in a death struggle with China; one would normally take it for granted that Germany would assist Japan in every way," wrote John Gunther, who visited in 1938. "But in Hankou I found the amazing spectacle of a variety of Germans helping China, the enemy of their ally. What is more, I found Russians—aviators mostly—in Hankou also working on the Chinese side, fighting in cooperation with Germans against Japan. I blinked. The German military mission, the Russian aviation mission, were headquartered within a few blocks of one another. . . . To preserve diplomatic proprieties, neither Germans nor Russians would admit that the others existed, and they never met officially. German help to China came in several ways. It was so conspicuous when I was in Hankou that young Dr. Trautmann, the son of the German Ambassador to China, arrived from Berlin with a German Red Cross unit. The Chinese announced that $500,000 worth of medical supplies were coming to China, donated by German factories and other organizations."

By the end of 1937, the Japanese had captured Nanjing, Chiang Kai-shek's capital city. There ensued a massacre of civilians lasting many weeks, which was called the "Rape of Nanking." About a quarter of a million people—the exact number will never be known—were murdered by large numbers of undisciplined Japanese troops. An official German eyewitness report quoted by historian John Toland described the ruthless efficiency of the Imperial Japanese Army as "bestial machinery."

The story of the first year of the Second Sino-Japanese War was one of relentless, unstoppable Japanese advances, contrasted with continuous Chinese routs and withdrawals. It would have been logical to assume that after such an epidemic of defeat, and the loss of one major population center after another, including two capital cities—Beijing and Nanjing—the Chinese would have given up. Certainly the Japanese expected this.

"Crush the Chinese in three months and they will sue for peace," Japanese minister of war Hajime Sugiyama confidently predicted at the start of the campaign. By all reasonable measures, the Chinese *were* crushed in three months. After six, nine, and a dozen months, they were *still* being crushed, but had yet to give up.

When his capitals fell, Chiang Kai-shek did not. He picked up and moved, relocating the seat of government three hundred miles west to Hankou (now part of modern Wuhan). After that city fell in October 1938, he moved again, nearly five hundred miles farther west, to another provisional capital, in Chongqing (then Chungking) in Sichuan (then Szechuan) Province. Chiang's only strategic advantage at this point was China's immense geographic scale, although Japanese strategy would never involve the occupation of China's entire landmass, but mainly of its coastline, its ports, and its major cities.

Chennault, meanwhile, relocated his own base of operations to Kunming, where he would remain for the next five years. The capital of Yunnan Province, Kunming is in mountainous southern China, with French Indochina to the south and the northern part of Britain's Burma colony to the west.

"When I first came to Kunming, it was a sleepy, backwoods Oriental town with a thin Gallic patina," wrote Chennault. "The French had pushed a meter-gauge railroad up from Indochina, across the tremendous Yunnan gorges to Kunming, and used the cool, dry, and invigorating climate of the Kunming Plateau as a refuge from the steamy heat of their colony. During the summer Lake Kunming was dotted with their champagne-stocked houseboats. Life in Kunming and its environs had changed little with the passing centuries. Squat brown tribesmen crowned with faded blue turbans carried on the provincial commerce, driving pack mule caravans loaded with salt, tin, and opium over narrow mountain trails. Creaking, ungreased pony carts rattled and groaned over Kunming's cobbled streets. Water buffalo, cattle, and herds of fat pigs were not uncommon sights between the pepper trees lining the main thoroughfare. Here and there the alien lines of a French villa loomed incongruously out of a welter of sooty tiled roofs and lofty olive-green eucalyptus trees."

Chennault set up training operations at Yunnanyi, about three hundred miles west of Kunming, and continued to import a handful of former Air Corps pilots from the United States. Among these was Claude Bryant "Skip" Adair, who would later play an important part in recruiting the Flying Tigers. A former bomber pilot, Adair was working as a pilot for Eastern Air Lines when Chennault hired him in late 1938.

O ther Americans in China were also on the move and in the same direction. Along with a general exodus of foreign legations from occupied Beijing, the American embassy caught up with the retreating Chinese government during its brief sojourn in Hankou, which Joe Stilwell colorfully described as "the bunghole of creation."

As the Japanese advanced, Bill Pawley moved CAMCO's operations first to Hankou, then to Hengyang (Hengzhou) in Hunan Province, and finally south into Yunnan following Chennault's move. It was here that he later established a CAMCO factory near Lei Yun (then called Loi Wing or Loiwing), a tiny village on the Burmese border, about twenty miles west of Ruili in Yunnan's Dehong Prefecture, and four hundred miles west of Kunming. Here he later exercised a license to build Vultee Model V-11 monoplane attack bombers, as well as a small number of Curtiss Model 75s, for the Chinese.

Meanwhile, Pawley was also promoting the Curtiss CW-21 Demon high-altitude interceptor that could be used to attack Japanese bombers above thirty thousand feet. With its water-cooled engines, it bore a resemblance to the earlier Model 75/P-36 Hawk. In fact, in an unprecedented move, Curtiss actually shipped the original prototype CW-21 to China in 1939, with which company test pilot Bob Fausel reportedly shot down a Japanese aircraft. More than two dozen unassembled CW-21s were ordered by China for assembly at Lei Yun.

The isolation of locations such as Kunming and Lei Yun in the interior far from the great swath of territory occupied by the Japanese was a two-edged sword of relative security and logistical impossibility. When the Japanese strategic plan to seize the ports was realized, the only means of supply were over mountainous terrain served by poor roads or no roads at all. For Chiang Kai-shek's air forces—the Soviet contingent and Chennault's mainly Chinese force—fuel and supplies were a constant operational dilemma, as they were not for the Japanese, who controlled all access to the seaports on China's eastern coast.

As 1937 gave way to 1938, and as Chiang Kai-shek's armies were collapsing under the weight of the Japanese assault, the British had undertaken the immense engineering challenge of building a seven-hundred-mile road across the steep and virtually impassible mountains from Lashio, Burma, the Burma Road's "Milepost One," to Kunming. It was a herculean task, not only building the road and navigating a steep, unpaved thoroughfare that was just nine feet wide, but also navigating the official red tape of His Majesty's government and general British skittishness about angering Japan by helping China.

By the time that Chiang and Chennault had relocated to their new bases of operation, the Burma Road was essentially the only land route between China and the outside world. Ultimately, much of the effort to supply China during World War II was by air, but the skies over much of China belonged to the Japanese.

Despite the IJA-IJN rivalry, logistical and equipment superiority had translated into the Japanese having maintained air superiority over Chinese cities and battlefields since the opening days of the conflict. They continued to launch regular and largely unhindered bombing raids on those cities and battlefields. Each of Chiang Kai-shek's provisional capitals routinely experienced the sound of Japanese aircraft engines and the concussions of Japanese bombs.

In 1940, the air force of the IJN began deploying the remarkable Mitsubishi A6M "Zero," which proved itself as the best fighter aircraft in the Far East and a warplane unmatched by anything in the Chinese arsenal. The Zero would have been a game changer had the game in China's skies not already been going Japan's way, but it certainly added weight to an already unstoppable winning streak.

There were occasional moments of Chinese success. On April 29, 1938—Hirohito's birthday—the Japanese had launched a major air attack on Hankou. Chennault divided his small defensive force, with one contingent engaging the escorting Japanese fighters in a dogfight aimed at compelling them to use up their fuel, while another attacked the unprotected bombers as they left the battle. The Japanese themselves reported losing more than thirty aircraft, virtually the entire strike force. Writing in the May 1939 issue of *Flying* magazine, J. Barton Underwood discusses the battle, noting that of the sixty-seven fighter pilots flying for Chiang Kai-shek that day, forty were Russians.

Chennault thought back to his days in the US Army Air Corps. He missed the quality of the equipment, and that of the infrastructure for both maintenance and training that he had taken for granted. He wished that he could somehow transfer this to Kunming and use it against the Japanese. He was already imagining a "foreign legion" of American pilots and aircraft flying against the Japanese.

Chennault was frustrated by both logistical and organizational issues, and by the lack of a substantial American response to the plight of the Chinese. Both he and Stilwell agreed on this one thing, and they were both outspoken in their belief that the United States must somehow take an active role in saving China from the Japanese—but at home, despite sympathy for the plight of the Chinese, especially after the Rape of Nanking, there was no stomach for involvement in a foreign war. In December 1937, after the fatal sinking by Japanese aircraft of the US Navy river gunboat USS *Panay* on the Yangtze River, there was talk, both in the United States and China, of an armed response, but after a Japanese apology, the crisis atmosphere evaporated.

As Chennault described it in his memoirs, "in the fat peacetime years it was as unpopular to discuss the realities of the Pacific . . . Japan had been chewing away at North China for four years, but nobody who counted thought it was any of our business."

In September 1939, when Germany invaded Poland and Europe went to war, the United States remained staunchly neutral, although Congress, through the Neutrality Act of 1939, did amend a ban on sales of arms to nations at war in an effort to aid Britain and France. In 1940, when France fell to Hitler's legions and Britain was locked in a death struggle with German bombers in the skies over London, empathy in the United States was aligned with the British, and public opinion began to drift. Americans still favored neutrality, but the isolationists, who insisted upon neutrality at all costs, grew increasingly isolated by a growing number who favored doing *something* to aid the beleaguered

Britons. The plight of the Chinese remained on the back burner, but the changes to the Neutrality Act would also apply to them.

Even before the 1940 presidential election, Franklin Roosevelt was already distancing himself from the isolationist movement. Early in the year, he had been very outspoken in calling for an American arms buildup, especially with unprecedented numbers of new combat aircraft, and in June he had fired his isolationist secretary of war, Henry Hines Woodring, and replaced him with Henry Louis Stimson—a Republican who had previously served William Howard Taft as secretary of war and Herbert Hoover as secretary of state.

Indeed, the Chinese, as well as Britain and France, could take comfort in a letter that Stimson had written to the *New York Times* in October 1937 in the wake of the Japanese invasion in which he had said "in America, occupying the most safe and defensible position in the world, there has been no excuse except faulty reasoning for the wave of ostrich-like isolationism which has swept over us and by its erroneous form of neutrality legislation has threatened to bring upon us in the future the very dangers of war which we now are seeking to avoid."

McGeorge Bundy, who edited Stimson's memoirs and who was himself a future counselor to Presidents Kennedy and Johnson, wrote that "Granting that American military action in Asia was probably 'impossible' and certainly 'abhorrent to our people,' and insisting, as he always had and would, that the final destiny of China must depend on China herself, [Stimson] nevertheless argued that the United States was not bound to 'a passive and shameful acquiescence in the wrong that is now being done.'"

By 1938, another cabinet secretary was at work facilitating aid to the British. A financier by trade, Secretary of the Treasury Henry Morgenthau Jr. had helped arrange the financing for Roosevelt's New Deal social programs in the 1930s, and he was playing a lead role in doing the same for the export of armaments, especially aircraft, from the neutral United States to declared belligerents in World War II, especially the United Kingdom and France. As such, he was much more heavily involved in shaping foreign policy than most treasury secretaries.

In 1938 and 1939, when the British and the French had come to the United States to buy arms, Morgenthau had facilitated their shopping. By the waning days of 1940, with France defeated, and the United Kingdom running out of money, they needed Morgenthau's skills as a dealmaker to thread the difficult diplomatic needle between neutrality and favoritism and facilitate the necessary loans through the Import-Export Bank, the federal government's export credit agency.

The British had found a friend in the staunchly anti-Nazi Morgenthau. Indeed, he was so zealous in his efforts to get warplanes to the British that he had incurred the wrath of Air Corps chief General Henry Harley "Hap" Arnold, who was angry that airplanes he felt were necessary for *his* service were going to the RAF.

With the 1940 election behind him, Roosevelt became increasingly proactive in his advocacy of matériel support for the countries standing up to Germany and Japan. He operated under the theory that if Britain and China could be aided in their current war efforts, then the United States could postpone a direct involvement in World War II that many considered inevitable but that the isolationists wanted to avoid at all costs.

On December 29, the president made his famous "Arsenal of Democracy" speech in which he cast American industry in the role of arms supplier to those opposing the Axis. He and his staff, especially Harry Hopkins, his principal adviser and troubleshooter, began work on the program that became the Lend-Lease Act. Passed by Congress and signed by Roosevelt in March 1941, it was crafted specifically to aid the United Kingdom, which was carrying on the war against Germany alone—while running out of money to continue buying war matériel on a cash-and-carry basis. It was Roosevelt's idea that the United States could "sell, transfer title to, exchange, lease, lend, or otherwise dispose of" weapons and matériel to any government whose defense the president deemed vital to the defense of the United States. The way it would work was the US government would purchase weapons from manufacturers and then deliver them to the United Kingdom. China was not originally envisioned as a Lend-Lease recipient, but was added to the program not long after it was enacted.

History remembers Roosevelt as an ardent champion of the British as a bulwark of democracy against the tyranny of Nazi Germany, but his support of China in a similar role versus Japan, which grew exponentially during 1941, is often overlooked. Indeed, when he met the president in Washington in December for the Arcadia Conference, their first conclave after the United States entered the war, Winston Churchill was startled by the extent of Roosevelt's empathy, and even a deep admiration, for China and for Chiang Kai-shek.

"If I can epitomize in one word the lesson I learned in the United States, it was 'China,'" Churchill wrote in the immediate aftermath of the conference.

In *Hinge of Fate*, the fourth volume of his history of World War II, Churchill recalled that "at Washington I had found the extraordinary significance of China in American minds, even at the top, strangely out of proportion. I was conscious of a standard of values which accorded China almost an equal fighting power with the British Empire, and rated the Chinese armies as a factor to be mentioned in the same breath as the armies of Russia. I told the President how much I felt American opinion overestimated the contribution which China could make to the general war. He differed strongly. There were five hundred million people in China. What would happen if this enormous population developed in the same way as Japan had done in the last century and got hold of modern weapons?"

Churchill replied that he was speaking of the present war, "which was quite enough to go on with for the time being. I said I would of course always be helpful and polite to the Chinese, whom I admired and liked as a race and pitied for their endless misgovernment, but that he must not expect me to adopt what I felt was a wholly unreal standard of values."

Roosevelt had already made up his mind about how China fit into the world, presciently viewing it as the Zhongguo, the Central Kingdom it once had been, and which it would realize its potential to be again, though many years farther in the future than Roosevelt imagined. The president was aware, certainly more so than Churchill, that the era of the great Eurocentric empires was coming to an end—sooner rather than later—and that China's future was that of a great power to be reckoned with. He was determined to treat it as such.

In the fall of 1940, Roosevelt had sent Thomas Corcoran, one of his most effective troubleshooters, on a secret mission to China to assess the situation. The man whom Roosevelt had affectionately nicknamed "Tommy the Cork," Corcoran was a Harvard Law graduate who had joined the Roosevelt administration in 1932 and had made himself indispensable as the key strategist of the New Deal and as the president's man behind the scenes in the smoke-filled rooms on Capitol Hill and everywhere else across Washington where deals were done.

Because of his Irish heritage, Corcoran was cool on the idea of aid to the United Kingdom—a fact that frequently brought him into conflict with Morgenthau—but he was enthusiastic about helping the Chinese. Tommy Corcoran agreed with Roosevelt that the United States should work behind the scenes to aid China, even if it might push the borderline of a violation of American neutrality and anger Japan.

"American prestige was never higher in China than during the months before Pearl Harbor," Chennault wrote in his memoirs, underscoring the prevailing mood at the time. "The generally favorable American press convinced Chinese leaders and masses alike that the

United States was sympathetic to their struggle for independence against the twin imperialisms of Europe and Asia. Increasing personal attention to Asiatic problems by President Franklin D. Roosevelt added concrete assistance to this sentimental support."

Late in 1940, as the desperate, cash-strapped British were heavily lobbying the Roosevelt administration for credit and aid to support their efforts against Hitler, Chiang Kai-shek sent his brother-in-law T. V. Soong to Washington, DC, as his personal representative to do the same, and to lobby for China's share of the "concrete assistance" of which Chennault wrote.

Soong arrived in the United States at a good time. At the end of September 1940, only six weeks before the US presidential election, Japan had joined Fascist Italy and Nazi Germany in the Rome-Berlin-Tokyo Tripartite Axis, which was clearly a gift to Soong because it placed Japan and Germany on the same side as American public opinion against Germany was hardening.

Well received in Washington, the articulate and erudite Soong lost little time in making himself well connected. The Harvard-educated emissary courted congressmen, cabinet secretaries, and dealmakers. As a businessman himself, he spoke the language of the industrialists from key industries with whom he crossed paths in his lobbying expeditions.

One by one, the newcomer from Shanghai worked his way through the roster of New Deal insiders, losing little time connecting with the right people. He met with Henry Morgenthau, and he reconnected with an old contact whom he had known in China. David Corcoran, who ran the international operations of Sterling Drug and had previously been with the Japanese office of General Motors, introduced Soong to his brother Tommy, who was at that very moment in the process of reinforcing Roosevelt's enthusiastic predisposition toward aid for China.

As Morgenthau was Britain's best friend in Washington, T. V. Soong found a friend in the increasingly anti-Japanese Tommy Corcoran, who operated with the personal blessing of the president. Indeed, it was with that blessing and the president's active encouragement that Soong and Corcoran proceeded to set up a new shell company, China Defense Supplies, Incorporated, as a mechanism for funneling money into the defense of China, and to process the acquisitions made possible by the cash-and-carry financing that Morgenthau was facilitating for Britain and now for China.

Tommy Corcoran, who had resigned from the federal government payroll to avoid the appearance of a conflict of interest, took only a "consulting" role as outside legal counsel to the new company. David, however, took a leave of absence from Sterling to become the president of the new firm. To add a patina of legitimacy to the venture, they invited Frederic Adrian Delano, the president's seventy-eight-year-old uncle, to act as cochairman along with Soong. Though long in the tooth, the Hong Kong–born Delano had extensive business experience, both in commercial trade with China and as the president of several American railroads. Indeed, much of the Delano family fortune had been made in the China trade, and he knew the lay of the land in the Far East business world as well as any American in Washington.

To function as the executive secretary of China Defense Supplies, Soong, Delano, and the Corcorans hired Boston attorney Whiting "Whitey" Willauer. A graduate of Princeton University and Harvard Law who had also served in the Justice Department, Willauer was the kind of Washington insider who could make things happen. His role in major covert operations, from prewar China to postwar Latin America, was only just beginning.

As China Defense Supplies was taking shape at offices in a redbrick building on V Street Northwest, Chiang Kai-shek sent his leading aviation advisers, P. T. Mao and Claire Chennault, to join Soong in Washington.

"You must go to the United States immediately," Chiang told Chennault in October 1940. "Work out the plans for whatever you need. Do what you can to get American planes and pilots."

At the time, with all the planes that American industry could produce for export—and then some—going to the United Kingdom, the former was a long shot. As for American pilots, this seemed even more improbable. Since 1937, the State Department had been urging Americans to *leave* China.

"The few American eyes focused abroad were centered on Europe where England was fighting for survival," Chennault wrote in his memoirs. "The Orient was completely forgotten. A sluggishly rising tide of public opinion was beginning to flow for aid to England. Hundreds of Americans were slipping across the Canadian border to join the RCAF and fight in Europe, but the idea of American volunteers in China seemed fantastic. Virtually everybody to whom I broached the subject told me, with varying degrees of courtesy, that I was insane."

Chennault had come to Washington with a concrete plan that went beyond just American planes and pilots. Back at the Air Corps Tactical School a few years before, he had formulated his doctrine of detection, interception, destruction. While planes and pilots were elements of the latter two, detection involved an elaborate early warning network he was already planning for the areas around key locations such as Chongqing and Kunming. He intended to use the advantages of interior lines of communication, combined with a radar and ground spotter warning network, just as the British had used during the Battle of Britain, to allow him to use his fighter aircraft to their maximum advantage.

When it came to these aircraft, Chennault's eagerness to upgrade the quality of the Chinese Air Force was considered not so much madness as naïveté, given that every aircraft that rolled off American assembly lines was spoken for—or *fought over*, given that the American armed forces were at odds with Morgenthau, who wanted more and more aircraft for Britain. Whether crazy or naïve, T. V. Soong asked the Roosevelt administration for five hundred aircraft, to which Henry Morgenthau rolled his eyes. John Morton Blum, quoting Morgenthau's diaries, wrote that this was "like asking for 500 stars." Instead, Chennault would have to settle for one hundred. One can imagine what Morgenthau would have offered if Soong had originally asked for a hundred.

When Chennault and Mao went shopping, Soong told them to "buy what you need and send me the bills." Armed with the "credit card" supplied to Soong by Corcoran with Roosevelt's blessing, Chennault and Mao headed off to Buffalo to visit a purveyor of warplanes well known in the Chinese market: Curtiss-Wright.

At the time, the best Curtiss warplane in China was the Model 75 Hawk, the P-36 analogue of which Bill Pawley had assembled a handful at his new CAMCO factory in Lei Yun. In Buffalo, however, the Model 75 had long since been eclipsed by the Model 81 Warhawk, a faster, more powerful fighter aircraft with a water-cooled Allison engine that the US Army Air Corps was acquiring under the series designation P-40. Meanwhile, through the end of 1940, 558 of these aircraft had also been delivered to Britain's Royal Air Force, where they operated under the name Tomahawk.

By the time the two men from China reached Buffalo, the incrementally evolving Warhawk/Tomahawk series had reached the point where the Model 81 series A2 (H81-A2) Tomahawk IIA was in production for the RAF, and a similar aircraft was being delivered to the US Army Air Corps as the P-40B. With its water-cooled engine, which Chennault felt was more vulnerable than an air-cooled engine, the Warhawk/Tomahawk family of aircraft was not exactly what Chennault would have liked—but it was significantly better than what he had in China, so he decided to spend T. V. Soong's money and buy a hundred of them.

"The P-40B was not an ideal airplane for the purpose required, but it was better than nothing and the only thing we could get at the time," Chennault complained, resigning himself to a fait accompli.

The only problem now was that there were no Model 81s of *any* variant available. Everything on the six Buffalo assembly lines at the time was earmarked to become a British Tomahawk.

With the encouragement of Corcoran, and even that of Morgenthau, Curtiss-Wright proposed a solution. If the British would permit the reassignment of a hundred of their Model 81s to China, the company would expand production and give them first priority on a like number of a more advanced variant (H81-B) that was equivalent to the US Army's P-40C. The British accepted the "Curtiss swap"—as it was called—in January 1941, pleased to have their order upgraded and, because of the opening of a new production line, not long delayed.

Chennault, meanwhile, was not pleased with accepting hand-me-down aircraft. "Most of the P-40Bs had already been fitted with British .303-caliber wing machine guns instead of American .30-caliber guns," he complained. "The problem of getting odd-size ammunition for these guns was one of our worst headaches. . . . All of the planes were supposed to be fitted with British VHF radio equipment [after they reached] England, so we got them without any radios. Unable to buy military radio equipment, China Defense Supplies, Incorporated, had to purchase ordinary commercial sport-plane radios, adding another hazard to our combat operations."

However, aircraft that were available almost immediately were superior to aircraft available at an unspecified future time, if at all. For the most part, the P-40s had already been manufactured and were receiving the last finishing touches before being disassembled and crated for shipment to the United Kingdom. They were on the docks at the Port of New York in February, and all that was left was to reroute the destination of the shipment to Rangoon (now Yangon), the capital and major port in the British colony of Burma (now alternately known also as Myanmar).

This fit into Chennault's schedule of having his air force in Kunming by early spring, where he could undertake a training program and begin air defense operations over Chongqing early in the summer.

However, there was one more catch that threatened to sink the whole deal. Though most of the transaction had occurred without him, Bill Pawley arrived on the scene as the Tomahawks were being crated and insisted on his usual 10 percent commission on Curtiss-Wright sales to China, which would have netted him, in Chennault's calculation, $450,000 (more than $7 million in today's dollars).

"Curtiss Wright refused to pay Pawley, alleging he had nothing to do with the sale," Chennault recalled. "Months were lost in futile negotiations until there was acute danger that the Chinese would lose the planes. Rather than pay Pawley, Curtiss Wright was ready to sell them back to the RAF. Secretary Morgenthau called a conference on April 1, 1941, for a showdown. The fight lasted all day. The Chinese were so desperate for the planes they offered to pay Pawley out of Chinese funds. . . . Morgenthau threatened to take over the Curtiss contract as a war emergency, but Pawley didn't scare. Finally the Chinese suggested a compromise whereby Pawley would be paid $250,000."

Pawley was also promised the contract to reassemble and maintain the P-40s at his CAMCO factory at Lei Yun on the Burma-China border. Of course, it was probably the only facility in or near China that could have handled the work.

The delay over the dickering had worked to Pawley's advantage, but it had cost Chennault valuable time.

EIGHT

American Volunteers
for China Skies

P ersonnel proved a tougher nut to crack," Chennault recalled of his need for qualified pilots to fly the P-40s that Soong had just acquired for him, and ground crewmen to maintain them.

In October 1940, when Chiang Kai-shek had ordered him back to the United States to "do what you can to get American planes and pilots," Chennault had already been thinking long and hard about a "foreign legion" of American pilots flying for China. He had watched the Soviets send complete Red Air Force squadrons into China, and he wanted to see the Americans doing the same. He imagined a unit comprised of volunteer American pilots akin those who flew in combat with the French Lafayette Escadrille in World War I, and those who were at that moment flying with the Eagle Squadrons of the RAF.

It was an idea more easily imagined than realized.

When he reached the United States, Chennault was hard pressed to find anyone in the US Army Air Corps—or anywhere else in the US Army—who considered such a scheme anything but preposterous.

However, fresh in the memory of everyone involved in considering Chennault's foreign legion scheme, was the number of international soldiers of fortune—including Americans—who had gone overseas to fight for one side or the other in the Spanish Civil War. Between 1936 and 1939, as General Francisco Franco's Nationalists fought, and eventually succeeded in overthrowing, the elected Republican government of Spain, at least thirty thousand foreigners from around the world, including those from the officially neutral United States, had enlisted in the International Brigades to aid the Republicans. On the other side, there were an even larger number of "volunteers" from Italy and Germany.

Along with these large numbers on the ground, both Germany, siding with the Nationalists, and the Soviet Union, who opposed them on the Republican side, sent sizable air forces. The Luftwaffe pilots of the Condor Legion, equipped with the latest German equipment, gave Franco's forces air superiority over the battlefield, while the Spanish Republican Air Force, like the Chinese Air Force, benefited from entire squadrons of Soviet planes and crews. There were also sizable numbers of French and American pilots. Some of the Americans flew with Soviet squadrons, but a half dozen American pilots formed a unit they called the "Yankee Squadron," under Soviet command.

During the Spanish Civil War, the Roosevelt administration had sympathized with the Republicans because they were standing up to forces backed by Hitler and Mussolini, but he had abided by a narrow interpretation of existing neutrality laws and never actively supported them.

A key difference with China was that Roosevelt now actively promoted covert intervention, even if it was quasi-legal. Recognition of a missed opportunity in Spain no doubt fueled the president's desire to actively aid China in 1941.

In comparing the Spanish Civil War experience with Chennault's call for volunteers, historian Herbert Weaver wrote that "the precedent in Spain might be dismissed as of doubtful validity, but to stand on the niceties of international law only to permit China to fall a complete victim of Japanese aggression was also a disturbing suggestion. The clinching argument was the inescapable necessity to provide aerial protection for Burma Road during the time needed for rehabilitation of the Chinese Air Force."

Though the civilians in the government were leaning one way, the American military leadership was opposed, if only because they did not want to see their equipment and manpower, still in short supply, siphoned off to serve under a foreign flag.

"The military were violently opposed to the whole idea of American volunteers in China," Chennault recalled, recognizing that his scheme was a clear violation of American neutrality. "I tried to convince them of the large return in tactics, intelligence, and equipment evaluation they would get from a small investment in personnel. Many countries had tested their air strength in combat through the device of volunteers under a foreign flag—the Russians in China and Spain; the Germans and Italians in Spain—but nobody in the Navy and Munitions buildings [the precursors to the Pentagon, which opened in 1943] would buy it."

US Army Air Corps chief General Hap Arnold told Chennault that he "couldn't spare a single staff officer then without endangering the Air Corps expansion program and that he would oppose vigorously any diversion of Air Corps strength to any other country." Indeed, he had frankly told Roosevelt the same thing with regard to the diversion to Britain of American aircraft, especially heavy bombers, which Arnold needed for the Air Corps.

However, Franklin Roosevelt, the stalwart champion of the United Kingdom's war effort, was now a zealous convert to being the same for China. To bolster Chiang Kai-shek's Nationalist government as a front-line defense against Japan's territorial ambitions was seen by the man in the White House as a worthy enterprise.

Having sent Tommy Corcoran to China in the fall of 1940, he sent his White House staff economist, Lauchlin Bernard Currie, on a clandestine fact-finding mission to China early in 1941. Born in Canada, Currie was a graduate of the London School of Economics and had served as an adviser to Henry Morgenthau during the 1930s. Currie returned to the United States as the Lend-Lease Act was being enacted, and he joined Corcoran in urging Roosevelt to include China as a beneficiary. In turn, Currie was named as the Lend-Lease administrator for China.

While the Lend-Lease mechanism would greatly improve the ability of Soong and Chennault to acquire hardware for the Chiang Kai-shek Air Force, it did nothing to provide for the American crews that Chennault so anxiously sought. The lack of support from American military leadership was only one of the problems that made personnel "a tougher nut to crack" for Chennault.

There was a whole Pandora's box of potential legal issues involved in American military pilots and maintenance personnel serving in the armed forces of a foreign state. Indeed, it would be illegal for active duty personnel to do so—most of the men in the Eagle Squadrons had never been pilots in the US armed forces—and even as civilians they would potentially be subject to loss of nationality if they swore an oath of allegiance to the armed forces of a foreign state.

However, Roosevelt wasn't one to be daunted by such tricky nuances. When the president got it in his mind that something was a good idea, he simply made it happen—regardless of whether he played by the book. When he wanted to essentially *give* arms to the British, he crafted Lend-Lease and nudged Congress to make it legal. Later, when Roosevelt became frustrated with the gross inefficiencies of the US military intelligence agencies, he would simply bypass the Army and the Navy and ask William J. "Wild Bill" Donovan to create the all-new Office of Strategic Services from scratch.

As Donovan would become his agent in the realization of Roosevelt's vision of the OSS, he had readily embraced Chennault's ideas of an aerial foreign legion as though they were his own. Chennault had needed airplanes, and strings were pulled. Chennault needed pilots, and Roosevelt made it happen. The American Volunteer Group (AVG) of the Chinese Air Force materialized into a reality, and the commander in chief created the mechanism by which pilots could be plucked from the US armed forces to serve with it.

"It took direct personal intervention from President Roosevelt to pry the pilots and ground crews from the Army and Navy," Chennault wrote in his memoirs. "On April 15, 1941, an unpublicized executive order went out under his signature, authorizing reserve officers and enlisted men to resign from the Army Air Corps, Naval and Marine Air Services for the purpose of joining the American Volunteer Group in China."

It was not so much an "unpublicized" as it was an "*unpublished*" executive order. It never appeared in the *Federal Register*. The latter lists the executive orders of 1941, numbered consecutively from 8625 through 9005, but the order cited by Chennault is not among them. In his book *Roosevelt's Secret War*, Joseph Persico says simply that the president "unhesitatingly approved" the plan. In fact, the approval was of dubious legality, a fact that disturbed Morgenthau. Others, from Hap Arnold to Henry Stimson, knew about it, but chose not to mention it in their memoirs.

However it was executed administratively, it was done on the sly— Chennault called it "strict secrecy"—with only a relatively few insiders having been briefed on the full scope of the project. Among them, of course, was Bill Pawley, who had inserted himself into the acquisition of the P-40s at Curtiss-Wright. As Chennault explained in his memoirs,

"Pawley suggested to Dr. Soong that CAMCO be used as a blind to hire personnel. A confidential contract was drawn up between CAMCO and China Defense Supplies, Incorporated, in which CAMCO agreed to handle all AVG financial matters at cost and provide complete maintenance and repair for our damaged aircraft at [Lei Yun] factory."

He may have almost derailed the P-40 sale, but Pawley was now making up for this by greasing the rails for Chennault's AVG. In keeping with the covert theme, fighter squadrons were called "advanced training units," and the fighter aircraft themselves were referred to as "advanced trainers."

The pilots would be hired as CAMCO "employees," with each man signing a one-year contract effective July 4, 1941 (the Independence Day date was for patriotic reasons). The contract called for the men to receive monthly salaries—ranging from $250 for ground crewmen to $750 for flight leaders—plus expenses routed through a Chinese bank account. The latter sum, for pilots hired as flight leaders, is worth about $12,000 in current dollars and was the equivalent to the price of a new car.

Reportedly, their resignations from the US armed services were filed along with an agreement of reinstatement without loss of precedence if the United States declared war. It was widely believed, and mentioned by Greg Boyington in his memoirs, that the resignations of those who had resigned from regular—as opposed to reserve—commissions were under lock and key and would simply be torn up when the man returned to seamlessly rejoin his branch of service.

As Chennault explained, "There was no mention in the contract of a $500 bonus for every Japanese plane destroyed. Volunteers were told simply that there was a rumor that the Chinese government would pay $500 for each confirmed Jap plane. They could take the rumor for what it was worth. It turned out to be worth exactly $500 per plane."

This, in effect, turned the former military officers into a cadre of bounty hunters. Such had been the case in Spain, where the Spanish Republican government had lured American fighter pilots with the ultimately empty promise—actually written into the contract—of $1,000 for every enemy aircraft shot down. Unlike the Spanish Republicans, Chiang Kai-shek's government actually *made* the bonus payments.

Technically, the AVG was to have been designated as the 1st American Volunteer Group, as Chennault was ambitiously planning for a 2nd American Volunteer Group. It would have been a bomber unit equipped with Lockheed Hudson and Douglas DB-7 twin-engine light bombers like those being produced in Southern California for the British, but which were to have been diverted to China. A 3rd American Volunteer Group, another P-40 unit, was also planned, but neither the 2nd nor 3rd was ready for deployment when the United States entered World War II later in 1941.

Already by June of that year, when the Air Corps formally became the autonomous US Army Air Forces (USAAF), the momentum to build up that force had reached a tempo that mitigated against the diversion of further resources to projects such as the AVG. Chennault had barely slipped under the wire, but he still had the president's enthusiasm on his side.

———————

When Roosevelt briefed top military brass on the fait accompli of the AVG scheme, they were naturally displeased with the idea of losing experienced pilots, but they *nevertheless* cooperated with the plan that authorized the recruitment of 100 pilots and 150 support personnel from the armed services. Secretary of the Navy Frank Knox and Air Corps chief Hap Arnold had both signed off on the program and opened doors for Chennault's recruiting team to have access to the air bases throughout the United States, "authorizing bearers of certain letters freedom of the post, including permission to talk with all personnel."

To head his cadre of "authorized bearers" Chennault picked a retired Air Corps pilot named Richard Aldworth. He was reputed to have flown with the Lafayette Escadrille during the early part of World War I, but there were contradictory accounts that he had not. For health reasons, Aldworth was not immediately available, so much of the recruitment task fell to other men whom Chennault had enlisted to work with him.

Chennault sent Rutledge Irvine, a retired US Navy lieutenant commander, to call on pilots at Navy and Marine Corps facilities. To work the Air Corps fields, he picked Skip Adair, who had just returned to the United States from his stint as chief instructor pilot at Yunnanyi. Adair would accompany Chennault when he returned to China, and function as the executive officer of the AVG.

It would be an understatement to say that base commanders and squadron commanders were irritated and suspicious when Irvine and Adair walked into their respective domains to convince some of the best potential combat pilots in the American armed forces to *quit their jobs.*

At North Island in San Diego Bay, Lieutenant Commander Clarence Wade McClusky, commander of Fighting Squadron 6 (VF-6), aboard the USS *Enterprise,* heard the knock of Rutledge Irvine at his door. He had been with the squadron since 1940, but in April 1941 he had only just assumed command. A year later, commanding the entire *Enterprise* air group, he was credited by Admiral Chester Nimitz with having "decided the fate of our carrier task force and our forces at [the Battle of] Midway," but that was still in the future. When Irvine crossed his threshold, McClusky was new on the job and startled with this strange request that carried the endorsement of Secretary of the Navy Frank Knox—and that of the president of the United States.

"President Roosevelt is intent on furnishing some kind of military assistance to China so that she can survive," Irvine explained when McClusky had reluctantly summoned his pilots into his office. "I am here to offer all pilots of VF-6 who are reserve officers the opportunity to resign from your service and join a volunteer organization in the Far East to defend the Burma Road against Japanese bombing attacks."

Irvine went on to tell them about China's precarious strategic situation and outlined the desperate need for the air defense of Chinese cities. Finally, he presented the salary and bonus details that had been approved for any pilot joining CAMCO, and then he handed out the application forms.

James Howell Howard was among those whom McClusky invited into his office to hear what the retired naval aviator had to say. He reminded Irvine that "there was a freeze on all reservists whose term of duty was up. In fact, reservists and National Guard units were being recalled to active duty."

Irvine assured him that since the program had been authorized by Roosevelt, it "would override any legal curb to prevent resignations."

A number of pilots thought that the scheme sounded foolhardy. Others were reluctant to risk their lives in China's war. Recalling his personal connections to China, Howard saw things differently.

"The chance of returning to my boyhood home in China, while defending the interests of America at the same time, was the opportunity of a lifetime," he recalled in his memoirs. "I couldn't have been in a better position at a better time. The nostalgia of going to China would be a strong incentive, but the overpowering reason was my yearning for adventure and action."

He also recalled that opportunities for advancement in pay grade within the US Navy, especially for people who were not Annapolis grads, was painfully slow. Like many who decided to sign up, the pay sounded good. For Ensign Bob Prescott, who was an instructor pilot at NAS Pensacola when Irvine came on base, the AVG sounded like an adventure.

Tex Hill was a bomber pilot when Rutledge Irvine came calling, flying SB2U Vindicators with VS-41 aboard the USS *Ranger* in the North Atlantic. When the ship came into port in Norfolk, Hill and his friend Ed Rector were among those whom their operations officer picked to meet the mystery man. As he had so often that spring, Irvine laid out the program in full detail.

Irvine patiently related the importance of the Burma Road as China's lifeline to the outside world, and China's desperate need for air defense. When Hill wondered out loud where Burma actually was, Rector, a better student of geography, chided him for his query.

"How is this deal supposed to happen?" Hill asked. "We're not at war with Japan yet or anything."

Irvine replied that this was true, but that the pilots who joined his volunteer organization would resign their commissions and go to work for CAMCO as civilians.

It was Ed Rector who said the word "mercenaries" out loud, though he softened that inconvenient term by adding that it "sounds rather exciting, doesn't it?"

Rector took an application form, and so did Hill. Like Jim Howard, he had been born in the Far East, and he had been looking for ways to be reassigned to the region. He had even requested a transfer to sea duty on the USS *Houston*, the heavy cruiser that was the flagship of the US Navy's Asiatic Fleet. Irvine had now given him a possible route back to a part of his life of which he had a great deal of curiosity, if no memory.

G reg Boyington was not contacted by one of Richard Aldworth's recruiters. He took matters into his own hands and tracked him down. Both Irvine and Adair had been stressing the confidential nature of the AVG program, but as about three hundred men at air bases throughout the country were being interviewed over the course of several months, the word had gotten around.

Boyington, who was by now a Marine Corps flight instructor at Pensacola, felt that his six years of experience in fighter aircraft made him a good candidate. In his memoirs, he did not mention specifically to whom he had spoken, only that he was a "retired Air Corps captain," who was in Pensacola interviewing selected pilots. By his description, which included a reference to the captain's World War I experience, it may be concluded that it was probably Aldworth and not one of his subordinates. He was apparently impressed with Boyington, and he suggested that he might qualify as a flight leader within the AVG.

The admiration may have been mutual, though Boyington perhaps had his tongue in his cheek when he wrote that "bravery above and beyond the call of duty was dripping all over his suite in the San Carlos Hotel there at Pensacola."

The hard-boiled flight instructor went on to say that "the captain tried to impress me with the high character of the men who were to be over me and under me. They were people who drank like gentlemen and paid their gambling debts. . . . Maybe he wanted them all for this dream group but had to settle for less. I don't know. But one thing for certain, I didn't tell him that he was hiring an officer who had a fatal gap between his income and accounts payable. . . . Nor did I tell him that I was a whiz at a cocktail party. All this spelled but one thing, I would be passed over for the rank of captain in the USMC, as surely as I was sitting there in the San Carlos. I had to convince the captain—and I did."

By his own recollection, Greg Boyington's resignation was processed within four days. Perhaps it was because only a handful of Marines were recruited. With other pilots, the process took weeks. Jim Howard was with the *Enterprise* operating out of Bremerton, Washington, on June 12 when he finally learned that his application had been approved and that he had the authorization to resign from the US Navy. Tex Hill got the word in the Atlantic Ocean bound for the Azores. For the ongoing U-boat patrols, VS-41 had just been transferred from the *Ranger* to the USS *Yorktown*, which had recently been reassigned from the Pacific to the Atlantic Fleet.

———————

As with Boyington, R. T. Smith heard about the AVG on the street before he ever met a recruiter—but while Boyington learned of the program on the rumor mill, Smith read about it in *Time* magazine!

The high level of secrecy that was supposed to have cloaked the project had begun to fray from the very start. Perhaps this was due to deliberate leaks somewhere along the line, or perhaps to the diligence of a journalist, left anonymous by the fact that *Time* did not publish bylines in those days. Of course, the United States was not yet at war, and the AVG was a civilian, not a military, program, so military security would not, theoretically, have applied. Perhaps the wily Roosevelt wanted the world to know that he was doing something dramatic to help China without saying so officially and he let something slip.

In any case, the June 23 issue of the magazine carried a story that told of "crack US Army Air Corps pilots" who had been given permission to resign to enlist in the Chinese Air Force to help protect the Burma Road from the Japanese. The article stated that "tall, bronzed American airmen" had already been "quietly slipping away" from American ports. No mention was made of US Navy or Marine Corps pilots, but the article did report that a hundred Curtiss P-40 aircraft had been delivered to Burma. The latter was *almost* true. One of the hundred had been lost when a crane dropped it into New York Harbor during loading.

R. T. Smith, still a flight instructor at Randolph Field near San Antonio, was having a drink in the living room at the bachelor officers' quarters and flipping through the magazine when he first learned of fellow military pilots resigning to fly against the Japanese.

"The full meaning of the story had hit me like an electric shock," he recalled in his memoirs. "I slammed the magazine down on the coffee table, spilling my highball in the process, and leaped up from the sofa."

Excitedly, he shared the article with fellow instructor Paul Greene, telling him "seriously, here's the answer to our prayers. You gotta read this!"

Both men had been griping that they were tired of the monotony of the Training Command and yearning for action in that way that young men in their early twenties so often do. Nevertheless, while Smith was ecstatic, Greene was circumspect, reminding his friend that this adventure could be an easy way to get killed.

Nevertheless, Smith set about trying to find out whom to contact to sign up to be one of the "crack US Army Air Corps pilots" who were going to get to take a crack at the Japanese. His first stop was the Officers' Club, where the current of rumor flowed as easily as the inexpensive bourbon. He asked around and found a man who said he knew a man who knew a man who knew something of substance of the rumor. By the end of the evening, Smith had a phone number in Washington, DC.

It was past midnight in the East when he and Greene phoned the number. The man whom they awoke from his slumber gave them the name of Claude Bryant Adair, to whom they promptly sent a telegram, detailing their experience and their interest in volunteering. Adair's reply was a terse invitation to meet him when he came to San Antonio on June 30.

When the three men met in Adair's room at the Gunter Hotel on the appointed date, he mixed them each a drink, told them to just call him "Skip," and then launched into his usual briefing about the plight of China and the reasons behind the formation of the AVG. He freshened their drinks, told them about Chennault, about Bill Pawley, and about how they would be civilians working for CAMCO. When he finished and asked them what they thought, Greene said "Put me in, coach," and Smith asked "What do we sign?"

However, the mood was dampened considerably when Adair asked them about their experience, and they had to admit that they spent their days flying trainers and that they had never flown a P-40. When he told them that the "Old Man," as he called Chennault, had mandated him to enlist only fighter pilots, they left Adair's suite in a state of devastation. Undaunted, they bounced back and went to see Adair unannounced the following day and proceeded to give him a full-court press. When it was over this time, Adair had their signed CAMCO contracts in his briefcase.

Not all those who asked for the coach to put him in was invited to sign a contract. On the face of it, Albert John "Ajax" Baumler of Bayonne, New Jersey, was the ideal candidate. He had earned his wings and his lieutenant's bars with the Air Corps in 1936, but had resigned his commission to fly with the Spanish Republican Air Force in the Spanish Civil War. Beginning in February 1937, he flew Polikarpov fighters with two separate Soviet-led squadrons, the Escuadrilla Kosakov and the 1st Escuadrilla de Moscas. In five months of combat, he scored confirmed victories against four Nationalist aircraft—three Italian Fiat CR.32s and a German He-51—while scoring a shared victory and a probable.

Baumler rejoined the Air Corps in 1938, but resigned again three years later, planning to join the American Volunteer Group. Given his recent air combat experience, especially among the others who had none, he was the kind of man whom Chennault was anxious to have. However, the State Department refused him a passport. It seemed that his having enlisted in a foreign military service in violation of the Neutrality Act prevailing in 1937 snagged him in an entanglement of Catch-22 red tape that would prevent him from defying American neutrality to fight for China. He joined the US Army Air Corps for a third time, but that was not to be the end of his story.

R obert Lee Scott Jr. was another man whose résumé made him appear ideal—at least on paper. To begin with, he was a West Point man, the cream of the crop among the growing officer corps within the USAAF. He had commanded the 78th Pursuit Squadron out of Albrook Field in the Panama Canal Zone, and he was currently an instructor pilot. However, there was an issue with his age. Scott had recently turned thirty-three, placing him well beyond the ideal that Chennault sought in his fighter jockeys. Then there was his status as part of the regular army, not the reserve, as was the case with the others "hired" by CAMCO for the AVG. Neither the War Department nor the State Department would allow the USAAF to cut him loose.

As he recalled, "the State Department sent me a rather curt letter reminding me that I was a member of the regular establishment and that by being so thoughtless as to offer my services to do aerial combat against the forces of a nation not a belligerent I had caused a division of our government considerable embarrassment. For the time being I hid my disappointment by flying day and night and attempting to lose myself in my job as a detachment commander in the Air Force expansion program."

———————

C harles Rankin Bond was no stranger to covert, off-the-book operations when he first talked to Skip Adair. While Bond was with the 2nd Bombardment Group at Langley Field, Virginia, he had met an officer named Curtis Emerson LeMay, who was the lead navigator for the 2nd's well-publicized long-range B-17 demonstration flights in the late 1930s.

Early in 1941, LeMay and Bond had been recruited to work with the Montreal-based Atlantic Ferry Organization, an unpublicized if not exactly "secret" outfit. The civilian forerunner to the RAF Ferry Command, it had been established in 1940 on behalf of the British Ministry of Aircraft Production to facilitate transfer of aircraft, ranging from Lockheed Hudsons to Consolidated B-24 Liberators from the United States to Britain. Known by its acronym "ATFERO," it was the brainchild of Morris W. Wilson, the Nova Scotia–born president of the Royal Bank of Canada, who had his picture on Canadian currency. Like the American Volunteer Group, ATFERO utilized American military pilots, though unlike the AVG, they did not have to resign their commissions. As LeMay later recounted, they only had to show up on the flight line or at ATFERO's headquarters in civilian clothes— which made it seem like a very cloak-and-dagger entity that sat lightly on the cusp of violating American neutrality.

In June 1941, Bond got a call from an old friend, Lieutenant Jacob "Jebbo" Brogger, who told him that if he still wanted to be a fighter pilot, and if he wanted to make some really good money, he should call

Skip Adair. Brogger had known Adair for some time and learned that he was recruiting fighter pilots to go to China to fly with a man named Claire Chennault. Bond had second thoughts, given that he had been a bomber pilot for nearly three years. Like Smith and Greene, he had no current fighter experience and had never flown a P-40.

"It did not take long for me to decide," Bond recalled in his memoirs of his decision to give it a try and phone Adair. "The lure of adventure in a foreign country on the other side of the world was exciting. More important, however, was the unique and ideal manner in which this opportunity served to satisfy my dreams: a chance to get back into fighters, a chance for combat experience which might help me secure a regular commission [rather than his current reserve commission], and a chance to earn fast money which would put me in a position to buy my parents a home."

Bond picked up the phone and called the number that Brogger had given him. Apparently he was able to pass muster with Adair during their phone interview. When they were finished, Adair gave him another phone number in Washington and told him "If you want to join the AVG, just call that number and leave your name and duty station."

The following day, he did as Adair had instructed, and within twenty-four hours, Bond had his answer. He was instructed to write a letter of resignation and await further instructions from CAMCO, his new employer.

NINE

Bounty Hunters and Farmers
Sail for China

W hen Claire Chennault walked into the imposing Mark
Hopkins Hotel on Nob Hill in San Francisco to meet the
American Volunteer Group pilot and ground crew re-
cruits for the first time, on July 7, 1941, he was painfully aware of it
being the fourth anniversary of the incident on the Marco Polo Bridge
that tipped the dominoes across China and led him to this moment.

"Nobody who saw that odd assortment of young men, looking
slightly ill at ease and uncertain in their new civilian clothes, could
have possibly imagined that in a few months they would be making
history," he wrote in his memoirs.

Jim Howard, who was among the men who gathered in San Francisco that week, recalled Chennault as "a crusty-looking man of average
height in his late forties."

Howard went on to say that "in the months to come, I would appreciate him for his one-man assault on what he despised and for his
unflagging support for what he firmly believed. He turned out to be a

man of convictions and integrity, and was filled with compassion for the underdog. In other words, he was fair, but no pushover."

Richard Aldworth was also present, and so too was Bill Pawley.

"Welcome to all of you who are about to embark on a mission to the other side of the world to defend American interests in that part of the globe," Aldworth told the men gathered in the crowded lobby of the Mark Hopkins. He introduced Pawley, who briefed them on what CAMCO was, what it did in China, and explained that they would be assembling the P-40s that the 123 volunteers gathered in the lobby would be flying, maintaining, or supporting in the field. He also added that an advance group of about 30 ground crewmen had sailed two weeks earlier aboard the SS *President Pierce* of the San Francisco American President Lines. These were the "tall, bronzed American airmen" whom *Time* magazine had reported to have been "quietly slipping away" from American ports in the previous weeks. Part of this group was Paul Frillman, a Lutheran minister and a former missionary to China, better known as "Padre," who was to be the chaplain of the AVG.

Howard noted that this was the largest of a half dozen AVG contingents that would be setting sail over the coming weeks, and that it included thirty-three pilots from all services, as well as a medical team of three doctors and a dentist, headed by a former Army doctor, Major Thomas C. "Doc" Gentry, who was to be the AVG's chief flight surgeon.

There were also two women on the medical team, nurses Jo Buckner Stewart and Emma Jane Foster. The daughter of a Pennsylvania Country doctor, Emma had been to China as an exchange student five years earlier. In a 2004 interview, she told Mike Barber of the *Seattle Post-Intelligencer* that "the most courageous thing I did wasn't in the war. It was when I left my home for the first time to go to China in the 1930s with people I never met before. . . . I was so scared and homesick for two days riding that train to the West Coast to get the boat. I wanted out of it, but my pride wouldn't let me. But after I got over it, I was never afraid again."

When someone asked Pawley when they would be getting their aircraft, he told him that crated aircraft had already reached Rangoon and that he had an assembly facility there.

"By the time you arrive in Burma your planes will be ready to fly," Pawley promised.

Howard recalled that someone asked Chennault for confirmation on a question that had already been asked and answered in interviews with recruiters, but that was on everyone's mind.

"Won't we lose our American citizenship if we fly against the Japanese at a time when we are not officially at war?"

Chennault replied that "the president has assured us that, as long as we fight for a country that professes democratic faith, your citizenship will remain intact. I might mention also that you will be officially part of the Chinese military so you won't be classified as a war criminal if you are captured. While this mission is considered secret, it won't be secret for long. I would like to remind you that the eyes of the world will be focused on this expedition, and its chances of success or failure depend entirely upon you. Therefore, it is imperative that all of us behave and act in such a discreet way, Americans will be proud of us."

Pawley then handed out the passports to his new CAMCO employees. These were issued in their real names, but on the line where each man's occupation was identified, nobody was accurately listed as a pilot or, perhaps more appropriately, by the title articulated earlier by Ed Rector, as a *mercenary*. Instead, they were bankers, clerks, musicians, or students. When he sailed with another group six weeks later, Greg Boyington was listed, with great irony, because nothing could have been farther from his persona, as a member of the clergy. Chennault still traveled under the passport identifying him as a farmer.

They each also received an envelope containing $100 in expense money, cash that would fuel numerous poker games over the coming weeks at sea.

The following day, Chennault caught the Pan American Airways Clipper bound for Hong Kong by way of Hawaii. He lamented the fact that the kerfuffle over Bill Pawley's commission had cost the program three valuable months, but at least the AVG project was finally on track.

Two days later, on July 10, the men set sail aboard the MS *Jagersfontein* of the Verenigde Nederlandse Scheepvaart Maatschappij (VNSM, or United Netherlands Navigation Company). It was a reminder both of the extensive Dutch maritime presence in the Pacific, and of the fact that the Netherlands—because of its sprawling colonial possession in the East Indies—had a crucial stake in the war that was looming in Southeast Asia. Their homeland may have been occupied by Hitler's legions a year earlier, but the people and troops in the Dutch East Indies were still very much allied with Britain and China and preparing to confront the feared and anticipated Japanese onslaught into their territory.

"Our departure was uncomfortably cold," Jim Howard recalled, noting the counterintuitive meteorological anomaly that always makes San Francisco colder in July than in November. "We were told to enjoy it since we would be wishing for this same cold weather in Burma. A loud blast from the ship's horn signaled to everyone within miles that the time for departure had arrived. . . . As she passed under the Golden Gate Bridge and disappeared in a blanket of fog, many showed signs of sorrow and anxiety. The curtain had fallen on those who may have had second thoughts. There was no turning back."

———

Despite the efforts that had been made to obfuscate the existence of the American Volunteer Group and its movements, their departure was far from secret. It was ominously reported by Radio Tokyo, which announced in advance that the *Jagersfontein* would be sunk along with its contingent of American mercenaries. It was not sunk, but the cat was obviously out of the bag. The Japanese probably had better sources even than *Time* magazine.

Two weeks later, the second major contingent of AVG pilots and support personnel converged on San Francisco. This time the rendezvous point was the seven-story Bellevue Hotel on Geary Street, which R. T. Smith and Paul Greene found "small, and filled with well-worn furnishings" that "would never be mistaken for the Mark Hopkins." A decade earlier, the Bellevue had been the model for the Belvedere Hotel in Dashiell Hammett's *The Maltese Falcon*, the place where Sam Spade met with Cairo. The Bellevue still exists, having been renovated as a boutique hotel called the Monaco.

Smith and Greene, who were traveling under passports identifying them as a plantation foreman and a salesman, respectively, had their covers blown almost immediately. They had barely had a chance to order a drink when a tall man at a neighboring table asked in a Texas drawl, "Hey, you fellas AVG by any chance?"

David Lee "Tex" Hill was sitting with Ed Rector and Bert Christman, all of them late of VS-41 aboard the USS *Ranger*. Before the war, Christman had achieved notoriety as a cartoonist and as one of the creators of the Sandman character for DC Comics. Between 1936 and 1938, when he had enlisted as a flying cadet, Christman was well known as the illustrator of the Scorchy Smith syndicated comic strip about a crime-fighting freelance pilot—a role to which Christman himself now aspired.

After a round or two of drinks, they all reported to the hotel's conference room, where Skip Adair greeted them and about twenty other pilots. He briefed them with the usual caveat that what was discussed inside the room should stay inside the room, but admitted that the Japanese "already know enough about what's going on, and they've made official protests to our State Department recently, so the less said about what we're up to, the better."

As he adjourned the meeting, Adair told them that their ship would sail a few days later, and in the meantime they should "keep your noses clean and your lips buttoned up," to which he added that "every man is to check in at the office in [room] 314 every day between one and five p.m. Incidentally, Mrs. Hamilton will be glad to help you with anything that requires typing; making out wills, mailing instructions, that sort of thing."

Wills?

Smith recalled in his memoirs that "The room seemed terribly quiet. It must have occurred to a number of us that we hadn't even thought about making out a will. . . . Flip a coin, heads or tails. But even had we known the odds in advance, it's doubtful that it would have changed our outlook. We were all aware of the danger to be faced, but it was a case of thinking, perhaps subconsciously, Sure, somebody's going to get killed, but it won't be me—the age-old philosophy that has sustained men in combat since wars began."

Smith, Greene, Hill, Rector, Christman, and the others sailed beneath the Golden Gate Bridge on the afternoon of July 24 aboard another VNSM liner, the MS *Bloemfontein*, a ship the Americans came to refer to simply as "the *Bloom*." Former US Navy pilots, used to life aboard aircraft carriers, awoke the following morning refreshed by the cool sea air. The former Air Corps men were a bit green in the face for the first few days at sea.

"It was a relaxed, congenial group, already bound together by the promise of still unknown and mysterious adventure that lay ahead," R. T. Smith observed. "And for the first time in a long while I felt completely at home; these were my kind of guys, all of them, seeking adventure and willing to accept the risks and pay the price."

The last batch of two dozen American adventurers included Charlie Bond and Greg Boyington, who filtered into San Francisco nearly two months later. Boyington recalled in his memoirs that his mother and stepfather came down to San Francisco from their apple ranch near Okanogan, Washington, to see him off and to return north with his car.

"There are other ways of paying off one's indebtedness," Grace Gregory Hallenbeck told her son in a vain attempt to talk him out of his adventure at the last minute.

"Oh, don't worry, Mom, I'll get by okay," he reassured her. "I haven't got an enemy in the world."

That was except for the million or so Japanese troops who were in China waiting for him.

"I didn't know anything about the Orient, other than what little I had learned in school," he admitted to himself.

As the earlier contingents of AVG airmen were greeted by the likes of Claire Chennault and Skip Adair, Bond, Boyington, and their group were met by the colorful Dr. Margaret "Mom" Chung. Born in Santa Barbara and educated at the University of Southern California, she had earned a reputation as a "physician to the stars" in Hollywood before opening a practice in San Francisco. An ardent and outspoken supporter of her parents' homeland after the Japanese invasion, she also developed an interest in American naval aviators that grew to include Marine and Air Corps fliers. "Mom" started an American aviators' club called the "Fair-Haired Bastards," and "adopted" some fifteen hundred pilots through World War II, inviting them to Sunday dinners at her home and giving each of her "Bastards" a silver ring with a jade Buddha. She was naturally very interested in the AVG.

At midmorning on September 24, when the men boarded MS *Boschfontein*, the VNSM sister ship of the earlier vessels, they received their send-off from Richard Aldworth. According to Boyington, he showed up "immaculate in a fresh uniform . . . shook hands with us, placing an arm around each, telling us how badly he wanted to go overseas with us." He then disembarked and drove away.

Whereas many of the AVG men wrote of a wistfulness as they sailed, Boyington was overcome by cynicism.

"When we left San Francisco, I knew that I was trying to escape my own common-sense reasoning," he recalled. "If this was strictly a service deal, our mission to further democracy didn't quite gel. And I knew it. . . . Just the same as cattle. The two ingredients necessary to accomplish this human sale were greedy pilots and a few idealists."

While he and his fellow pilots had been pub-crawling through San Francisco for the several days prior to sailing, Boyington had relished telling people that he was, as his passport erroneously identified him, a member of the clergy. Naturally, when he sat down for dinner on his first night at sea, he continued the ironic charade.

"At my table were two men and a woman doctor," he remembered. "But what I did not know, not until after I finished shooting my mouth off, was that the other three members of my table were honest-to-goodness missionaries. And furthermore, there were 55 of them aboard—men and women. How phony I felt. My orders on what to say, my passport, couldn't possibly cover my feeling of embarrassment. If only I had let them talk first!"

Naturally, the missionaries had figured Boyington out before he spoke, but they played along and snared him at his own game. A few days later, one of the real missionaries asked if he would give the sermon at the services on the following Sunday. He declined, but later wished he had accepted the invitation.

———

The Pacific crossings were punctuated by concern—more than fear—of being intercepted by the Japanese, or even by German surface raiders who were rumored to be stalking Dutch ships in the Pacific. There were nightly blackouts that lasted until sunrise, and many pairs of eyes scrutinized the horizon until nightfall. The first of the ships to depart, and the one that carried the lion's share of the AVG personnel, the *Jagersfontein* had been escorted west from Hawaii by two US Navy cruisers, but the other ships had traveled alone.

For more than a month, each of the Dutch ships made its way slowly and indirectly to the Far East, crossing the international date line, crisscrossing the equator, making port calls in Australia and Manila, and extensive layovers in Batavia (now Jakarta, Indonesia), the capital of the Dutch East Indies. In Singapore, each group of AVG volunteers was wined and dined by the Chinese consul general at the legendary Raffles Hotel.

By all accounts, the food that was served aboard the ships was not merely good, but also extraordinary, and the AVG men got along reasonably well with their fellow passengers while trying to maintain the fiction that they were *not* combat pilots going to war. Along the way, several AVG volunteers decided that they did not want to be combat pilots, and jumped ship at an enticing tropical port. Since they were no longer military pilots, they were not deserters—except in the eyes of Chennault; they had just defaulted on their one-year employment contracts.

In Surabaya, on the Dutch East Indies island of Java, Charlie Bond ran into two men who had gone over on one of the earlier ships and who were now trying to make their way home.

"They are throwing in the towel and returning to the States," he wrote in his diary of October 20. "They painted a bad picture of the organization and raised doubts in my mind: what am I getting myself into? I'm still looking forward to getting into the cockpit of a P-40."

As the weeks dragged on, cabin fever set in. R. T. Smith recalled "the cramped quarters, and now the heat and humidity as we crossed the equator again, plus the constant presence of others, the same faces day after day, were starting to get to us. We were becoming considerably more testy with each other, more apt to take offense at some imagined slight."

The boredom was offset mainly by nonstop card games. A Chinese-language professor aboard the *Jagersfontein* held classes for a dollar, but only thirty-five signed up. Jim Howard, who enrolled to brush up on a language he had known as a child, recalled that only a half dozen students were still in class at the end of the voyage.

At the succession of ports, the men sought out the companionship of the local female population, and there were even side trips with hired cars from Surabaya to Bali, where the bare-breasted Hindu girls—made iconic by their having been featured in *National Geographic*—were a contrast to the somewhat more modest Muslim girls in neighboring Java.

"These young women were very congenial," Boyington wrote of the hospitality girls he met in Singapore. "They would ask you if you cared for a drink. And you would say, 'Yes, scotch and soda,' which was the drink in that part of the world. So then she would take a large brass key and unlock a carved teak cabinet and pour you a glass of good scotch and fill it with chilled soda. No ice. She doesn't join you in a scotch and soda. She doesn't care to drink, she says, because drinking in a hot climate like Singapore is not good for one. And before the evening is over, you begin to realize the same thing. . . . To this day, and I'm not trying to be naive, either, I don't know how to describe the status of these lovely creatures: In some cases I am sure that it is not what one would ordinarily assume."

Meanwhile, though, sparks also flew between the sexes aboard ship. On the *Jagersfontein*, Jim Howard admitted developing an attraction for nurse Emma Jane Foster, "with tousled red hair reaching to her shoulders, deep blue eyes. . . . I found her breathtaking. I couldn't take my eyes off her. I'm sure she must have felt slightly embarrassed for she tried to avoid my gaze."

Having spent a year in China as an exchange student before the war, she was well aware of the situation into which she was sailing. Nicknamed "Red" by the pilots, she later became the wife of another AVG man named John Petach.

Aboard the *Boschfontein*, Tex Hill was engrossed in a romance that kept him in high spirits for weeks. As R. T. Smith observed, "there was a missionary woman of about 30, single, reasonably attractive and built along the lines of Dorothy Lamour, whom Tex was doing his damndest to convert. She, of course, was trying equally hard to make him see the light and give up his fun-loving ways. I'm not sure how the contest finally came out, but knowing Tex, I'd never have bet against him. At least they seemed pretty chummy by the time they finally parted company in Singapore."

A fter seven weeks of transit time, the men who had embarked on the first two of the Dutch ships reached their destination by mid-September. The *Jagersfontein* anchored in the broad and muddy Irrawaddy Delta south of Rangoon, but the *Bloemfontein* dropped its passengers in Singapore, where the AVG men had to transfer to the Chinese-registered coastal steamer *Penang Trader*. The *Boschfontein* finally arrived in Rangoon on November 12.

Bill Pawley sent his brother Ed to meet the *Jagersfontein*, but he and Skip Adair were both on the dock when the *Penang Trader* and the *Boschfontein* came in. Each contingent got a welcoming speech that included the phrase "only 160 miles to go," an envelope filled with Burmese rupees, and dinner and drinks at the Silver Grill, a nightclub that had become a sort of aviators' bar for the RAF pilots posted to Rangoon.

The "160 miles" referred to the last leg of their journey, which was to be made aboard a rickety, narrow-gauge railroad to Toungoo (now Taungoo), which was to be the first operational base of the AVG. Located on the Sittang River due north of Rangoon and due south of Mandalay, Toungoo was a city of about twenty-five thousand, where the local economy revolved around the hardwood lumber industry.

The delays earlier in the year that had pushed Chennault's timetable back three months had pushed the schedule into the monsoon season. Having originally planned to finish his training during the spring at Kunming, he had intended to undertake air defense operations over Chongqing by the summer. However, the heavy rains turned his unpaved landing strips into swamps and sent him knocking on British doors, asking for the use of paved RAF fields in Burma to use as his training fields.

When Chennault and P. T. Mao sat down with British officials in Rangoon, they were told that the United Kingdom was not yet officially at war with Japan and the British hoped to avoid provocations and keep it that way. Indeed, as late as the summer of 1941, the prevailing British point of view was that Japan would not attack Burma unless somehow provoked. Mao argued that because Japan had not declared war in the ongoing Sino-Japanese War, the AVG could not be considered belligerents in the context of violating British neutrality. It cost Chennault another three months, but in October, the attorneys in His Majesty's government in London finally concurred with Mao's opinion.

With the caveat that the American volunteers could not conduct *combat* training activities at RAF bases in Burma, the British gave the AVG a green light.

TEN

The Old Man of Toungoo
and His Buccaneers

The RAF's Kyedaw Airfield, eight miles from Toungoo, had a four-thousand-foot paved runway but little else. The ninety-nine P-40s that had reached the Port of Rangoon in June were supposed to be there when the first large contingent of pilots arrived in mid-September, but ninety-five of these were still in varying states of disassembly at the CAMCO shops at Mingaladon Airport, near Rangoon—and two had been lost in a fatal midair collision between two veterans of the USS *Ranger* on September 8. John Gilpin "Gil" Bright parachuted to safety, but John Armstrong had become the AVG's first fatality.

By the end of the month, about three dozen P-40s had reached Toungoo. The deliveries were made by AVG pilots who would take the train down to Mingaladon and fly them back. The only other aircraft possessed by the AVG was an old Beechcraft Model 18 twin-tailed light transport that was used by Chennault to commute between Toungoo and Kunming, and to fly up to Chongqing to confer with Chiang Kai-shek.

The DC-2 and DC-3 airliners of the China National Aviation Corporation (CNAC), owned jointly by the Chinese government and Pan American Airways, served these locations and also carried a great deal of freight—both officially and unofficially—for the AVG. Just as the tip of China's air combat spear was a fighter group composed of American civilians, the heavy lifting of strategically vital airlift in southern China was in the hands of a cadre composed mainly of American civilians.

The AVG had also received three Curtiss CW-21 Demon high-altitude interceptors of the type that Bill Pawley had planned to begin manufacturing at Lei Yun, but never did. These three, imported from the United States substantially complete, were the only CW-21s, aside from the original prototype, that ever flew over the Asian mainland. Chennault had planned to use their high-altitude capabilities for reconnaissance flights over Japanese positions. Another two dozen Demons were delivered to the Dutch in the East Indies, but only a handful of these ever saw action.

Aside from the runway, the facilities at Toungoo were more like a cruel practical joke than an air base.

"Toungoo was a shocking contrast to a peacetime Army or Navy post in the United States," Claire Chennault recalled in his memoirs. "The runway was surrounded by quagmire and pestilential jungle. Matted masses of rotting vegetation carpeted the jungle and filled the air with a sour, sickening smell. Torrential monsoon rains and thunderstorms alternated with torrid heat to give the atmosphere the texture of a Turkish bath. Dampness and green mold penetrated everywhere. The food, provided by a Burmese mess contractor, was terrible, and one of the principal causes of group griping. Barracks were new and well ventilated, but along with the air came every stinging insect in Burma.

There were no screens or electric lights and not a foot of screening to be bought in all Burma. We learned that the RAF abandoned Kyedaw during the rainy season because Europeans were unable to survive its foul climate."

Perhaps worst affected was Fred Hodges, who had a serious dread of insects that went beyond that of the others. Despite this, and the ribbing of comrades who nicknamed him "Fearless Freddie," he gritted his teeth and never let his phobia get the best of him.

One of the best illustrations of life in Toungoo was penned by Greg Boyington, who wrote "the heat was so fatiguing that, as one example, I couldn't get enough energy to jump out of my net-covered bunk while some of the other pilots were busy in the grass barracks near my bunk killing a cobra."

Nevertheless, of more than a hundred pilots and a larger number of support personnel who mustered in Toungoo and beheld the deplorable conditions, only a handful exercised the option to resign and leave.

The British, who had built the Kyedaw airfield, had been helpful, but only to a limited extent. Without them, the AVG would not have had a hard-surfaced runway and aviation fuel to use it, and the British did supply Burmese mess staff to run the kitchens and Gurkhas to guard the perimeter, but they provided no screening to keep pests from flying, crawling, or slithering through the windows of the barracks. The RAF operated Curtiss Tomahawks, but mainly in North Africa and none in Southeast Asia, so they had no spare parts inventory from which the AVG could beg, borrow, or steal.

Chennault got along well professionally with the head of the British Far East Command in Singapore. Air Marshal Sir Henry Brooke-Popham was the first RAF officer to lead a major joint command, and as a fellow airman, he did everything he could—as meager as it was, given his own resources—to assist Chennault and the AVG. However, he was seventeen hundred air miles away with responsibility for an entire theater, and as things heated up across Southeast Asia, his plate was overflowing.

When it came to dealing with the RAF in Burma, Chennault had to endure the obstacles that flowed from what he perceived as the snobbery and petty jealousy of Group Captain E. R. Manning of 221 Group. The RAF senior officer in Burma, he resented the AVG for their being civilians, for being Americans, and for their intrusion on what he perceived as his proprietary turf. He especially resented Chennault's independent status. He had demanded without success to have the AVG placed under his command for the air defense of that turf. Manning, who was an Australian, had both Australians and New Zealanders, as well as Englishmen, serving under him, and he felt that the Americans should as well.

Chennault, meanwhile, was frustrated with Manning's unwillingness to cooperate with the AVG and to accept Chennault's professional recommendations for defending Rangoon from a potential Japanese air attack. The RAF had no early warning network such as Chennault had constructed to protect Chiang Kai-shek and Kunming. When he recommended that Manning build a network of air spotter posts, Manning dismissed the suggestion out of hand. It was still the prevailing belief that Japan was unlikely to challenge the British in Burma.

———

When they first arrived at Toungoo, most of the AVG men had yet to meet Chennault, and when they did, the reaction was universally one of confidence in his ability to lead the adventure upon which they were about to embark. It was an enterprise that many had come to feel would be quixotic—but meeting Chennault made it seem somehow practical and doable.

Chennault was, by all accounts, the kind of leader who not only led, but also inspired those who followed. Almost universally, they referred to him as "the Old Man," a term of respect and endearment that has always been a common appellation in the armed forces for referring to a leader who is well liked. To his face, they called him "Colonel," the honorary title that had followed him since he arrived in China. Many believed that he had been commissioned as a colonel in the Chinese Air Force, which he had not. The hierarchy of "ranks" that did exist within the civilian AVG read as job descriptions—squadron leader, vice squadron leader, flight leader, and wingman.

Bond wrote in his diary that "the Old Man still has a military air about him. With his tan RAF bush jacket and sun helmet, he impresses us as a commander rather than a director or manager. I like the Old Man."

"What do you think?" Ed Rector asked Tex Hill after they met Chennault for the first time.

"Seems to me like that's a guy who knows what the hell he's doing," came the reply, to which Rector nodded in agreement.

As Hill's biographer Reagan Schaupp wrote, "Chennault was a unique man in a unique situation. . . . Almost no one had ever been given the autonomy to train a group of combat pilots in his own particular tactics, but that was exactly the chance Chennault had with the AVG. If it lacked the most modern planes or veteran fighter pilots, he did not care. It was his group. Few other men, if any, could have held together the maverick AVG at all, let alone have accomplished anything noteworthy with them. But it never occurred to the confident Chennault that the group would do anything but succeed. He had been a natural leader from boyhood, one of the greatest the United States ever produced. His courage was unquestioned; the men saw it firsthand. He never asked them to do anything that was outside his own experience."

"For those of us who had arrived on the 15th of September, our first glimpse of Claire Lee Chennault was some three or four days later," R. T. Smith recalled in his memoirs. "He came flying in aboard the little twin-engined Beechcraft that had been provided for his use by the Chinese government, and that evening had dinner at the pilots' mess. He made a brief welcoming speech for our benefit, and later we all met him in person."

Smith went on to say that "much has been written about Chennault's appearance, which seemed to invite clichés such as 'face chiseled from granite,' etc., many of them quite appropriate. . . . He was not a man to waste words, and his manner was rather gruff but not unpleasant. He spoke in a low voice, with a Louisiana Cajun-country drawl that took a bit of getting used to before being completely understood. He was a physically active man, loved to hunt and fish, and often took part in our softball games late in the afternoon. He would play cribbage by the hour when possible, hated losing and seldom did."

"I was genuinely impressed," Greg Boyington recalled tersely. "In fact, seeing Chennault, and listening to him talk, was the only thing about this deal I had seen so far that did impress me."

Conversely, as he watched them arrive, the Old Man was unimpressed with his "boys."

"Pilots looked far from promising as they checked in at Kyedaw," Chennault wrote in his own memoirs. "The long boat trip and Dutch shipboard menus had left many flabby and overweight. They all appeared wilted during their introduction. . . . It was a rude shock to some of the AVG pilots when they matriculated in my postgraduate school of fighter tactics at Toungoo. Most of them considered themselves extremely hot pilots; after a long sea voyage bragging to fellow passengers about their prowess as fighter pilots, many of them were convinced they

were ready to walk down the gangplank at Rangoon and begin decimating the Japanese Air Force."

Classes at the Old Man's "postgraduate school of fighter tactics"
began immediately after a critical mass of pilots had reached Burma.

"I had been working on my plans to whip the Japanese in the air
for four years, and I was determined that, when the American Volunteer
Group went into battle, it would be using tactics based on that bitter
experience," he recalled. "I taught them all I knew about the Japanese.
Day after day there were lectures from my notebooks, filled during the
previous four years of combat. All of the bitter experience from Nanking
to Chungking was poured out in those lectures. Captured Japanese
flying and staff manuals, translated into English by the Chinese, served
as textbooks. From these manuals the American pilots learned more
about Japanese tactics than any single Japanese pilot ever knew."

———————

As the pilots settled in, Chennault began organizing his 1st American Volunteer Group into three squadrons on the basis of eighteen aircraft assigned to each. Other flyable aircraft on hand served as
replacements and backup aircraft as necessary. Each of the squadrons
was numbered, and also nicknamed. All of the AVG P-40s were marked
with the Nationalist Chinese insignia—the white sun of the Nationalist flag on a dark blue roundel—but they now also got their informal
squadron markings.

The 1st Pursuit Squadron, because they were first, were nicknamed "Adam and Eves," and were commanded by Robert "Sandy"
Sandell, late of the Army Air Corps. Charlie Bond designed an insignia for the squadron that pictured Eve chasing Adam around a
big red apple wrapped in a snake. Chennault told him to get rid of
the apple because it looked too much like the Japanese "meatball"

insignia. He didn't want any mistakes in the heat of battle. The apple was painted green.

The 2nd Pursuit Squadron was placed under the command of John "Scarsdale Jack" Newkirk, a naval aviator who had flown F4F Wildcats aboard the USS *Yorktown*. While there was a mix of pilots in both squadrons, former Air Corps men dominated the 1st, and the 2nd was populated by ex-Navy pilots, whom the Air Corps men called "water boys."

Because the AVG was destined to fight in China, the 2nd became the "Panda Bears," and Bert Christman, the well-known prewar cartoonist, took on the job of painting a personalized panda on each of the squadron's P-40s. Scarsdale Jack's panda wore a top hat, while Tex Hill's wore a Stetson and sported a pair of six-shooters.

When the 3rd Pursuit Squadron was activated, it took the handle "Hell's Angels" after the 1930 Hollywood movie about air combat in World War I (the motorcycle club of the same name was not formed until 1948). It was led by Arvid "Oley" Olson, who had previously been with the Air Corps' 8th Pursuit Group. Each plane was painted with a devilishly red female angel.

It was about the middle of November when the men began painting the distinctive and well-known shark teeth on the engine cowlings of their aircraft. The paint scheme had previously been used on both British and German aircraft, and pictures of a shark-faced Tomahawk of RAF Number 112 Squadron in North Africa appeared on the cover of an issue of the *Illustrated Weekly of India* that found its way to Toungoo. Someone—both Bert Christman and Erik Shilling are mentioned in various accounts—suggested that the AVG should adopt such markings. As Chennault pointed out, "with the pointed nose of a liquid-cooled engine it was an apt and fearsome design." Over time, it became customary within the AVG to use the term "shark" when referring to their aircraft in two-way radio transmissions.

B ecause Hap Arnold had agreed to allow Chennault to poach Air Corps pilots but *not* staff officers, the AVG was a lean organization, light on administrators. Everyone from the pilots to the ground crew to the parachute riggers had a specific job directly related to the mission. Chennault's senior staff consisted only of Skip Adair and a man named Harvey Greenlaw, who had been a flight instructor at Brooks Field in Texas when he first met Chennault in the late 1920s.

Born in Wisconsin in 1897, Greenlaw had attended West Point, graduating near the bottom of the Class of 1920. As was the rule in the lower echelons of class rankings, Greenlaw had been assigned to the infantry, but over time he was able to gradually migrate through the US Army organization to the Air Corps. Having advanced no farther than first lieutenant, he left the service in 1931. After a stint as one of the handful of American flight instructors who had been hired by the Chinese Air Force before the Chennault era, he returned to the United States, where he went through a series of vocations from working as an oil company pilot to managing a bismuth mine in Mexico for his father-in-law.

Greenlaw returned to China in about 1937 as a sales rep for North American Aviation, reconnected with Chennault, and became his de facto chief of staff and all-around deputy—though by various accounts, he seems to have been most adept at delegating his own responsibilities to others. Chennault had officially assigned Jim Howard to the job of operations officer, but Greenlaw saw to it that he was listed as such on the roster. As Howard recalled of Greenlaw, "many of us couldn't tell just what it was that he was supposed to do." Greg Boyington described him as "the self-made executive officer [who] called himself Lieutenant Colonel Greenlaw, although no one else would."

Few accounts of the AVG fail to mention Olga Sowers Greenlaw,

Harvey's charismatic wife, whom Jim Howard later described as "startlingly attractive." R. T. Smith thought she looked like movie star Paulette Goddard, "only with a better figure."

She was the type of woman who had a presence who made her seem mysterious, despite the fact that she was a ubiquitous fixture around the AVG at both Toungoo and Kunming, and later the keeper of the AVG's daily log. Because her name was Olga, there were rumors that she was a White Russian exile whom Greenlaw had met in Shanghai, and this underscored her mystique. In fact, she had been born in Mexico of an American father and a Serbian-Mexican mother, and she grew up in Los Angeles—which is where she met Greenlaw. She was an intimate friend to many of the pilots, and unverifiable rumors still circulate that she was also a lover to several.

The Greenlaws lived off the Kyedaw base in the town of Toungoo, where they entertained pilots in a house that functioned as a de facto officers' club. Olga called it the Hotel Greenlaw, a name that was also applied to a later house the couple occupied in Kunming. As she recalled in her memoirs, "I couldn't turn around without stepping on a Flying Tiger."

Olga, along with nurses Red Foster and Jo Stewart, were among a mere handful of women in an organization that best resembled a fraternity house. As the Old Man was fostering discipline in the air, his management of the men on the ground was, in his own words, "not calculated to inspire anything but distrust in the orthodox military mind. The military observers regarded the group as an undisciplined mob. Official reports that went back to London and Washington and circulated around Rangoon were pretty bad. . . . My ideas on how to handle a group of high-spirited, adventurous volunteer fighter pilots and ground crews departed radically from military tradition."

R. T. Smith recalled that "the absence of 'rank' as it existed in the Army or Navy permitted a much more democratic atmosphere, which in the case of our little group worked very well and was seldom abused. Actually, I think it tended to keep us on our toes."

"Tex had to admire Chennault's approach to unit discipline," Reagan Schaupp wrote of Tex Hill's thoughts on the subject. "There were plenty in the AVG who, having recently 'escaped' the military, wanted no part of the rules and regimen the services had imposed on them. Others, though, liked military structure and discipline; they wished the Old Man would enforce more rules. Chennault decided a democratic approach was best. He let the men gather and determine among themselves the hours of operation for the bar, time for 'lights out,' and other issues that affected everyone. Chennault wisely concluded that rules the men made themselves would be much more effective—and better enforced."

Off-post, discipline was essentially nonexistent. As Olga Greenlaw recalled, "because there was nothing to do in off-hours the boys got into considerable trouble. Some of it was funny and harmless; some of it was not."

If Toungoo developed a reputation for being more like the hideout of a pirate band than a military base, that was because it *was*. The Old Man's buccaneers were not military men but civilian hired guns, and they behaved accordingly.

With this raucous reputation came publicity. What foreign correspondent passing through Burma in the fall of 1941 could resist a visit to the lair of the AVG? With the publicity came the news items that appeared in newspapers back home and around the world, and the last tenuous vestiges of secrecy that had been intended to cloak the project faded. The journalists who visited Chennault's frat house found rich pay dirt in the colorful irreverence of his merry band.

W hile strictness on the ground was lax, it was just the opposite in the air, where Chennault demanded the utmost precision and attention to detail. He worked them hard, those men who had enrolled in his "postgraduate school of fighter tactics," imposing a curriculum that stressed the doctrine of "detection, interception, and destruction" that he had formulated a decade earlier at the Air Corps Tactical School. He hoped to turn his band of misfits into the best fighter pilots in the Far East inside of two months.

Though the monsoon season had ended in October, and his airfields around Kunming had dried out, Chennault kept the AVG at Kyedaw to take advantage of the hard-surfaced runway for his training.

Beginning classes at 7:00 a.m. with a lecture, he then took them into the air and drilled them hard to "fight in pairs. Make every bullet count. Never try to get all the Japanese in one pass. Hit hard, break clean, and get position for another pass."

He taught them to use the advantages that the P-40 had against the weaknesses of the Japanese aircraft. "You can count on a higher top speed, faster dive, and superior firepower," he told them. "The Jap fighters have a faster rate of climb, higher ceiling, and better maneuverability. They can turn on a dime and climb almost straight up. If they can get you into a turning combat, they are deadly."

The P-40 also had the advantages of self-sealing fuel tanks and armor protection behind and below the cockpit, though this added to the weight and reduced maneuverability.

From his experience in China, Chennault related that the enemy fighter pilots always tried the "same tricks" repeatedly and that his men should not fall for these tricks in a dogfight, adding, "God help the American pilot who tries to fight them according to their plans."

"It was no easy task," Chennault recalled. "I had to teach my pilots all the tricks of their enemy—how to use their own equipment to the best advantage, and how to fight and live to fight again another day.

This last factor was extremely important since, with a group so small and replacements so uncertain, we simply had to reduce our own combat losses well below average, at the same time boosting the enemy's high above what he was prepared to absorb."

He drilled them relentlessly, in the air and on the ground, until they were at one with their shark-faced warplanes, and combat maneuvering was reflexive second nature, repeatedly admonishing them to "never worry about what's going to happen next, or it will happen to *you*."

———————

On December 7, 1941, R. T. Smith wrote home, telling his parents that "I've been holding off in writing to you as I thought surely we'd be in China by now. We've been under instructions to be ready to leave on an hour's notice for about ten days. All I can say is that we—half of us, at least—are ready. There will be sixteen from my squadron flying up when we go, and about the same from the others. Naturally we're all anxious to get going, and irked at the delay. There is no news to report here, except that the Englanders are reinforcing [Burma's] borders. Things are getting tenser and tenser, but nobody knows what'll happen, or when."

Across the international date line at Pearl Harbor in Hawaii, it was still December 6, and "when" was now very, very close.

ELEVEN

The War Comes
to Southeast Asia

As the American Volunteer Group had long since given up the pretense of a covert operation, Japanese moves in the fall of 1941 were made with but scant lip service to the notion of secrecy. It was obvious that a major thrust into Southeast Asia was coming. This was despite the fact that the Japanese final decision to undertake such an offensive had only been made in July, at the same time that Claire Chennault was staring at crated Tomahawks on the Rangoon docks and trying to find a paved runway on which to base them.

However, this is not to say that the advocates in Japan of such a strategy were not ready to implement plans of long standing. Even before the turn of the twentieth century, Japanese strategic thinking had been defined by two divergent schools of thought, which were expressed as two points on an expansionist compass: Hokushinron, the Northern Road, and Nanshinron, the Southern Road. Beginning with the Sino-Japanese War in the 1890s and continuing into the 1930s and the second Sino-Japanese War, the Northern Road doctrine had dominated Japanese foreign policy and had taken Japan into Manchuria, northern China, and into border wars with the Soviet Union. The Southern Road would lead Japan toward Southeast Asia, a place where the Europeans—Britain, France, and the Netherlands—had been the colonial powers for more than a century, but where Japanese foreign policy and adventurism had little prior experience.

By the 1930s, with control of the Japanese government in the hands of military officers and civilian militarists, there came a revival of the ancient *Hakko ichiu* doctrine that envisioned "the eight corners of the world under one roof," and specified that this roof was Japan. From this came the idea, articulated by Foreign Minister Hachiro Arita in 1940, of a bloc of Asian nations under Japan's roof and free of Western powers. He called this bloc the Greater East Asia Co-Prosperity Sphere (Dai-to-a Kyoeiken). Embracing Nanshinron, the Southern Road, the Co-Prosperity Sphere became the template for the occupation of Southeast Asia.

Just as there was a contrary, but complementary, yin and yang in the geopolitical role of Hokushinron and Nanshinron, there was a duality in the Greater East Asia Co-Prosperity Sphere. It was promulgated by Japan as the altruistic ambition of replacing white masters with Asian—read *Japanese*—masters. However, when a totalitarian empire uses the word "Co-Prosperity," the "prosperity" described can easily be transparently understood as its own. Japan needed the vast resources of Southeast Asia, especially the great oil reserves of the Dutch East Indies, to fuel its expanding domestic economy, as well as its war machine in China. Oil was vitally important. Japan had no domestic reserves and depended, ironically, on the United States. With the Export Control Act of 1940, the Americans, to punish Japan for actions in China, had drastically reduced exports.

The Dutch East Indies, today's Indonesia, constituted the world's fourth-largest oil exporter. They were low-hanging fruit—lightly defended by the colonial administration of a country occupied by Germany in 1940, and they were within easy striking distance of the Japanese war machine.

"It took no special intelligence to know that the situation was rapidly building up to the boiling point in Asia during the fall of 1941," Chennault recalled. "It is impossible to assemble and equip a major military expedition in complete secrecy. The Japanese were never an exception to this rule. . . . When the United States slapped the oil embargo on Japan in the summer of 1941, it was evident to all who had been following the Sino-Japanese war closely that the Japanese would have to strike soon for oil or crawl back into their shell. During the fall there was a wealth of evidence that the Japanese preparations for the offensive were underway. . . . It was no secret that the stage was being set for a drive to the Dutch East Indies as the minimum objective and an all-out offensive to drive the Western powers from the Pacific as the maximum possibility."

———

On December 8, 1941—which was still December 7 at Pearl Harbor—the hammer fell. In his diary, R. T. Smith wrote, "Boy, did all hell break loose today?!"

The Japanese stunned the world with simultaneous air attacks from Pearl Harbor to the Philippines, and with ground attacks from Hong Kong to the Malay Peninsula.

In the mid-Pacific, a tiny American-owned atoll called Wake Island also came under Japanese air attack that day. Located 2,284 miles west of Pearl Harbor and 3,067 miles east of Manila, Wake was used primarily as a refueling stop for the transpacific Clipper flying boats of Pan American Airways. Indeed, one such aircraft was parked in the atoll's lagoon when the Japanese attacked, having flown in from Honolulu the previous day. While eight of a dozen US Marine Corps fighter planes based on the island were taken out of action by enemy bombs, the Clipper survived and was able to take off for Hawaii.

Against the backdrop of all the momentous events taking place that day, this incident would be hardly worth mentioning but for the fact that this aircraft was carrying the last load of supplies—spare parts and tires—that would ever be shipped across the Pacific to the American Volunteer Group. Needless to say, the consignment never arrived. Accompanying the shipment was USAAF Lieutenant Albert "Ajax" Baumler, the Spanish Civil War veteran pilot who had attempted to join the AVG earlier in the year only to be screened out by a sieve of red tape. Still anxious to catch up with the group, Baumler had missed this opportunity by just a day because of the attack on Wake Island. Life does not often give us second chances, but within half a year, Baumler would be given a third.

The Japanese also marched into the Kingdom of Thailand on December 8, which capitulated after a mere twenty-four hours of token resistance. Known officially as Siam until 1939, it was the only independent country in the region at the time, and was under the rule of a figurehead monarch and Field Marshal Plaek Phibunsongkhram, who occupied the seat of prime minister. Known generally as "Pibul" or "Phibun," he was a great admirer of totalitarian governments such as Hitler's Germany, and he quickly turned Thailand into one of Japan's best friends in Asia. Most of the Imperial Japanese Army Air Force aircraft with which the AVG would do battle over the coming weeks would be flying from bases in Thailand. Meanwhile, Indochina, a colony of German-occupied Vichy France, was also now available as a base for air and naval operations by the Third Reich's Japanese allies.

At Toungoo, news of the Pearl Harbor attack came in a shortwave broadcast from KGEI in San Francisco that was picked up by the base radio operator. "The airwaves vibrated," noted Olga Greenlaw, "with rumors and contradictory reports."

In his memoirs, R. T. Smith recalled being in the breakfast line when he heard the news, but Greg Boyington remembered that it was still dark outside and that there was a mad scramble by the men to get to their aircraft and get airborne so they were not caught on the ground by a Japanese attack. A few managed to take off, but the scramble was curtailed under the theory that in the darkness, collisions were more likely than accurate bombing by the enemy.

Within twenty-four hours, war had been declared by the United States, and issues of neutrality quickly faded. The men of the AVG in their shark-faced warplanes were still swashbucklers, but with the United States now a combatant, they were no longer outlaws—although they still worked for a foreign power and not the US armed forces.

Nor were they immediately *combat* pilots. Chennault ordered several reconnaissance flights over Thailand, but nearly two weeks would pass before the AVG tasted action. Chennault decided that wartime urgency trumped his concerns about having not finished his training program, and ordered his men to make the long-overdue move to their permanent home at Kunming.

During the first week of Southeast Asia being a theater of World War II, things went remarkably well for the Japanese. The drive of their Twenty-fifth Army south through the Malay Peninsula was like the proverbial hot knife through butter. Only two days after the Japanese had neutralized the US Navy Pacific Fleet at Pearl Harbor, IJNAF bombers sank the battleship HMS *Prince of Wales* and the battle cruiser HMS *Repulse*, which the Royal Navy had sent to Singapore to conduct operations against the Japanese fleet. After one day of token resistance,

Phibun's capitulation brought the Japanese Fifteenth Army racing through Thailand toward the Burmese border.

The threat of a Japanese invasion of Burma, which the British had thought unlikely, suddenly seemed probable. E. R. Manning, Chennault's antagonist and the commander of the RAF contingent in Burma, who had coveted the AVG earlier, went back to the Old Man in an effort to cajole him into placing his squadrons under RAF command.

Even Air Marshal Brooke-Popham in Singapore, who had previously been understanding of Chennault's position, now lobbied for the AVG to be part of his command. He went so far as to take up the matter with Chiang Kai-shek. Chiang naturally wished to have the AVG remain committed to the defense of China, but he was also aware that the Port of Rangoon was an essential part of the lifeline of Lend-Lease supplies upon which China depended. Indeed, virtually everything that was trucked north on the Burma Road came across Rangoon's docks. Chiang deferred to Chennault.

Though the Old Man refused to place the AVG under the RAF chain of command, he did agree under pressure to give Manning the services of the 3rd "Hell's Angels" Squadron for the air defense of Rangoon and its vital port. "I fought vigorously to withdraw the AVG from what I considered an unnecessarily exposed position," he wrote. "Only the heavy pressure of the Anglo-American Combined Chiefs of Staff and the Generalissimo prevented me from doing so."

Chennault regarded Manning's combat tactics as "suicidal," adding that "by serving under his command, I would have lost my own authority over the group and forced my pilots to accept his stupid orders. . . . All during the period we were negotiating for transfer of all or a part of the AVG to Rangoon, Manning refused to allow me to enter his fighter-control room or become familiar with any of the facilities that we were supposed to use jointly in the air defense of Rangoon."

On December 12, the Hell's Angels relocated south to the Mingaladon airfield, while at Toungoo, the AVG was pulling up stakes and packing to leave. As their equipment and ground personnel traveled overland aboard trucks by way of the Burma Road, the men of the 1st and 2nd Pursuit Squadrons flew up to Kunming on December 18—one day after Japanese bombers had raked that city, killing four hundred people.

The 1st Pursuit Squadron took off first, with Sandy Sandell leading them, flying at about twenty-one thousand feet to avoid the mountains. Chennault had flown up earlier in his Beechcraft 18 with the Greenlaws and other members of his staff aboard, and CNAC aircraft had been pressed into service to carry other personnel and equipment.

As Boyington recalled in his memoirs, Sandell was "responsible for taking us a little over six hundred miles of unfamiliar terrain to the north and east of Toungoo. The weather, as far as cloud formations, was definitely against him. Neither Sandy nor any of the others had ever flown into inland China. As we continued to fly northward, the mountains became higher, and the terrain was by far the most rugged I had ever witnessed. At that time the maps of this territory we were forced to use, for lack of anything better, happened to be very inaccurate indeed. We found that points of reference, in some cases, were off a hundred miles or so. But I had to give Sandy all the credit in the world. He found the 6,000-foot-high valley, and the three lakes nestled within, amid the surrounding high mountains and the layers of stratus that covered them."

The P-40s of both squadrons reached Kunming, but the three CW-21 interceptors were lost when they attempted to cross the mountains into China. Erik Shilling had crash-landed when his engine failed, and as no radios had been installed he couldn't tell the other pilots to keep going, and they wrecked their aircraft attempting to land with him.

On the morning of December 20, as the pilots were waking up

in the massive converted university dormitory known as "Hostel Number One," Chennault was able to note that there were thirty-four combat-ready P-40s, with "a fighter-control headquarters hooked into the Yunnan warning net and the Chinese code rooms that were monitoring Japanese operational radio frequencies and decoding enemy messages. . . . It was this kind of lightning mobility that was necessary to realize a full potential of airpower. . . . It was this ability to shift my combat operations 650 miles in an afternoon and 1,000 miles in 24 hours that kept the Japanese off balance for four bloody years."

The AVG did not have to wait long for their baptism of fire.

Sandell and more than a dozen men of his Adam and Eve Squadron awoke in the predawn darkness on their first morning in China, complaining of the chilly weather on the high plateau, but at the same time thankful to be away from the sticky, debilitating heat of the Burmese jungle.

Their first patrol, launched at 6:00 a.m., was routine and fruitless, but back on the ground four hours later, they got word of the real thing. Chennault's elaborate early warning net reported ten Japanese bombers entering Yunnan airspace from the direction of Hanoi in Indochina.

This was the decisive moment I had been awaiting for more than four years," Chennault wrote of December 19 in his memoirs, "American pilots in American fighter planes aided by a Chinese ground warning net about to tackle a formation of the Imperial Japanese Air Force, which was then sweeping the Pacific skies victorious everywhere. I felt that the fate of China was riding in the P-40 cockpits through the wintry sky over Yunnan. I yearned heartily to be ten years younger and crouched in a cockpit instead of a dugout, tasting the stale rubber of an oxygen mask and peering ahead into limitless space through the cherry-red rings of a gunsight."

Sandell and the men of the 1st Pursuit Squadron *did* leap into the wintry sky over Yunnan that morning to taste the stale rubber and the exhilaration of their own first aerial combat action—and that of the American Volunteer Group.

The squadron dashed southeast from Kunming, leveled off at twenty thousand feet, and soon spotted ten pale green, twin-engine Kawasaki Ki-48 bombers. Panicking at the sight of the shark-faced warplanes, the Imperial Japanese Army Air Force pilots immediately jettisoned their bomb loads and made a 180-degree turn, but the AVG sharks gave chase. Even at 225 miles per hour it took them about ten minutes to catch the enemy.

"I charged all my guns and turned on my gun sight and gun switch," Charlie Bond wrote in his diary, noting that he was diving to attack from above. "The Japs were in a tight formation. As we closed in, they lowered their 'dustbin' rear-sighting guns to defend against us. As a result they slowed down. I was tense but more excited. I was about to taste combat. I thought in terms of shooting down airplanes and gave no thought to the fact that there were men in those ships."

At about a thousand feet above and an equal distance to the left, he rolled into his attack and squeezed the trigger.

"Damn it, nothing happened!" he thought.

"In my excitement, I had checked it so many times that I had turned it off!" Bond admitted. "I was closing in fast on the outside bomber and not firing. I broke off violently—down and away and then back up to my original position for another attack. I went in for a second attack, and all guns were blazing this time. I saw my tracers enter the fuselage of the bomber. At the last second I broke off, and then I felt a quiver in my control stick but thought nothing of it."

He later discovered bullet holes in his right aileron, right stabilizer, and rudder.

"I attacked again and again," he recalled. "Two bombers began to lag behind, trailing smoke. Many of the other guys were after those two ships, so I concentrated on the main formation. I could see only seven. Three evidently had gone down, but I could not yet claim that I shot one down. Some of our guys followed the bombers down and watched them explode against the mountains."

Realizing that the squadron was 200 miles from Kunming and that they had burned a lot of fuel in high-speed maneuvering, Sandell finally called off the attack and began leading his men away from the fracas. Though they were lost for a brief time on the return, they all made it home from their first fight. The only plane lost was that of Ed Rector, who ran out of fuel and successfully crash-landed.

"As the P-40s dived to attack, everybody went a little crazy with excitement," Chennault recalled of that day. "All the lessons of Toungoo were forgotten. There was no teamwork—only a wild melee in which all pilots agreed that only sheer luck kept P-40s from shooting each other. Pilots tried wild 90 degree deflection shots and other crazy tactics in the 130-mile running fight that followed. Hell's Angel Fritz Wolf of Shawano, Wisconsin, shot down two bombers and then cursed his armorer because his guns jammed. When he landed and inspected the guns, he found they were merely empty."

That day saw a victory for the AVG in more ways than one. Beyond merely being the defeat of an enemy bomber formation, it was a vindication of Chennault's doctrine of detection, interception, destruction. Much of the credit is due to the often overlooked network of ground spotters and radar sites that Chennault had erected to guide the interception.

As Chennault wrote in his memoirs, "our tactics were to use every advantage of interior lines of communication, the warning net, seasonal weather, range of our planes, and the Japanese orthodox combat habits to retain the initiative, jab the Japanese off balance with surprise thrusts at widely separated targets, and keep their numerically superior forces on the defensive." This would summarize the tactics of the AVG for the remainder of their time in combat.

In the debriefing on the afternoon of December 20, the pilots calculated that they had shot down four of the bombers. In fact, they had shot down three, but they had badly damaged a fourth one that did crash before returning to its base near Hanoi.

"Well, boys," Chennault recalled telling his men, "it was a good job but not good enough. Next time get them all."

TWELVE

Stale Bread
and Fair Weather Friends

A s the majority of the American Volunteer Group moved north into China, Oley Olson and the Hell's Angels of the 3rd Pursuit Squadron were at the airfield at Mingaladon on the edge of Rangoon. Here they joined the RAF contingent consisting of a handful of Bristol Blenheim light bombers in Number 60 Squadron and about thirty worn and obsolete American-made Brewster Buffalo fighters in Number 67 Squadron, of which only about half were flyable. The latter were flown mainly by New Zealanders. At the end of January, the RAF contingent would be reinforced by Hawker Hurricanes—a fighter that had earned fame and respect during the Battle of Britain in 1940—that were flown in from India. However, in December, there was no urgency to improve the quality of RAF equipment. The British were still operating under the illusion that the inferior Buffaloes would be adequate opponents for Japanese fighters.

The facilities at Mingaladon were the best that the AVG men had yet worked from. There were multiple hard-surfaced runways and the types of infrastructure that one would expect from an airport serving a major city such as Rangoon. Now known as Yangon International Airport, it has been one of the major airline hubs in Southeast Asia since the war and is still the capital city's major airport. At the time the AVG operated there, it was the hub of a series of dispersal fighter fields around Rangoon that were to be used if Mingaladon was under attack or threatened. These fields, nicknamed after liquor brands, included "Johnnie Walker" and "Haig and Haig."

In early December, when the Japanese had stunned the world with simultaneous attacks from Hawaii to Hong Kong, and from Bangkok to Singapore, they had not yet included Burma in the tactical plan for their airpower. They had virtually wiped out American air assets in the Philippines within the first forty-eight hours of the war but had not ventured over Toungoo. They had attacked the British throughout Malaya and had sunk the pride of the Royal Navy in the Far East, but they had not yet touched the vital Port of Rangoon, the keystone of China's Burma Road lifeline.

This was not for want of air bases. The Japanese had access to excellent airfields across Thailand, thanks to Prime Minister Phibun's fondness for the Japanese. Coincidentally, the bases around Bangkok, only 350 air miles from Rangoon, were the same that would house American B-52s and F-4s during the Vietnam War three decades later. Thai-based Japanese high-altitude reconnaissance aircraft had been observed over Burma for months, but more than two weeks passed between Pearl Harbor and the first air raid on Rangoon.

As the anticipated Japanese air attacks on Rangoon failed to materialize in the early weeks of the now-declared war, the AVG men at Mingaladon watched as prewar complacency continued to dull the judgment of their opposite numbers among the RAF.

R. T. Smith observed that they "seemed much more relaxed about the precarious situation we were all in than seemed warranted. Every day at mid-morning and mid-afternoon they took their tea break no matter what, while our guys continued working their tails off in the hot sun. This somewhat lackadaisical attitude prevailed even after the shooting started, and in time led to some marked differences of opinion, often expressed verbally, and was the beginning of considerable friction between the AVG and the British."

On December 23, this all changed.

A large number of enemy bombers were closing on Rangoon, but the defenders did not get the kind of advance warning that the men at Kunming had enjoyed two days earlier because RAF boss E. R. Manning had ignored Chennault's recommendation to build a network of spotters.

"As I anticipated, the radar-phone combination of the RAF warning system failed to provide adequate warning," Chennault recalled of the failures of a structure that could not now be fixed. "Numerous AVG interceptions were made only after the enemy finished bombing and was leaving the target due to the inadequate warning."

The enemy strike force was much larger than the AVG had faced near Kunming earlier in the week. The enemy had flooded Thailand's airfields with more than a hundred bombers and many fighters to support them. Today alone, there were five dozen bombers, twin-engine Mitsubishi Type 97s, which the Imperial Japanese Army Air Force designated as K-21s and classed as "heavy" bombers, though they were the equivalent to American medium bombers. They did, however, have twice the bomb capacity of the Blenheims, which were the only Allied bombers available in Burma.

The plot was thickened by the fact that their target was neither Rangoon nor its port, but the airfield at Mingaladon. Fortunately, two flights of P-40s and most of the RAF's Buffaloes managed to get airborne so they would not be caught on the ground.

"Check your gun switches," George "Mac" McMillan calmly told his seven-ship flight over the radio once they were airborne. "Here we go."

In his memoirs, R. T. Smith recalled "our handful of little P-40s peeling off to attack, following Mac's lead as he dove toward the right flank of the first bomber formation and began firing. And now it was my turn, diving and turning to line up my gunsight with plenty of 'lead' at a bomber, squeezing the stick-trigger and hearing the crackling sound of my four .30 caliber wing guns and the slower, powerful thudding of the two .50s in the nose, like twin jackhammers ripping up pavement; and the pungent smell of cordite filling the cockpit, a good smell. Now aware that dozens of guns from the bombers were firing back, tracers criss-crossing the sky in every direction, black smoke and flames streaming from the left engine of a bomber up ahead, and all the while that creepy-crawly feeling at the back of the neck, knowing their fighters must surely be about to pounce down on us at any moment, sneaking up in the blind spot to the rear, set for the kill."

Indeed, the bombers were escorted by Nakajima Ki-27 Model I-97 fighters, which the AVG pilots routinely referred to by their model number. The AVG men also reported encountering the very similar Mitsubishi Type 96 fighter, which served with the Imperial Japanese Navy as the A5M. It is unlikely the AVG met these aircraft because they never reached squadron service with the Imperial Japanese Army. Both the 96 and 97 types were obsolete, fixed-landing-gear aircraft, but as R. T. Smith articulated, they were "every bit as maneuverable as Chennault had said." To this, he added that "outnumbering us as they did, it was hard to get a shot at one before another was on my tail and I was forced to do a half-roll and dive away."

The bombers that attacked Mingaladon were only the first wave. The IJA Air Force made up for two weeks of having left Rangoon alone with a second wave that rained bombs on the city and its port.

"I picked out this one bomber, got directly behind him and just under his prop wash, and opened fire at about 200 yards," Smith said, describing that moment when he became a fighter pilot. "I could see my tracers converging on the fuselage and wing roots as I rapidly overtook him but kept firing until he blew up right in my face. His gas tanks exploded in a huge ball of flame, the concussion tossing my plane upward like a leaf. I fought for control, flying through the debris, felt a thud as something hit my left wing, let out a shout of triumph into my oxygen mask. . . . I was elated beyond words, but there was little time for self-congratulation. With one victory in hand, I wanted more, and God knows there were plenty left."

He and Mac McMillan joined forces to attack another bomber and left it trailing smoke but they were jumped by three Japanese fighters that took an intense interest in Smith. He gave them the slip, but two Americans were not so lucky. Neither Hank Gilbert nor Neil Martin came home that day. Paul Greene was also shot down, but he bailed out. As he dangled in his parachute, Japanese fighters did their best to finish him off, but he survived to fly again.

The RAF and AVG pilots flew patrols again on Christmas Eve, but the Imperial Japanese Army Air Force did not appear again until about noon on Christmas Day. In his diary, Smith wrote that thirteen P-40s met three waves, each consisting of twenty-seven bombers, Ki-21s again, supported by thirty fighters. It was reported that some of the infamous Mitsubishi A6M Zeros were among the fighters, though the Zero served with the Imperial Japanese Navy. The aircraft in question was almost certainly the Nakajima Ki-43 Hayabusa (Peregrine Falcon), visually similar to the Zero and often misidentified as such in Allied battle reports.

Of the two dozen Japanese aircraft downed by the AVG that day, Smith and Chuck Older were each credited with two Ki-21s and a Ki-43, while McMillan downed three bombers and Eddie Overend claimed two. The AVG got its first ace on that Christmas Day, when

Robert "Duke" Hedman became one of a handful of fighter pilots in history to score all five of the requisite aerial victories in a single day—four bombers and a Hayabusa.

For the moment, there was plenty to celebrate, including the fact that the AVG was flying an aircraft that turned out to be ideally suited for the task at hand. Even Claire Chennault, who had grumbled about having to accept the P-40, realized that the AVG had lucked out.

"Whatever its later shortcomings, the Curtiss-Wright P-40 was an excellent fighter for the battles over Rangoon, all of which were fought below 20,000 feet," he admitted in his memoirs. "At those altitudes the P-40 was better than a Hurricane and at its best against the Japanese."

However, the already badly outnumbered AVG lost two P-40s that day over Rangoon, including the one flown by McMillan. Given up for dead, the pilots had actually survived crash landings, and walked or hitchhiked back to Mingaladon. The RAF 67 Squadron lost five of their Buffaloes and four pilots while downing four Japanese aircraft.

For the AVG, the excitement of Christmas Day gradually waned as food and ammunition dwindled and as the bacteria in the water laid some of the men low with dysentery. In the city, with fires burning out of control and civilians dead from strafing attacks, morale was also a casualty. In his memoirs, Chennault wrote that the air raids "put the torch of panic to Rangoon. Those who were rich enough to do so fled for their lives to India. Native Burmese rioted, looted, and began potting stray Britons. All the native cooks and servants fled from Mingaladon, leaving the AVG without a mess. For two days they lived mainly on stale bread and canned beer, of which there seemed to be an ample stock."

As the AVG men watched the skies, nervously reacting to false alarms and waiting in the strength-sapping 115-degree heat for the next raid, the IJAAF, stunned by their lopsided losses against the AVG, suspended further attacks on Rangoon through the end of the year.

Had they known this, the Americans could have relaxed, but after two substantial aerial battles, it was better to be safe than sorry. This required continued aerial patrols because of the inadequacies of the early warning network, about which Chennault had been complaining to Manning for months.

———————

The conventional wisdom promulgated by and accepted by conventional wise men from the RAF headquarters in Rangoon to the halls of power in Washington held that the "unprofessional" AVG would not outlast its first week or so in combat. The news reports circulating back home and around the Far East told of a frat house of undisciplined mercenaries but gave no inkling of an effective fighting force. Indeed, there would be no inkling to give until the Hell's Angels of the 1st Pursuit Squadron had a chance to show what they could do.

Ironically, one of those who had embraced the notion of their being doomed amateurs was a man who should have known better—William Douglas Pawley. After everything that transpired, one would have thought it was in Pawley's best interest, from the perspective both of appearances and good business practice, to maintain good relations with the AVG. The AVG was money in his pocket. Indeed, the contract that he had with the Chinese government called for CAMCO to provide maintenance support to the AVG at their facility at Lei Yun. However, as early as November, Chennault had come to be deeply disappointed with the service that Pawley delivered.

"As damaged planes began to pile up during training at Toungoo, I made repeated requests to Pawley for men and materials from his Loi-Wing [Lei Yun] plant to repair them," Chennault wrote in his memoirs. "A few CAMCO men were sent to Toungoo but it was decided to do only emergency work there and to ship badly damaged planes over the Burma railroad to Lashio and thence by truck, up the Burma Road to the Loi-Wing factory. A number of P-40s were shipped to Loi-Wing, but after they arrived, little work was done on them."

It was Chennault's perspective that Pawley was doing little to earn the commission money that was going into his pocket.

In December, as the military situation across the Far East rapidly unraveled, things got even worse. Chennault recalled bitterly that in December, Pawley issued an order to his American employees at Lei Yun "forbidding them to touch an AVG plane, and followed this with a radio to me that, as of January 1, CAMCO would do no more repair work on AVG P-40's. I replied that Pawley's inability to do this work was regretted, but we would manage without him. . . . I have always suspected that Pawley, like the Japanese, thoroughly believed the British and American intelligence reports that the AVG would not last three weeks in combat. At any rate on the occasions when he had a chance to provide the AVG with badly needed assistance, Pawley exhibited what I considered a remarkable lack of cooperation. It was only after the AVG's combat record had made the organization world famous that Pawley made strenuous efforts to have himself identified with it."

THIRTEEN

To Do *Something* in This War

At the end of December, Chennault decided to rotate his exhausted 3rd Squadron out of Mingaladon, and send in the rested 2nd Pursuit Squadron. By New Year's Eve, seventeen P-40s of Scarsdale Jack Newkirk's Panda Bears were on the ground at Mingaladon, and Oley Olson's Hell's Angels had reached Kunming with their ten flyable aircraft.

Relations with the RAF, which had been strained at best, changed markedly when the insecure and unimaginative Group Captain E. R. Manning was replaced as RAF commander in Burma by the aggressive and determined Air Vice Marshal D. F. Stevenson, who had been sent out from the United Kingdom to shake things up. Stevenson's previous command had been RAF Bomber Command Number 2 Group, which had been tasked with daylight raids on coastal shipping and heavily defended objectives in occupied Europe, during which he had been criticized for pushing his crews relentlessly and for incurring heavy losses, albeit at substantial cost to the Germans.

Before dawn on January 3, 1942, after two days of false alarms, Newkirk decided—partly to break the tension and partly out of sheer cockiness—to "take the war to the enemy" by flying a four-ship patrol into Thai airspace to hit the IJAAF on the ground. With Jim Howard flying as his wingman, Newkirk was also joined by Tex Hill and Bert Christman, though Christman had to turn back early in the mission because of engine trouble.

The remaining trio headed south by southeast, flying low to avoid Japanese radar. They reached their target, Tak Airport near Raheng, north of Bangkok, just as the sun crested the horizon.

As Howard recalled, "we nosed down two hundred yards apart, throttles wide open. . . . A couple of dozen Nakajima 97 [Ki-27] fighters were circling the field and turning up their engines on the ground. Apparently we had caught them as they were forming up to hit Rangoon again. There were only three of us, but we had the advantage of speed and surprise. If we could just get in and out before they could react, we might catch them with their defenses down—we hoped."

Newkirk broke off to attack one of the circling Nakajimas, while Howard began strafing the Japanese aircraft lined up on the field below. Another of the Japanese fighters that was in the air turned in pursuit of Howard, but Tex Hill lined up on him and quickly shot him down. In turn, Newkirk shot a Nakajima off Tex's tail.

"I roared down the line of idling aircraft with my thumb on the firing button all the way," Howard wrote in his memoirs. "The machine guns left a wonderful line of destruction the length of that array of fighters. I hauled back on the stick for the getaway. . . . As the nose came up, a dull thump shook my fighter. With mine the only plane strafing ground targets that day, every Japanese gun on the field was pointed right at me on the second pass. Smoke poured from the cowling, and the screaming Allison went dead. My prop idled down until it was just a windmill. I had been hit by ground fire. In the distance

I could see the two specks that were Newkirk and Hill racing for home."

Howard found himself all alone over an enemy airfield without power and too low to successfully bail out.

It was the worst of nightmare scenarios.

He radioed the others that he was hit and going to attempt a crash landing. His airspeed was barely above stalling when he heard his Allison V-1710 engine give "a tentative cough," so he advanced the throttle and it restarted.

"I realized that I wasn't out of the woods yet," he continued. "Nakajimas appeared on either side of me. We flew straight and level for what seemed endless moments. Then it dawned on me that they hadn't even noticed me or my predicament. The Japanese pilots apparently had their gaze fixed on the ground, engrossed in the confusion and disaster that had befallen their fellow pilots. My engine was now operating at full power so I applied maximum throttle and soon left my 'escort' behind."

The historian C. Douglas Sterner, the curator of the *Military Times* "Hall of Valor," has proposed that this spur-of-the-moment and ultimately successful mission was the first preplanned American offensive action of World War II. Of course, the three pilots were all civilian soldiers of fortune, and not active duty military personnel.

At the time, the only elements of the USAAF engaging the Japanese were the handful of aircraft of the Far East Air Forces (FEAF) that had survived the initial attacks in the Philippines. They were able to launch an occasional attack during January as they withdrew gradually, first to the southern Philippines and then into the Dutch East Indies. Commanded by Major General Lewis Brereton, FEAF consisted mainly of a few P-40s and some B-17s. Numerically, the FEAF was no better off than the AVG.

On the day following the Tak raid, the Japanese returned the favor, storming over Mingaladon at daybreak to avenge the damage done at

Tak. Newkirk launched fourteen of his sharks in two waves, and as he reached twelve thousand feet, he realized that two groups of bombers were inbound, one targeting Mingaladon and the other heading for downtown Rangoon. He then peeled off with eight fighters to go after the latter strike force, and ordered Jim Howard to intercept the others.

After a head-on attack at a combined closing speed of 500 miles per hour left two bombers trailing smoke, Howard's men pulled into a steep climb and rolled out to dive on the fighters escorting the bombers. Five of these were fatally hit in the ensuing few moments. The bomber formation had been sufficiently disrupted to prevent major damage and they were struck again by Howard's Pandas as they lumbered eastward from Mingaladon.

After the January 4 battle, the Japanese shifted to a spate of nighttime attacks, though Jim Howard, in his memoirs, mentions a daytime engagement two days later in which at least two Pandas were compelled to make crash landings, and Bert Christman had to bail out of his stricken P-40. Only Ken Merritt managed to score in the battle.

Part of the Japanese rationale for the night attacks was certainly that it divided the forces of the AVG and RAF by necessitating day and night air patrols and ground alerts. On the night of January 7–8, Jim Howard was airborne with Gil Bright and Pete Wright, while Tex Hill, Ed Rector, and Ken Merritt arrived at the airfield in the predawn darkness to be prepared to relieve them. Hill and Rector walked to the flight line, while Merritt remained asleep in their car.

Meanwhile, the others had unsuccessfully engaged a flight of Japanese bombers and returned to base. As Wright was lowering his landing gear on final approach, a damaged hydraulic line exploded all over him, filling the cockpit with hydraulic fluid, blinding him. He was confronted with trying to wipe his eyes and clean his windshield while landing and hoping that he did not run out of hydraulic fluid to control his flaps. The P-40, initially centered on the runway, drifted to the right, coming down in the wrong place at the wrong time, and crashing straight into the car where Merritt was asleep. Wright survived, but was badly shaken upon learning of the fluke that had killed Merritt.

Later the same day, another pilot, Charlie Mott, was shot down during a strafing mission over Tak Airport. He survived, but wound up among the thousands of Allied POWs who were used as slave laborers in the construction of the Burma Railway, a project that included the infamous "Bridge on the River Kwai."

"On one of these they had 18 single-engined bombers and about 50 fighters," Gil Bright wrote of the battles during the first week of January in a letter to his parents in Reading, Pennsylvania. "I managed to get a bomber. I got a fighter a day or so later in another raid. On all these jobs, we have had only about fifteen planes in the air, which is a source of amazement to the correspondents. They think it great stuff that we, although greatly outnumbered, can knock off so many planes. The secret, of course, is in letting the enemy beat himself. With our faster planes we can let them mill around until they break their own formation up. Then we get the strays. The bombers never stay with their escort, so they don't make out very well either."

⸻

The next major battle over Rangoon came on January 23, the one-month anniversary of the first attack on the city, and in coordination with the long-anticipated Japanese ground invasion of Burma that had begun with a series of incursions over the preceding few days and a larger move the day before. Jim Howard later said that the Japanese had "started a new series of large-scale raids, as if trying for the knock-out blow." That *was* their idea.

As he explained to his biographer Reagan Schaupp, Tex Hill recalled two Japanese attacks that day, with the first wave of fighters coming in the morning, with he and Frank Lawlor scrambling to meet them. As Hill reached the flight line, Lawlor was in a P-40, and the only other flyable fighter belonged to Jim Howard, so he took it. At that moment ground crews were sweating to get additional P-40s airworthy as quickly as possible.

"What have we got, Frank?" Hill asked over the radio as he followed Lawlor to twelve thousand feet.

"Many bandits southeast . . . that's all we know."

"One o'clock low, Frank," Hill reported as he rolled to attack more enemy aircraft than he could ever remember seeing at once. "Got 'em."

Both P-40s ripped into the Japanese fighters. Hill remembered firing a burst, missing, then firing a second burst into the tail of an I-97 and a third into the cockpit as it turned. Lawlor, meanwhile, shot up a series of I-97s while ducking into and out of a bank of cumulus, sending three spiraling to earth.

On his second pass, Hill took a deflection shot at another I-97, ripping off its wing just as he felt rounds impacting his own wing.

Lawlor claimed his fourth kill of the day just as several other P-40s joined the fight, and Hill made his way back toward Mingaladon having downed two of the enemy fighters. Meanwhile, Bob Neale, who had served with Tex Hill as a bomber pilot aboard the USS *Saratoga* before joining the AVG, also downed an I-97 that day. It was the first of an eventual thirteen aerial victories that would make Neale the highest-scoring AVG ace.

"Hope you took good care of her," Jim Howard said, looking at his P-40 as Hill taxied to a stop.

"I think she held up all right, considering the odds," he replied with a smile, climbing out of the cockpit.

Doing a walkaround, Howard scolded Hill for damaging his P-40 as they counted the bullet holes. To this, Hill reminded Howard that the last time they flew together, on the January 3 mission to Tak Airport, he had saved Howard's life.

The second wave of Japanese fighters and bombers appeared about an hour and a half after the first, presumed to be timing their attack to catch the AVG sharks on the ground, licking their wounds. However, the ground crews were racing and achieving extraordinary results. The Japanese entered Rangoon airspace with the wounds already having been licked—which had included getting Howard's P-40 patched up in record time.

Howard now took his P-40 back from Hill and spearheaded the attack, which included both AVG P-40s and RAF Buffaloes, as well as a few RAF Hurricanes that had recently arrived.

"I put the formation in trail and started my head-on attack," he wrote. "I sprayed my bullets at three bombers bunched together. As I pulled up, I could see that one was on fire and headed down. [Robert "Moose"] Moss, who had been flying my wing, got his by flying under the formation and aiming at a plane at the tail end of the group."

In his memoirs, Howard wrote that Jack Newkirk, the squadron leader, was in Rangoon that day, "organizing the transfer of supplies up the Burma Road to Kunming," so Howard led the second intercept. Other accounts, including Hill's, have Newkirk present, and note that he destroyed at least one Japanese fighter before having his own plane severely damaged and forced into a crash landing.

"Disregarding the fighters, we kept up attacks by seesawing from one side to the other," Howard wrote. "It was another case of decimating the enemy, but it cost us two P-40s and one life. As Bert Christman bore into a formation of bombers, he was jumped by several Nakajima fighters, who sent him spinning down in flames."

In fact, he managed to bail out, but was shot dead by Japanese pilots who fired at him as he hung helpless beneath his parachute.

Christman, who had survived the loss of two other P-40s, had seemed to have led a life as charmed as that of Scorchy Smith, the character he drew for prewar comics, but his number had finally come up. The Scorchy Smith strip would survive, in the hands of several other artists, until 1961.

The IJAAF returned in strength the following day, and once again, the AVG rose to exact a toll. Tex Hill was airborne, flying as wingman to Bob Neale and intercepting an echelon of Ki-21 bombers. One of a pair of RAF Buffaloes targeted the same slice of the bomber formation and downed one, while a stream of Bob Neale's gunfire tore one of the unarmored bombers in half. Neale went on to shoot down one of the escorting I-97 fighters, while Tex Hill claimed two bombers. These, on top of two the previous day and the one over Tak on January 3 that saved Jim Howard's life, made Hill an ace.

The losses of AVG aircraft were mounting, though most of the pilots who were shot down lived to fight another day. Aircraft damaged in earlier training accidents at Toungoo were being gradually repaired, but there remained a shortage of operational P-40s. Chennault decided that it was time to send in reinforcements, so eight men from the 1st Pursuit Squadron "Adam and Eves," led by Sandy Sandell, flew down from Kunming on January 25, with a refueling stop in Lashio on the Burmese side of the border, to beef up the Pandas. Among them were Charlie Bond and Greg Boyington.

This brought the effective strength of the AVG over Rangoon to about twenty P-40s, depending on maintenance schedules. In his diary, Bond noted that the RAF maximum strength at the time was four Buffaloes and as many as eight Hurricanes. Accommodations at Mingaladon left undamaged by the Japanese were limited, so Bond and

George Burgard were put up at the home of a Danish oilman named Jensen.

At first, Boyington stayed at the base, where a roped-off unexploded bomb remained in the middle of the barracks, but he later was invited into the home of a British businessman named Bill Tweedy, who occupied a hilltop villa with a staff of servants who treated the former Marine aviator like nobility.

As Boyington recalled of their first night at Mingaladon, "we spent most of the night in the RAF officers' mess, there on the field. We drank with them, RAF and AVG alike. We coaxed all the information we could out of the pilots who had seen action, anything pertaining to the performance of Japanese aircraft we would be up against. As we talked and drank, this information became all the more important, for the ceilings and walls around us in this mess bore mute evidence that this was no game. The Nips were playing for keeps. Although this mess had been spared by the bombs, it was perforated by machine gun fire. One even had to watch his elbows upon the bar, or he was apt to pick up splinters."

When Boyington asked how the alerts were announced, one of the other AVG men told him that "long before the RAF gets around to announcing the alert, you will see two Brewsters take off in a westerly direction, regardless of the wind sock. That's the signal."

This was cruel jab at the New Zealanders of 67 Squadron. The Japanese attacked from the *east.*

In his memoirs, Boyington wrote that his own baptism of fire came soon after he arrived at Mingaladon. He complained that his flight leader (unnamed in his account) had positioned the flight beneath forty to fifty I-97s, giving the enemy the altitude advantage with their backs to the sun. With the sun in their eyes, it was hard for the Americans to see the Japanese fighters. Suddenly, the Japanese dived, forcing the Americans into half-blinded evasive action.

"Soon I spotted a pair of Japs off to the side of me, so I added throttle and started to close in behind them," Boyington recalled. "One of these two pulled almost straight up, going into a loop above my P-40 about the same instant I started my tracers toward the other. I knew that I had to break off firing and commence turning."

Because the I-97 could outmaneuver a P-40, Boyington experienced extreme g-force as he tried to outturn his opponent.

"I was sufficiently blacked out not to be able to see whether my bursts had gotten the I-97 I had been firing on," he wrote. "I had pulled myself plumb woozy."

He broke off, using the P-40's power to dive away from the enemy aircraft.

When he pulled out, he spotted another Japanese fighter. When he tried again, he had a firsthand experience of how nimble the enemy aircraft were.

"As I approached this Nip fighter, he also permitted me to get close enough to where my tracers were sailing about him," Boyington wrote, continuing his account. "Then I witnessed this little plane perform one of the most delightful split S's I had ever seen, and then I discovered that I was turning again with some of his playmates. . . . 'To hell with this routine!' I thought, and dove out. Bonus money of the fantastic variety fluttered to the ground like so many handbills, and with them the last of my illusions. . . . I hated myself so badly I didn't even bother to write up my first combat report, for this could have happened to others—but not to me. Self-pity had always been one of my greatest indulgences anyhow."

In his diary, Charlie Bond reported this air battle as having taken place on January 29. He notes that the Japanese were flying Mitsubishi Model 96 fighters, but these were not operated by the IJAAF and were easily mistaken for the Nakajima I-97s reported in other accounts. In any case, there were no discrepancies when it came to the recollections of Bond and Boyington of the maneuverability of the enemy fighters.

"Suddenly we spotted a swarming beehive of Japanese I-96 fighters about ten o'clock low," he wrote in his diary. "We dove in. I was breathing hard as I charged my guns. Gunsight switch on. I was almost vertical in a dive. The Jap fighter I picked out began turning tightly in a horizontal plane. I missed him by a mile. Aware of their maneuverability and tactics to get on our tails, I continued my dive on down a few thousand feet further. As I started pulling up I partially blacked out. . . . I picked one that was flying straight and level, but as I closed in, he turned sharply. I missed again as I rammed on past."

Bond wrote of "a swarming mass . . . twisting, turning, diving, and maneuvering to get position."

And so he did, lining up on the rear, six-o'clock position of a Japanese fighter at about 250 yards, recalling that "my tracers tore into his cockpit and engine. Suddenly I was right on him. I had to raise my left wing to get over him as I zoomed past. His cockpit was flaming. I squealed in delight, laughing aloud."

Picking out two Japanese fighters that were isolated from the pack, Bond brazenly tore after them, but they pulled into Immelmann turns and were suddenly on a head-on trajectory with him.

"As we passed each other, I saw smoke trailing from one of the fighters, and he disappeared in a dive down into some clouds," Bond recalled, chalking up the second victory for the day and for his career. He picked another Japanese aircraft as his potential third, but this pilot managed to outmaneuver him, so Bond decided to call it a day.

The AVG downed a dozen Japanese aircraft that day, including one each for Noel Bacon, John Dean, Tex Hill, Whitey Lawlor, Bob Little, and Jack Newkirk—and the three fighters that made Sandy Sandell an ace, while the RAF bagged two. The outnumbered handful of Allied pilots were making the enemy pay.

That night, Mr. Jensen, Charlie Bond's landlord, congratulated him over a few drams of scotch, and Bond told his diary that "I thought to myself how content I was now that I had done something in this war."

FOURTEEN

Flying Tigers in Asian Skies

News of the American Volunteer Group victory over the mountains of remote southern China on December 20 and the continuing combat victories by the grossly outnumbered Americans over Rangoon rippled around the world, playing well in the American media, where there had been no good news in the long weeks since Pearl Harbor that had been marked by substantial Japanese victories and humiliating Allied losses. Even if they were civilian bounty hunters flying shark-faced aircraft with Chinese markings, the David and Goliath exploits of the AVG buoyed the American spirit.

It was at about this time that they became the "Flying Tigers."

The name, which is probably the best-remembered American air group nickname of World War II—and indeed of all time—did not originate within the unit to which it applied, though the origin is uncertain. Daniel Ford, who is the world's preeminent AVG historian, believes that it originated in Washington with China Defense Supplies, having been coined by David Corcoran or T. V. Soong. In later years, Corcoran used his role in helping to organize the Flying Tigers as an item in his résumé—it was also in the first line of his *New York Times* and Associated Press obituaries in 1990—so this is clearly a possibility.

One thing is certain: Claire Chennault himself did *not* coin the phrase, and at first, he was quite mystified by it.

"My men were astonished to find themselves world famous as the Flying Tigers," Claire Chennault wrote in his memoirs. "How the term Flying Tigers was derived from the shark-nosed P-40s I never will know. At any rate we were somewhat surprised to find ourselves billed under that name."

One of the first mentions of the term in the media appeared in the December 29, 1941, issue of *Time* magazine under the title "Blood for the Tigers." Published a week earlier than its cover date, the article described the December 20 "Flying Tigers" victory over Kunming. In keeping with the magazine's practice, there was no byline, but the piece was almost certainly penned by Theodore H. White, *Time*'s correspondent in Chongqing, who later went on to become the Pulitzer-winning, best-selling author of *The Making of the President 1960*, the first of a successful election recap series that he wrote over two decades.

White had gotten to know Chennault, and was an occasional visitor to Kunming. In his article, he accurately described the origins of the AVG, that "lean, hardbitten, taciturn" Chennault had "rounded up US volunteers to fly 100 new P-40s purchased from the US." He also correctly reported the loss of four Japanese bombers in that battle. The term "Flying Tigers" may or may not have been inserted by an editor in New York who had been in contact with China Defense Supplies.

However, an Associated Press item datelined from Chongqing on January 26, 1942, announced that "the Chinese press bestowed the name of 'Flying Tigers' today on pilots of the American Volunteer Group in recognition of their recent exploits against the Japanese." Indeed, the term was widely used in Chinese newspapers early in 1942.

The following day, the United Press wires carried an item datelined Rangoon that used the term to describe the AVG having escorted RAF bombers against the Japanese. Wherever and with whomever it originated, the name was suddenly everywhere.

In Hollywood, David Miller was directing a film for Republic Pictures about a group of American volunteer airmen in the Far East that was loosely based on the AVG. It starred John Carroll and Anna Lee, along with John Wayne in his first war movie. At the beginning of 1942, it was a project in search of a title. Originally it was to have been called *Yanks over the Burma Road*, but when MGM announced another film titled *A Yank on the Burma Road* for February release, Republic went back to the drawing board. They toyed with the working title *Yank over Singapore*, but the news reports flooding out of Kunming and Rangoon gave the studio a precious gift. Released on October 8, 1942, the film *Flying Tigers* was a hit, and John Wayne had found his niche. P-40s and company test pilots borrowed from Curtiss-Wright added some authenticity, though the combat scenes were done with models. In their memoirs, the AVG men gave it low marks for realism and accuracy. R. T. Smith called it one of the worst movies of all time.

While the "Flying Tigers" name may or may not have originated with David Corcoran or T. V. Soong at China Defense Supplies in Washington, Chennault himself confirms that the Flying Tiger insignia *did*—or at least the order did. The actual artwork, a cartoon tiger jumping out of a "V for Victory," was one of more than twelve hundred unit emblems created during World War II by the artists at Walt Disney Productions. As the procedure worked, units were able to contact Disney directly to request whatever they wanted, whether it be a Disney character—Donald Duck was featured in more than two hundred insignias—or something else.

According to Wanda Cornelius and Thayne Short, writing in the April 1979 issue of *American History Illustrated*, China Defense Supplies approached the Disney organization, where illustrator Roy Williams was assigned the task. They interviewed Williams, who explained that he did the final artwork based on a preliminary sketch by fellow artist Hank Porter. Each man was personally responsible for dozens of other insignias during the war years.

According to Chennault, the cartoon tiger did not reach the Flying Tigers until early summer 1942, but Charlie Bond mentioned the emblem in his diary on March 12. The bulk shipment of airplane decals and uniform patches, supplied courtesy of China Defense Supplies, probably took a bit longer. Olga Greenlaw recalled that a package of enameled pins bearing the tiger insignia arrived in Kunming early in April and that the pilots were initially put off by a cartoon character that reminded them of "something we used to buy at the five and ten back home." Gradually, though, they took to the insignia and started wearing it. Madame Chiang Kai-shek reportedly loved it the moment she first saw it.

The notoriety of the Flying Tigers made them seem larger than life, a few dozen airmen holding the Empire of Japan at bay, but at the beginning of February 1942, they were a remarkable success story at the center of a vast continent of bad news. In the seven weeks since Pearl Harbor, the US Army in the Philippines—except for the doomed men who had holed up in the Bataan Peninsula and on Corregidor— had been defeated and those islands occupied by Japan. Hong Kong was also in Japanese hands, and so too was all of Malaya, and the demise of Singapore was but a week away. On Borneo, the resources of the world's fourth-largest oil producer were in Japanese hands, as was the great refinery center at Balikpapan, the Ploesti of the Far East.

It seemed—at least to the popular media—as though Rangoon, despite its precarious position, could be protected indefinitely by the superhuman warriors with the shark-faced P-40s. Journalists flew halfway around the world—across Africa and India—to visit the men of

Mingaladon and craft the narrative that inspired Republic pictures to put John Wayne into a shark-faced P-40.

———

The AVG men themselves alternated their alerts and scrambles with all-night parties at the Silver Club in downtown Rangoon, where the booze flowed freely, female companionship was readily available, and where time seemed to have stood still in some endless continuation of prewar colonial reality.

Back on the Mingaladon side of reality, there had been more air raid alerts than significant air raids in the week or so leading up to February 5, but that night four waves of Japanese bombers came over, targeting the Allied air base.

"I nearly fell out of my bed, the bombs were so close," Charlie Bond confided in his diary. "I thought they knew exactly where I was and were going just for me! It was the first time I got a bit scared of bombs. There were four raids in all. Not much damage in town; it was obvious they went for our planes at the field when we saw the damage that morning on arriving at the parking area. Made me wonder just how much they knew about our dispersal plans at night."

Several hours later, with the sun high in Burmese skies, the Allies scrambled a half dozen P-40s and a pair of Hurricanes against a Japanese force above that turned out to include thirty-five fighters. The enemy had the dual advantages of the sun to their backs, and greater altitude, which can, for a fighter pilot, always be converted to speed.

"Pilots had been coming out of the sun since World War I, and so did we," Greg Boyington recalled. "But to make certain that no one sucked me in for a sun approach, or if he did and I couldn't avoid it, I used a trick to keep track of him: I closed one eye, holding the tip of my little finger up in front of the open orb, blocking out just the fiery ball of the sun in front of my opened eye. I found that it was impossible for an enemy to come down from out of the sun on a moving target without showing up somewhere outside of my fingertip if I continuously kept the fiery part from my vision. This is mentioned only because I assumed that others were doing the same thing, but the war was over before I knew that most of the pilots I talked to didn't."

This technique paid off, with two kills, and he bore in for another.

"The third fighter didn't go down quite so easily, it seemed, and something made me feel squeamish," he later wrote. "Air fighting had become impersonal, for there was no personal contact except on this one occasion. . . . On this occasion I had sent a burst into this little fellow. He had an open-cockpit fighter. The plane didn't burst into flames, and it didn't fall apart, but was definitely going down, out of control. As I flew right beside him, I could see his arm dangling out of the cockpit, flapping in the slipstream like the arm of a rag doll, and I knew definitely he was dead. For no other reason, or maybe because we were supposed to bring a claim back in our teeth to get credit, I sent another long burst into his plane and literally tore it up. That was the only time I ever felt squeamish about the entire affair."

Charlie Bond, who attacked the same slice of the fighter formation as Boyington, closed on an I-97 and opened fire just as the Japanese pilot did a snap roll, forcing Bond to take evasive action.

"There were too many other enemy aircraft in the area to stay glued to him, so I made several passes on other ships but did not get in many effective bursts," Bond told his diary. "Too damn excited, I guess. I saw tracers coming at me several times, but I received no hits. I had to dive out once when a Jap got too close on my rear, and when I leveled off and climbed back up, I lost the enemy fighters."

As he attacked another Japanese fighter, he failed to see an I-97 that had gotten behind him, but this pilot overshot him, and Bond managed to get away just as Bob Neale arrived.

"I figured one of us would get the Jap," Bond wrote. "Bob and I fought that little devil some five to ten minutes. He must have known he was done for, but he was a game little guy, and he would turn eastward in an attempt to get away every chance he had. Bob started one of his attacks, and as he closed in, the Jap pilot turned sharply and ended up flying straight at me. All my guns were firing as we barreled on at each other head-on. He started pulling up and I followed as long as I dared, then broke off in a screaming dive out. He flipped around in an amazing turn and followed me down. I had my throttle jammed fully forward—one glimpse at the instrument panel showed 52 inches of manifold pressure. I hoped the engine would stay together. But what the hell! It was either the engine or me. Looking back I saw Bob's ship on the Jap's tail. That was some comfort. I was in a vertical power dive and skidding like mad, since I did not bother [with] the rudder trim. Bob told me later that the I-97 turned out to be duck soup. I set him up for Bob, and the unintended cooperation paid off. I ribbed Bob about getting half the [$500] bonus. He just grinned."

On February 6, Air Vice Marshal D. F. Stevenson, the RAF commander in Burma, had sent a congratulatory telegram to Chennault, noting that the AVG had now destroyed a hundred enemy aircraft in the defense of Rangoon.

At Kunming, the situation was quite different. The presence of Chennault and his staff gave the base a pretense of military uniformity, though the Old Man himself spent much of the winter in his sickbed because of flare-ups of the chronic bronchitis that kept him from ever visiting his men in Mingaladon.

Uniformity also meant uniforms, and during January, Chinese officers' uniforms were issued to the pilots. As with their civilian flying gear, the "wings" the pilots wore on their uniforms were those they had earned while in the US armed forces—although Chinese Air Force wings were presented to the pilots by P. T. Mao on the last day of the month.

Tactically, the situation was also different. Japanese air raids, instead of being a nightly concern, were rare. Once, the Japanese had felt confident about launching raids against Kunming and Chongqing, but December 20 had changed that. The Flying Tigers had changed that. What the world knew about shark-faced P-40s as media hype, the Imperial Japanese Army Air Force knew as a painful reality. Whereas most of the scrambles from Mingaladon brought the Flying Tigers into clouds of two dozen or more Japanese fighters, those from Kunming were mainly against lone reconnaissance aircraft, flying high enough to escape.

There were a few exceptions, but the AVG pilots found the Japanese bomber formations flying north toward Chongqing were more likely to scatter and retreat when intercepted than were the Japanese bombers targeting Rangoon. In turn, the dispersed bombers provided isolated targets more easily preyed upon by the Tigers. These missions were also complicated for the enemy by their distance as balanced against the range of the IJAAF fighters. The base from which the Japanese launched their air raids against Chongqing, such as the one interrupted by the AVG on December 20, was at Gia Lam near Hanoi in French Indochina, which was twice as far as the Japanese bases in Thailand were from Rangoon.

Late in January, Chennault and P. T. Mao decided to turn the tables on the Japanese and run strike missions against Hanoi and the Port of Haiphong, targets that would be familiar to a later generation of American pilots in another war. The missions went out on the mornings of January 22 and 24, with Flying Tigers from the 1st Pursuit Squadron escorting Soviet-made Ant-40 "SB" (Skorostnoi Bombardirovschik) high-speed bombers. Chennault was not alone among the men of the AVG who yearned to have received the Douglas A-20 attack bombers that had been earmarked for the *2nd* American Volunteer Group but that had been commandeered by the USAAF on the flight line at Santa Monica.

They refueled at Mengzi, 100 miles south of Kunming, and headed south. R. T. Smith wrote in his diary for January 24 that "we all felt it was our last flight—going 150 miles into enemy territory and expecting to encounter Jap fighters 4 or 5 to one is no picnic. Possibility of being forced down and held prisoner, etc. or shot, was what worried us most."

It was an unusual potpourri, Americans in Chinese uniforms escorting Chinese crews in Russian airplanes attacking French cities occupied by the Axis partner of the country that had defeated France.

The SB was the same size and had the same range and speed as the Bristol Blenheim that the RAF operated out of Mingaladon to attack Japanese fields in Thailand, but while the RAF had fewer than a half dozen serviceable Blenheims, the Chinese had gotten another hundred, a rush order received just before the signing of the April 1941 Soviet-Japanese Neutrality Pact that had ended the long-running cooperation between the Soviets and Chiang Kai-shek.

In both cases, the missions were a bust because of heavy cloud cover over the targets. However, five days later, when Smith revisited Indochina as part of a four-ship photoreconnaissance mission over Japanese-held territory led by Oley Olson, the weather was clear and no enemy fighters bothered them at twenty-two thousand feet.

The proximity of Kunming to Chiang Kai-shek's capital at Chongqing meant that the AVG received frequent visits from General P. T. Mao and other Chinese dignitaries. While the men at Mingaladon pursued the raw diversions of the Silver Grill, those in Kunming dined at elaborate banquets with Chinese generals.

Mao, always flanked by a pair of hunting dogs and a small entourage of senior officers, visited often, and at least once in mid-January, he went duck hunting with Chennault, an activity that was a favorite pastime for the Flying Tigers at Kunming. In her memoirs, Olga Greenlaw recalled that the duck dinner that night "surpassed expectations" and proved a welcome break from "pork chops and beans." By all accounts, the food in Kunming was a cut above the fare that the men at Mingaladon had available.

FIFTEEN

Blood and Fire over Rangoon

During the last week of January 1942, even as the huge Japanese air offensive against Rangoon was occupying the attention of the Flying Tigers, General Shojiro Iida's Fifteenth Imperial Japanese Army ground offensive was pushing into Burma and toward Rangoon. The resources available to the British Burma Army, commanded by Lieutenant General Thomas Hutton, a former staff officer with Britain's General Headquarters India, were as inadequate on the ground as those of the RAF were in the air.

The distance from the Thai border was only about 150 miles, but there were a series of rivers flowing southward out of central Burma that would slow the advance. The first battle took place at the confluence of the Salween and Thaungyin Rivers, but it was little more than a holding action, and the British simply abandoned Moulmein (now Mawlamyine), one of the largest cities in eastern Burma. The problem of defending river crossings is that the defenders have the river to their backs. Abandoning irreplaceable supplies, they retreated by boat on

January 31, coincidentally at about the same moment that the last British Empire defenders—mainly Indian—were abandoning Malaya and retreating across the Johor Strait into Singapore. After a two-day holding action at the narrow and indefensible Bilin River, the British Empire defenders of Burma retreated under cover of darkness to the broad Sittang River, which was perceived by the strategic planners on both sides as the key defensive point between Thailand and Rangoon, and Iida's last significant obstacle.

As February arrived, the ferocity of the air assault on Rangoon abated, although there was the occasional raid against Mingaladon, and Japanese bombers ranged as far north as the old AVG haunts at Toungoo, which was still being used as a maintenance and repair facility.

The complexion of the operations changed considerably as the AVG found themselves moving from defense to offense. With the Japanese strike missions tapering off in a calm before an anticipated later storm, Stevenson began sending his handful of Blenheims against targets behind Japanese lines in Thailand, as well as to many locations such as Moulmein that were now behind Japanese lines in Burma.

As the Flying Tigers of Kunming had been called upon to escort Chinese bombing missions over Indochina, the Flying Tigers of Mingaladon were asked to escort Stevenson's Blenheims.

Jim Howard recalled having led several escort missions to rail centers in Thailand, mentioning that these were "milk runs that weren't very productive—seldom were the targets hit and enemy fighters failed to rise to the bait. The primitive area of northern Thailand had no real industrial bombing targets, yet the RAF stubbornly went through the motions by sending their Blenheims out on useless bombing runs as if to satisfy someone at higher headquarters that something was being done. If they had attacked the two or three airfields where Japanese planes were concentrated, their results could have been substantial.

Enemy fighters might have been drawn into the fray, thus presenting the guns of our AVG fighters with suitable targets."

Stevenson was doing what he knew. His last job, with Number 2 Group of Bomber Command, going back to April 1940, had been sending RAF Blenheims against targets behind German lines in Belgium and France as those lines moved ever westward, and ultimately to Calais, within sight of the White Cliffs of Dover.

Howard added that "we were thankful that Chennault was our leader, free as he was from any obligation to satisfy the whims of a detached and isolated higher command."

The American Volunteer Group squadron leaders also made a significant impression upon their men, and are often mentioned respectfully in their postwar accounts. However, the loss of Robert "Sandy" Sandell of the 1st Pursuit Adam and Eves seemed to have touched many people to a greater degree than the passing of many others.

It was on February 7 that it came, not as a blaze of glory at twelve thousand feet, but in a freak accident at five hundred feet when a repair job to damaged tail surfaces failed.

"I actually watched and was horrified," Charlie Bond remembered. "What a loss to us and what a shame to lose a man like that while we are engaged with the enemy. Sandy was up on a test flight of his P-40. He had been having some trouble with the controls of his ship and was checking it out thoroughly. On one pass near the field he went into what looked like the start of a slow roll, but he was awful low. . . . He rolled all the way over on his back and that was far as he got. He lost altitude very quickly and went right in."

Greg Boyington did not see the crash, but recalled in his memoirs that some RAF men told him, contrary to what Bond had seen, that it "appeared as though Sandy had spun his airplane deliberately, at fairly high altitude, and then appeared to be having difficulty in recovering. But eventually the plane recovered completely and was in a steep dive. At fairly low altitude Sandy apparently hauled back on the stick too rapidly when pulling out of the dive, and his P-40 half rolled slowly, going into the ground in an inverted attitude."

While Sandell was in Kunming, Olga Greenlaw had developed a deep affection for the young flier from San Antonio. She wrote at length in her memoirs about the last time she had seen him. Shortly after he had flown as part of the January 24 bomber escort mission to Indochina, he came into the operations office where she was, and invited her to join him at an art show at the YMCA, where they turned out to be the only non-Chinese. They discussed his buying her a watercolor painting, but when he said he thought it was too small for the price, she said she did not like it either, so they went to her house. As she recalled, he offered to trim her hair, and she accepted.

As was so often the case during the war, talk turned to when the war was *over*, and Sandell told her at length about his dream of settling in Northern California and becoming a cattle rancher. Over tea after the haircut, which she was surprised to find "very becoming," he told her that he would be leaving for Mingaladon. He then handed her his flight jacket and told her to put it on, which she did.

Complimenting her on how good it looked on her, he told Olga that the jacket was hers now.

When she protested, he said, "But maybe I won't come back."

"Sandy, you are acting damn silly," she replied. "What's come over you, anyway?"

"Good-bye, Olga," he said, hugging her. "Take care of yourself. Think of me now and then."

When he left, tears were streaming down her cheeks as she touched the wings still pinned to the jacket and said to herself "Oh, Sandy. Dear, silly Sandy."

Not everyone shared Olga Greenlaw's fondness for Sandell. Jim Howard, who was at Mingaladon the day he died, wrote that "while the personnel of the Adam and Eve Squadron were shocked to learn of the death of their commanding officer, unfortunately they weren't going to miss him very much. In fact, they felt that he belonged properly in an old-fashioned Army cavalry unit, leading a charge with drawn sword, instead of leading a squadron of high-strung young fighter jockeys. Only a few days before, Sandell's squadron mates had signed a petition asking for a new leader. As one of the reasons, they cited his order forbidding pilots from socializing with ground crewmen. This was reminiscent of the class snobbishness found among elite European military cadres in the nineteenth century. Americans had long since given up on these petty distinctions."

Olga was aware of the disgruntlement, but in her hour of grief, nothing detracted from her recollections. In her memoirs, she wrote of having heard the steps of someone walking into her room on the morning that Sandell died, but when she turned, no one was there.

At Mingaladon, Bob Neale succeeded Sandell as commander of the 1st Pursuit Squadron. In his diary, Charlie Bond noted that Neale was "a jovial guy . . . well liked by the pilots and men and is a fine pilot." Jim Howard called Neale "a good leader who set his men an example, as testified by his ability to beat the Japanese in the air." Neale had become an ace the day before he became the squadron commander.

Neale also found himself as the leader of the whole AVG contingent at Mingaladon, because Jack Newkirk and the Pandas of the 2nd Pursuit were now being rotated back to Kunming. Neale's deputy was to be Greg Boyington. "He has a lot of [prewar] experience in fighter aircraft, probably more than or as much as anyone in the AVG," Charlie Bond wrote of Boyington. "I am sure that this was the major factor that led to his being selected as vice squadron leader."

However, it was to be a rocky relationship between Neale and Boyington because of the latter's proclivity for showing up on the flight line without having sobered up from one of his marathon drinking sprees. Throughout his career, there was probably no American combat pilot anywhere whose stellar performance in the air was in sharper contrast to utterly atrocious misbehavior on the ground.

The private lives of Flying Tigers while they were not flying was not entirely a madhouse of uncurbed debauchery. Among many, there was a craving for normalcy and a nostalgia for the mores and manners of the civilization they had left at home and to which they expected to return. As Sandy Sandell had shared his dreams of a California cattle ranch as part of his postwar reality, Panda Bears flight leader John "Pete" Petach and red-haired AVG nurse Emma Jane "Red" Foster had decided that they wanted to *share* their postwar reality. They had been courting, as it was called in those days, almost since they first met aboard the *Jagersfontein* on the Pacific crossing so many months before.

"Pete hemmed and hawed. Red tried to keep calm and couldn't," Olga Greenlaw wrote of their coming to her for advice. "They wanted to get married. I told Pete to go and talk to the Old Man. Pete went out, falling all over himself. He was only 22 years old, and I could well understand how he would feel facing the colonel with such a problem. We all knew the colonel thought that war was no time for wedding bells. Red was a bit nervous waiting. She told me she and Pete had been contemplating marriage for some time, but were afraid of the colonel."

"Don't be afraid of him," Olga said with a laugh. "He understands young people—he has eight kids of his own."

"Do you think he'll give his consent?" Red asked.

Olga nodded.

Petach returned later with a thumbs-up. They were married in Kunming on February 16.

In fact, Chennault, who had a reputation as a ladies' man, was also becoming involved romantically. She was the much younger Chen Xianmei, better known as Anna Chan, a correspondent for *Hsin Ming Daily News*, whose sister worked in Chennault's headquarters in Kunming.

As the Japanese Fifteenth Army made its way slowly but inexorably westward, the mood at Mingaladon grew increasingly apprehensive. At the same time, there was still that sense that so often prevails on the eve of doom that the worst-case scenario is so dreamlike it cannot be real.

On the evening of February 11, Neale invited Charlie Bond to join him at a dinner that Stevenson gave in his quarters.

"There was an unusual number of the higher-ups at the party," Bond recalled in his diary. "Between drinks and dinner we learned a lot about what the war situation was in our area. One rumor was interesting: an American B-17 outfit was due here on 20 February. We are supposed to get more fighters. Things look bad for Singapore; Japs are already on part of the island. The worst news was learning that many Japs have crossed the Salween River just northeast of here. I wonder how long we can hold out?"

Four days later, the great fortress that was Singapore surrendered to General Tomoyuki Yamashita's Twenty-fifth Imperial Japanese Army.

The B-17 outfit never came, and the AVG received no new aircraft that month. The Japanese were indeed across the Salween, and closing in on the Sittang, the last major obstacle before Rangoon.

Hutton's army in Burma consisted primarily of the inexperienced and outnumbered Indian troops who made up the 17th Infantry Division. That unit was under the command of Brigadier Sir John George "Jackie" Smyth, who had earned a Victoria Cross for bravery in action in World War I. Smyth's troops had fought a series of holding actions that slowed but never stopped the Japanese. Hutton ordered Smyth to stop the Japanese at the Sittang, but therein lay a conundrum. To stop the enemy advance, Smyth would have to dig his troops in on the eastern bank and destroy the metal railway bridge that crossed the Sittang. This, in turn, would trap his troops and their heavy equipment on the wrong side of the river. When he asked permission for a partial withdrawal, Hutton refused. The Japanese caught up with the Indians at the Sittang on February 19, and the battle raged for four days.

"On our way to quarters tonight we could see towering flames of a huge fire on the docks on the Irrawaddy River in downtown Rangoon," Bond wrote on February 21. "Apparently the British are destroying the dock area in preparation for evacuation of the city. We passed several Indian infantry units on their way to the front and many trucks filled with supplies. . . . I wondered how long we would hold out. . . . It's so funny to say I am not afraid. I don't have time to be afraid. I just try to shoot down an airplane without getting another one on my tail."

On February 23, when Jackie Smyth blew up the bridge on the Sittang River, it was a bad decision, but it was the only possible decision. Most of Smyth's command was marooned on the eastern side of the river, and those who managed to get across had abandoned their weapons. The defeat on the Sittang cost Smyth his command and left his successor, Major General David Tennant "Punch" Cowan, with a 17th Division that was 60 percent depleted and dangerously short of weapons and other equipment. Meanwhile, Hutton was also sacked, replaced by Sir Harold Alexander. By now, this was a bit like rearranging deck chairs on the *Titanic* because Rangoon was doomed.

"The Burmese members of our [domestic] help disappeared without notice one day," Greg Boyington recalled. "Their action frightened so badly our Indian servants, who were definitely not pro-Japanese, that they announced they would be on their way to India on foot. Ed Liebolt, one of our pilots, forced down with engine trouble on the outskirts of Rangoon, was expected back, surely, for [Dick Rossi] had seen Ed get out of his wheels-up landing in a rice paddy and commence running. However, Ed Liebolt never got back, so we can only assume the Burmese had killed him. We discovered that the Burmese had turned pro-Japanese in a hurry."

Smoke from the fires in the dock area rose a mile high. The flames turned night into day and the rumble of the conflagration was punctuated with the incessant tinkle of breaking glass as the looters emptied the city's storefronts.

Fritz Wolf, a 1st Pursuit Squadron flight leader who returned to Kunming at about this time reported to Chennault that "fresh food of any kind is completely lacking. We are living out of cans. Water is hard to get. Most of the city water supply has been cut off. . . . There are continual knifings and killings. Three British were killed near the docks a few nights ago. Stores are all closed. At least 25 blocks of the city are burning furiously."

"The citizens of Rangoon are leaving by the thousands," Charlie Bond wrote in his diary. "Our hosts at the billets tell us to take anything we want when they leave. They consider it lost and would rather we have it than the Japanese. Some of the pilots have radios, beautiful carvings, food, liquor. . . . While on his way to the city, Bob Smith was stopped by a Dutchman in a truck who loaded him down with brandy, rum, beer, and other types of liquor. He gave Smitty the address of his store in the city and told him to take anything he wanted. . . . All of the convicts, lepers, and insane are being turned out of their institutions and given freedom. Looting is out of all reason."

Of conditions at Mingaladon, Wolf reported that the P-40s "are almost unflyable. Tires are chewed up and baked hard. They blow out continually. We're short on them, and battery plates are thin. When we recharge them, they wear out within a day. There is no Prestone oil coolant in Rangoon. British destroyed the battery-charging and oxygen-storage depots without any advance warning to us so we could stock up. We are completely out of auxiliary gear shifts and they are wearing out in the planes every day."

Bob Neale received a terse message from the Old Man in Kunming that read "Expend equipment. Conserve personnel utmost. Retire with last bottle oxygen."

Neale ordered Jim Cross, Mickey Mickelson, and Edgar Goyette to fly up to the RAF field at Magwe (now Magway), about 250 air miles north of Rangoon, to be prepared to fly top cover for the ground evacuation of AVG ground personnel and equipment that was already under way.

The Japanese were over the city again on February 25. In his diary, Charlie Bond estimated that eleven AVG P-40s and eight RAF Hurricanes met a force of about forty IJAAF fighters and a dozen bombers.

"The Jap fighters were as aggressive as we were," he recalled. "We headed straight at each other, each with all our guns blazing. At the last second he pulled up and I did the same thing at the same time. (It is more natural concerning g-forces to pull up than push over.) I reacted unconsciously as I shoved forward on the stick violently. My seat belt was damn tight for combat, but my head still hit the top of my canopy. We shot past each other, him above me. I rolled and pulled violently to the left, straining my head over backwards to pick him up. He, too, was in flames. Yeow!" By the time the day was over, Bond had claimed three of the aggressive I-97s. Adding these to the pair he had downed on January 29, Bond was now an ace.

The following day, attacking a formation of fifteen bombers and as many as thirty fighters, he downed yet another, but moments later, he came close to finding himself added to the score of an IJAAF pilot. As he wrote, "when I looked back I saw two Jap fighters smack-dab on my tail. Their guns were spitting smoke. Again, quickly into a split-S with full throttle. They followed. All I could do was hunch up behind my armor plate and wait for my acceleration to pull me out of their firing range. None of the bullets hit my fuselage, but I got a few in the left wingtip."

February 25–26, 1942, marked the climax of the air battle of Rangoon. Whatever could be said of the hopeless rout on the ground, the Allies, especially the Flying Tigers, still owned the sky.

In addition to Charlie Bond's victories, George Burgard, Bob Little, Bob Neale, R. H. "Snuffy" Smith, and Bob Prescott all scored multiple kills over doomed Rangoon.

As Claire Chennault summarized that forty-eight-hour period in his memoirs, "there were only 15 Allied fighters to meet the attack by 166 enemy planes. They fought off three raids on the twenty-fifth with the AVG bagging 24 Jap planes. The next day was even worse, with 200 enemy planes over Rangoon. The AVG, now reduced to six P-40s, bagged 18 Jap fighters to bring their two-day total to 43 enemy aircraft without loss to themselves. In those two days of almost constant air fighting Neale's detachment turned in one of the epic fighter performances of all time. With the best of equipment it would have been a brilliant victory, but under the conditions Neale and his eight pilots fought, it was an incredible feat."

It was also a last hurrah. On the ground, the situation was hopeless, and the British knew it. As Chennault went on to say, "on the night of February 27 the RAF removed the radar set from Rangoon without previous notice to the AVG. For Neale that was the last straw. The next morning he sent four of his remaining six P-40s to cover the route of the last AVG truck convoy to leave Rangoon."

The British finally abandoned Rangoon on March 6, with the last of their colonial administration following the tens of thousands of refugees on the road north to Magwe and Mandalay. It took the Japanese the better part of the next two days to reach and occupy the city, now virtually abandoned by the British, some of whom had lived there for several generations.

In his summary report, Air Vice Marshal D. F. Stevenson observed that while the ratio of RAF aircraft to Luftwaffe attackers in the Battle of Britain had been one to four, the ratio of Allied fighters to Japanese aircraft over Rangoon was closer to one to fourteen. Wrote Stevenson, "up to the last moment the P-40s of the AVG and the Hurricane force were able to provide a state of absolute air superiority over this wide and vital area against a considerable weight of air attack. . . . Air superiority was achieved over Rangoon and maintained until it fell on 8th March. The AVG—first in the field—fought with ready devotion and resolute gallantry."

The skies were now devoid of Allied aircraft. The IJAAF could at last fly with impunity in skies once owned by the shark-faced hawks. Japanese bombers that had, only a short time before, bombed the airfield at Mingaladon now landed on its runways and made it their own. However, if to retire from the field undefeated can be considered a victory, then the Japanese had not won the Battle of Rangoon Skies, and they took the airfield by mere default.

"Although the AVG was blooded [fought their first battle] over China, it was the air battles over Rangoon that stamped the hallmark on its fame as the Flying Tigers," Chennault wrote. "The cold statistics for the ten weeks the AVG served at Rangoon show its strength varied between twenty and five serviceable P-40s. This tiny force met a total of a thousand-odd Japanese aircraft over southern Burma and Thailand. In 31 encounters they destroyed 211 enemy planes and probably destroyed [another] 43. Our losses in combat were four pilots killed in the air, one killed while strafing, and one taken prisoner. Sixteen P-40s were destroyed. During the same period the RAF, fighting side by side with the AVG, destroyed 14 enemy planes, probably destroyed [another] 33, with a loss of 22 Buffaloes and Hurricanes."

In August 1940, when the fighter pilots of the RAF had fought the Luftwaffe to a standstill and saved Britain from invasion, Prime Minister Winston Churchill had told the House of Commons, "Never in the field of human conflict was so much owed by so many to so few."

In February 1942, awed by the gallantry and effectiveness of the American Volunteer Group, Churchill cabled Sir Reginald Hugh Dorman-Smith, Britain's colonial governor in Burma, telling him that "the victories of these Americans over the rice paddies of Burma are comparable in character, if not in scope, with those won by the RAF over the hop fields of Kent in the Battle of Britain."

SIXTEEN

We Cannot Hold Burma
Without Chinese Help

I n Burma, the Flying Tigers occupied what might have been called
a parallel reality. In the skies in which *they* did battle, they achieved
incredibly lopsided victories and wrought disproportional damage
upon the Japanese. In that *other* reality, all across the land, skies, and
seas of Southeast Asia and the East Indies, it was the Japanese who were
invincible.

In the ten weeks that the AVG ruled the skies over Rangoon, the
Japanese had captured all of Malaya and virtually all of the Philippines,
Singapore, and Rangoon. In January 1942, the Allies had optimistically
created the joint American-British-Dutch-Australian Command
(ABDA) to coordinate the defense of Southeast Asia from the Japanese.
Within two months, ABDA was essentially wiped out on the ground.
At sea, meanwhile, the Imperial Japanese Navy had sunk virtually the
entire combined American, British, and Dutch naval force in Southeast
Asia in a series of battles in and around the Java Sea.

When the last AVG P-40 departed from Mingaladon, most of the

Dutch East Indies were in Japanese hands—and a couple of days later, the Dutch finally surrendered their vast colony of 17,500 islands with its great oil reserves and state-of-the-art refineries.

With this conquest behind them, the Imperial Japanese Army could reorient its land armies to tightening its noose on the swath of northern Burma still in Allied hands, and to the distant Solomon Islands, which Japanese strategic planners expected to capture with ease and thereby to tighten the noose on Australia.

In northern Burma, as in the land battles in southern Burma and the Malay Peninsula, the British Empire forces were completely outclassed by the Imperial Japanese Army. However, this coincided with a reluctance by the British leadership to want to work with others. Just as the RAF had initially been reticent to coordinate with the AVG without dominating it, the British were also disinclined to coordinate their defensive needs in Burma with their nominal allies the Chinese. Chennault points out in his memoirs that Chiang Kai-shek, who was desperately anxious that the Burma Road be kept open, had offered to intervene to help save the Port of Rangoon from the Japanese advance. The Chinese Fifth and Sixth Armies in Yunnan could have come south, but the British declined. To Chennault, this seemed counterintuitive. To the British, it was practical.

The British institutional self-image was built around their long military tradition and their view of the superiority of their professional leadership. In *Hinge of Fate*, Winston Churchill had succinctly outlined this position, writing that he had told President Roosevelt at the beginning of 1942 that he felt "American opinion overestimated the contribution which China could make to the general war" and that the president "must not expect me to adopt what I felt was a wholly unreal standard of values."

Of course, after the embarrassments of Malaya, Singapore, and Rangoon, the British necessarily became more humble.

Churchill was as willing to acquiesce to the idea of his forces fighting alongside the Chinese, as the RAF in Rangoon had been willing, ultimately, to work with the AVG. However, this was in contrast to the perspective of his military man in the region, General Sir Archibald Wavell, who held fast to the narrative of British military superiority. Wavell, who had achieved success against the Germans in North Africa, had gone east in July 1941 to assume the post of Commander in Chief, India—with responsibility for Burma as well. After a two-month stint as commander of the short-lived and ill-fated ABDA Command, he resumed command of British forces throughout India and Burma on March 7, even as the Japanese were swarming into Rangoon.

Wavell only reluctantly accepted Chinese help, and only after it was too late to save the vital Port of Rangoon. When Churchill called him on his hesitation, Wavell wrote back that he had accepted two divisions of the Fifth Chinese Army, telling the prime minister that he did not want the Chinese Sixth Army "moved to Burmese frontier, as it would be difficult to feed."

In turn, Churchill pointed out the strategic implications of his diffidence, reminding him that "in the American view China bulks as large in the minds of many of them as Great Britain. The President, who is a great admirer of yours, seemed a bit dunched at Chiang Kai-shek's discouragement after your interview with him. The American Chiefs of Staff insisted upon Burma being in your command for the sole reason that they considered your giving your left hand to China and the opening of the Burma Road indispensable to world victory. And never forget that behind all looms the shadow of Asiatic solidarity."

To this, Wavell replied scornfully that "I am aware of American sentiment about the Chinese, but democracies are apt to think with their hearts rather than with their heads, and a general's business is, or should be, to use his head for planning. I consider my judgment in accepting the Chinese help I did (two divisions of Fifth Army) and asking that Sixth Army should be held in reserve in Kunming area was quite correct, and I am sorry that my action seems to have been so misunderstood. I hope you will correct [the] President's impression if you get opportunity."

Reflecting on the chain of disasters that had been befalling the British Army across Asia, Wavell told his boss "I agree British prestige in China is low, and can hardly be otherwise till we have had some success. It will not be increased by admission that we cannot hold Burma without Chinese help."

Nevertheless, when the Japanese drive against northern Burma did sputter to a halt, there were many more Chinese boots on the ground than British.

While most of the British boots on the ground in Burma in the dark early days of 1942 held the feet of Indian colonial troops, the officer who would lead the Chinese armies was an *American*.

Joseph Warren Stilwell had returned to the United States from his third extended tour of duty in China in August 1939, less than a month before World War II began. While he was aboard the ship on which he and his wife were returning Stateside, he received a teletype informing him of the startling news that he had just been promoted to brigadier general.

Winds of change were blowing through Washington, and one of them had elevated George Catlett Marshall—whom Stilwell had first met in Tientsin in 1926 and knew at Fort Benning in the 1930s—to the post of acting chief of staff of the US Army. Marshall had been a great admirer of Stilwell and had recommended a general's star for him ahead of nearly three dozen more senior colonels. On September 1, 1939, exactly the same day that Germany invaded Poland, Marshall formally became chief of staff.

Stilwell went first to the 2nd Infantry Division in Texas, and in July 1940, he went out to California to reactivate and command the 7th Infantry Division at Fort Ord.

By the spring of 1941, with Claire Chennault and T. V. Soong making the rounds of Washington and Buffalo, and Lauchlin Currie and Tommy Corcoran making the rounds at Chiang Kai-shek's stronghold in Chongqing, the tide of eagerness to support China's war against Japan was rising.

George Marshall and the senior leadership of the US Army recognized the importance of aiding China, but as the United States was not yet at war, they had done little to further this end. They had already opened a dialogue with their opposite numbers on the British General Staff, but nothing had been done vis-à-vis China. Plans for the US Army to help China fight Japan had yet to be formalized, nor was the service coordinating with the civilians running the Lend-Lease program. Meanwhile, Chennault and Soong had been moving around Washington actively poaching US military personnel for their unofficial private air force.

On July 3, one day before the date on the contracts that the American Volunteer Group pilots signed, Marshall approved the creation of an American Military Mission to China (AMMISCA), which would supersede the role of the US military attaché in Chongqing. Two weeks earlier, Lieutenant Colonel William Mayer, the outgoing military attaché, had recommended such a move in a memo to Brigadier General Eugene Reybold, the acting chief of staff for logistics (G-4). He suggested that his successor should be a general officer who would be charged with both advising and assisting Chiang Kai-shek. Mayer mentioned Stilwell by name, as well as John Magruder, who had served as attaché both before and after Stilwell.

Marshall picked Magruder. Stilwell, who had earned the nickname "Vinegar Joe" during a stint at Fort Benning, was seen as the sort of no-nonsense combat commander who was needed as a field commander. Marshall still saw Stilwell's value to the US Army as a man who should be used to lead a division or a corps into battle.

On December 7, 1941, still commanding troops in California, Stilwell suddenly found himself on what many feared was the front lines. In the wake of the Pearl Harbor attack, it was widely assumed that the West Coast of the United States would be attacked soon, and Stilwell's command was the only regular army division available to cover the thousand-mile coastline from the Mexican border to the mouth of the Columbia River. To make matters worse, Stilwell's boss, General John Lesesne DeWitt, the commander of the Fourth Army and the Western Defense Command, was on the verge of panic. "Jittery John" DeWitt imagined spies and saboteurs under every bush, and heard Japanese bombers over his headquarters at the Presidio of San Francisco. DeWitt also knew that Stilwell's men had less than a day's worth of ammunition on hand.

The Japanese invasion never materialized, and Roosevelt, Churchill, and their chiefs of staff met in Washington for the Arcadia Conference over the turn of the new year to discuss the nuts and bolts of offensive action against the Axis. One plan called for an American invasion of northwestern Africa to relieve pressure on the British, who were fighting the German Afrika Korps across the continent in Libya and Egypt. It was code-named Operation Gymnast, and Marshall's first choice to command it was Joe Stilwell.

In the meantime, Chiang Kai-shek was growing impatient. Roosevelt and Churchill had integrated him into the Allied fold by designating an Allied China Theater, with Chiang as its commander, but he now insisted on an American military officer to function as a chief of staff, a man of sufficient stature to facilitate his getting the aid he felt China deserved, and to help him organize his army. He was disappointed in Magruder, who was increasingly pessimistic, and angered by British condescension that was manifest in the attitudes of men such as Archibald Wavell, who considered Chinese troops to be inferior. The bottom line was that Chiang wanted an American general to command his army. The only question was *who.*

Stilwell was the obvious choice, but he declined, telling Marshall that Chiang and his staff would remember him as the "small-fry colonel they kicked around" when he was an attaché. Lieutenant General Hugh Drum, commander of the US First Army and Pershing's understudy in World War I, was offered the job, but he declined because he thought it beneath him. He expected to be asked to lead American forces in Europe, a call that never came.

As it turned out, the northwestern Africa invasion was postponed to November 1942, renamed Operation Torch, and commanded by a general named Dwight Eisenhower.

When Secretary of War Henry Stimson asked Stilwell a second time, Stilwell told him to ask Chiang Kai-shek. According to Stimson's diary, the reply was that "General Stilwell's coming to China and assuming duty here is most welcome."

According to Charles Romanus and Riley Sunderland in their book *Stilwell's Mission to China*, the memos then circulating in the War Department "suggested that the Chinese wanted a senior American officer in Chungking who would accept what he was told by the Chinese at face value and in effect be another Chinese envoy to the United States." Chiang Kai-shek would get more than he bargained for.

Stimson and Marshall both now supported Stilwell as the obvious choice for the China post. So too did USAAF commanding general Hap Arnold. Though Stilwell would later come into a tangle of disagreements with Chennault, Arnold would always give Stilwell the benefit of the doubt because he had been picked by Marshall, and Arnold maintained an unwavering respect for Marshall's decisions. As his grandson, Robert Arnold, told this author, Marshall's "stamp of approval was about as good as it got."

After a round of Washington meetings, Stilwell, wearing the three stars of a lieutenant general, accepted the job on January 23, 1942. He left for Chongqing on February 11, a journey that took more than two weeks.

He reached Kunming on March 4, where he was greeted by Chennault and met some of the Flying Tigers, about whom he wrote in his diary that "they look damn good." It was only their second meeting. Stilwell and Chennault had first met, coincidentally in Kunming, on New Year's Eve 1938, when Stilwell was the military attaché, and Chennault was training the Chinese Air Force. This time the stakes were bigger, though the roles were similar. Stilwell still represented the mainstream US Army, while Chennault was a civilian, a mercenary leader, an American warlord in China.

Stilwell embodied an old-line strictness, and he clearly resented Chennault for his independence from the US Army command structure—and this became a topic of conversation. Stilwell arrived with confirmation that it was the intention of Stimson and Marshall, as well as of Arnold, that the activities of the American Volunteer Group should be integrated into the USAAF command structure as soon as possible. In his memoirs, Chennault mentions that such a move had been authorized as early as December 30, 1941, and it had certainly been a topic of speculation from Mingaladon to Washington. While it was only natural that the USAAF should want to possess the most effective—and certainly the most famous—American air combat command in the world, Chennault's attitude was that his soldiers of fortune had been doing okay on their own so far—with *no* help from the USAAF. He saw no reason to change, but assured Stilwell that he had an open mind about the idea.

In his diary, Stilwell wrote that he "had a long talk with [Chennault] and got him calmed down. He agreed to induction and said he'd be glad to serve under me. That's a big relief. . . . He'll be okay."

Stilwell flew on to Chongqing the following day, and had his first meeting in his new role with Chiang Kai-shek on March 6.

In Chongqing, Stilwell would find himself wearing a number of hats, including that of chief of Chiang's joint Allied staff, of President Roosevelt's personal representative to Chiang Kai-shek, and of Lend-Lease administrator. In addition, he was given the role of de facto theater commander in a vast amalgam of smaller command units—including the China Theater—that were not officially combined into the larger China-Burma-India (CBI) Theater until June 22. Even then, this organization was subordinate in the hierarchy of the Allied command structure to Wavell's India Command, as it would be under its successor, the South East Asia Command (SEAC), formed in 1943.

Because of his plethora of new titles and interwoven command responsibilities Stilwell had to navigate the labyrinth of Chongqing palace intrigue, a task that ill suited his temperament. He may have been Chiang's chief of staff, but he was not Chiang's *only* chief of staff. He shared this distinction with He Yingqin (then spelled Ho Ying-chin), better known simply as "General Ho," a longtime Chiang ally, who was the senior man in the Chinese Army. As Romanus and Sunderland note, his "actions soon suggested to Stilwell that he saw in the arrival of an American as chief of staff of the Generalissimo's joint staff the introduction of a rival center of power and influence and a direct challenge to his own position. This rivalry, tempered by the requirements of the military situation, produced a state of affairs in which Ho and Stilwell sometimes co-operated amicably and sometimes sought each other's removal."

"Stilwell appeared to be uniquely qualified for the China post," Claire Chennault wrote in his memoirs of the man whom he respected but never liked. "He had served two previous tours of duty in China and spoke Mandarin moderately well. He was a long-time close personal friend of Chief of Staff George Marshall and had the unqualified support of the War Department. However, Stilwell brought with him three things that served him ill during his difficult assignment in Asia: a strong prejudice against airpower coupled with a faint suspicion of any weapon more complicated than a rifle and bayonet; a 'treaty-port' attitude toward the Chinese, regarding them as inferiors incapable of managing their own affairs without foreign direction; and a complete disregard of the diplomatic facets of a top military post in a coalition war."

Stilwell had barely unpacked his luggage when Rangoon fell, so the notion of intervening to save Burma was one that required quick action. However, as Stilwell realized better than any other Westerner, the Chinese Army was not an uncomplicated entity to command and control. It was, as Stilwell understood, and as Romanus and Sunderland described, "a coalition of armed factions and provincial levies, whose loyalties were local and personal rather than national, plus a hard core of about 30 divisions personally loyal to the Generalissimo. This situation created many delicate problems of domestic politics for the Generalissimo, which he was not disposed to brush aside. . . . For Stilwell to persuade the Generalissimo to commit the Chinese Army or any major portion of it to offensive action was not easy."

Though the only USAAF airmen operating in a combat role in either China or Burma were the USAAF alumni flying with the American Volunteer Group, the USAAF was working to define the inevitable role that it would play in the theater and under Stilwell's command. There were a scattering of projects ongoing. With the Burma Road threatened, one project would involve the buildup of cargo-

Area of Operations for the American Volunteer Group.

Claire Lee Chennault in 1943 as a US Army Air Force major general and commander of the China Air Task Force. USAF

Generalissimo Chiang Kai-shek, the iconic leader of wartime China. LIBRARY OF CONGRESS

Captain Claire Chennault, Sergeant Luke Williamson, and Sergeant Billy MacDonald were the US Army Air Corps aerobatic team known as Three Men on the Flying Trapeze. They are seen here at the National Air Races in Cleveland in 1935. USAF

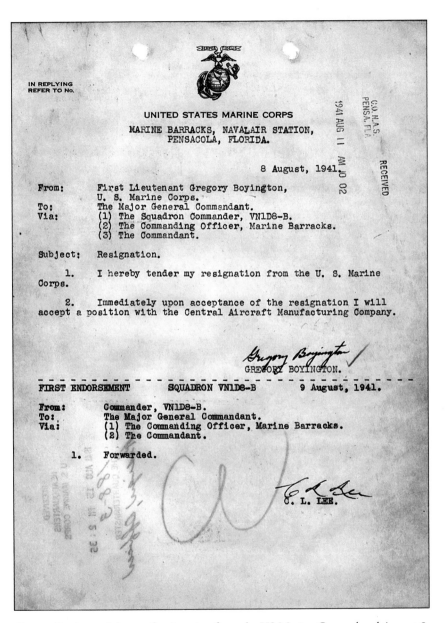

UNITED STATES MARINE CORPS

MARINE BARRACKS, NAVAL AIR STATION,
PENSACOLA, FLORIDA.

1941 AUG 11   C.O. N.A.S.
PENSA. FLA

AM 10 02   RECEIVED

8 August, 1941

From: First Lieutenant Gregory Boyington,
         U. S. Marine Corps.
To: The Major General Commandant.
Via: (1) The Squadron Commander, VN1D8-B.
         (2) The Commanding Officer, Marine Barracks.
         (3) The Commandant.

Subject: Resignation.

1.   I hereby tender my resignation from the U. S. Marine
Corps.

2.   Immediately upon acceptance of the resignation I will
accept a position with the Central Aircraft Manufacturing Company.

GREGORY BOYINGTON.

FIRST ENDORSEMENT   SQUADRON VN1D8-B   9 August, 1941.

From: Commander, VN1D8-B.
To: The Major General Commandant.
Via: (1) The Commanding Officer, Marine Barracks.
         (2) The Commandant.

1.   Forwarded.

C. L. LEE.

Gregory Boyington's letter of resignation from the US Marine Corps, dated August 8,
1941. When it was accepted, he was free to take a job as an aerial bounty hunter with
the Central Aircraft Manufacturing Company (CAMCO). NATIONAL ARCHIVES

An American Volunteer Group P-40B (H81) prepares for takeoff.

John "Scarsdale Jack" as a US Navy aviator before his resignation. He commanded the AVG 2nd Pursuit Squadron Panda Bears and was one of the group's highest scoring aces.

William "Black Mac" McGarry scored more than ten aerial victories with the AVG 1st Pursuit Squadron, known as the Adam and Eves. SAN DIEGO AIR & SPACE MUSEUM

The wheel chocks are pulled as an American Volunteer Group P-40B (H81) begins its takeoff roll. SAN DIEGO AIR & SPACE MUSEUM

Born in China, James Howell "Jim" Howard quit the US Navy and flew with the AVG 2nd Pursuit Squadron Panda Bears. He later joined the USAAF, earned a Medal of Honor in the skies over the Third Reich, and retired as a general.
SAN DIEGO AIR & SPACE MUSEUM

Ken Jernstedt was one of the highest scoring aces with the Hell's Angels of the AVG 3rd Pursuit Squadron. SAN DIEGO AIR & SPACE MUSEUM

Chuck Sawyer, Bob Neale, and Jim Howard of the AVG 2nd Pursuit Squadron Panda Bears. Neale commanded the squadron after the accidental death of Robert "Sandy" Sandell, and went on to become the highest-scoring ace among the Flying Tigers.

This college dormitory in Kunming, China, became "Hostel Number One," the home and headquarters of the American Volunteer Group for most of its time in service.

William "Black Mac" McGarry in the cockpit of his aircraft. He was shot down in the infamous strafing attack on Chiang Mai. He was observed to have successfully bailed out, but he was never seen again. SAN DIEGO AIR & SPACE MUSEUM

Colonel Robert Lee Scott Jr. was one of the USAAF pilots who flew missions with the American Volunteer Group. After the Flying Tigers disbanded, he commanded the 23rd Fighter Group, considered to be a successor organization to the AVG. USAF

carrying capability to transport supplies across the Himalayas from India by air.

Another USAAF endeavor, which had gotten a cool reception in Washington when Chennault had proposed it before Pearl Harbor, but which was now getting serious attention, was the notion of using China as a base for long-range bombing missions against Japan. Jimmy Doolittle's mission to bomb Japan with B-25s launched from an aircraft carrier was in the planning stages, but it would be a one-off. It was hoped that basing bombers in China would provide the possibility of a sustained effort.

Early in 1942, two separate missions were initiated that called for squadron-size contingents of long-range heavy bombers to attack Japan from bases that could theoretically support ongoing operations. The aircraft would fly across the South Atlantic, across Africa and the Middle East, and then from India into China. They would be based in or around Chengdu, but use more primitive fields closer to Japan as staging bases for strikes on Tokyo.

The best known of these was the Halverson Project (HALPRO), named for the mission commander, Colonel Harry A. "Hurry-Up" Halverson (born Halvor Halvorson), which involved two dozen B-24 Liberators. The second mission, led by Colonel Caleb Vance Haynes, departed from the United States with a dozen B-17 Flying Fortresses in March. However, both projects were terminated. After the fall of Rangoon, the planners in Washington decided that bomber bases inside China could not be supplied without the Port of Rangoon.

Halverson's B-24s made it as far as North Africa, and were diverted to another mission—bombing the great petrochemical refinery facility at Ploesti, Romania, which supplied most of the refined petroleum for the Third Reich. Caleb Haynes and his B-17s reached India before their Tokyo mission was scrapped. Both he and the aircraft were reassigned to the new USAAF Tenth Air Force, an umbrella organization created for the area that would later become the China-Burma-India Theater. On March 5, Major General Lewis Brereton—late of the USAAF Far East Air Force (FEAF)—arrived in New Delhi, India, to take command of the Tenth. Before Haynes reached India, the Tenth consisted of only *eight* tactical aircraft—B-17s that had escaped from the Philippines. Brereton put these to work flying supplies from Calcutta to Magwe, and carrying refugees on the return flights.

As historian Herbert Weaver wrote of the Tenth opening for business in India, "such were the meager beginnings of an organization forced to operate at the end of a longer supply line than that of any other existing American air force [though not longer than that of the AVG], over distances within its theater that exceeded considerably those embraced by the bounds of the United States, and in an area possessed of few of the industrial facilities upon which air power is directly dependent."

———————————

Chennault was invited by Chiang Kai-shek to sit in during one of the generalissimo's first meetings with Joe Stilwell.

"They were impressed with his three-star rank, his command of their language, and his appearance as a lean tough campaigner," Chennault recalled in his memoirs. "Madame Chiang was bubbling over with good spirits after the initial conferences with Stilwell. She took Stilwell and myself by the arm and led us out onto a terrace outside the conference room. As we paced up and down the terrace arm in arm, she told us how happy she was that at last China had the help of two American military leaders, how Stilwell and I must work smoothly together, and what high hopes she had for the joint Sino-American war effort under our direction."

Vinegar Joe Stilwell had apparently won the hearts, if not the minds, of the Chiangs and the tacit acceptance of Claire Chennault. It remained to be seen whether he could, with Chinese help, hold Burma for the Allies.

SEVENTEEN

Make Them Pay

As March 1942 wore on, as Stilwell negotiated the maze of Chongqing palace intrigues, and as the British said good-bye to Rangoon, the balance of power in the skies over northern Burma was tipped decidedly in favor of the Japanese. By most estimates, the Allied air forces across the Far East were outnumbered five to one. With the Imperial Japanese Navy Air Force engaged in flying top cover for Japanese land and naval forces in the Solomons, New Guinea, and elsewhere to the east, the Imperial Japanese *Army* Air Force could throw the weight of its resources into defeating the AVG and the RAF in Burma.

As Chennault explained, the "battles over Rangoon were deliberate clashes between two air groups at altitude, both seeking a decision in the air. Over northern Burma the character of battle shifted to continual attempts to catch the opposition on the ground and shooting sitting ducks. The Japanese had suffered too grievous losses in the air battles to want any more, and we had too few serviceable planes to deal more crippling blows to huge enemy formations in flight. This later became a characteristic of the Pacific war; the most decisive air battles were fought when attackers caught the enemy by surprise on the ground."

While the Japanese had their choice of air bases all across Thailand and southern Burma, much of the Allied air contingent was operating out of the RAF base at Magwe. The old RAF/AVG base at Toungoo was available, but as the Japanese armies marched north, it was increasingly close to the front lines.

Magwe was problematic in that it was still under construction when the war began, so many of its facilities were unfinished. The radar system that the RAF pulled out of Rangoon had been reinstalled at Magwe, but it covered only the southeastern approach. Magwe was also the only substantial base in that part of northern Burma and was therefore being used as a hub for the immense and often chaotic aerial evacuation of British personnel and civilians to India. In addition to the RAF Blenheims and AVG P-40s lined up in the blowing dust to use its crowded runways, CNAC transports were flying in and out constantly, adding to the traffic jam atmosphere of the place.

In the post-Rangoon era, the AVG pilots were first to take the fight to enemy air bases. On March 19, two Flying Tigers, Ken Jernstedt and Bill Reed, flying a patrol over the growing IJAAF facility around Moulmein, made seven low-level strafing runs over two Japanese-occupied former RAF airfields, destroying at least fifteen fighters, three bombers, and a transport plane. The Japanese, who had not anticipated such an attack, were caught completely off guard. There was no anti-aircraft fire.

The former Allied base at Mingaladon received a visit from RAF Blenheims, escorted by Hurricanes, the next day. Japanese fighters managed to claw their way into the sky and shoot up the British bombers, but the Hurricane pilots claimed a dozen IJAAF planes in the sky, while sixteen were reported destroyed on the ground.

On March 21 and 22, the IJAAF struck back with their biggest bombing raids in many weeks. These missions were not a fast retaliation for the March 20 raid on Mingaladon, but had been in planning for some time. Coincidentally, part of the intended strike force had been destroyed at Mingaladon.

More than 260 Japanese aircraft were thrown into a maximum effort that washed over Magwe in wave after wave. With the radar able to cover such a narrow slice of the perimeter, there were only a few minutes' warning on the first day, and the Japanese achieved the element of surprise just after dawn on the second. Two flights of 3rd Pursuit Squadron Hell's Angels managed to get airborne on the first day, with Cliff Groh and Parker Dupouy each taking out one of the attackers.

The devastation on the ground at Magwe was enormous. All of the dwindling inventory of RAF Blenheim bombers, loaded with fuel and bombs, were lost on the ground the first day, along with most of the RAF Hurricanes. The Hurricanes that survived the assault were flown to the RAF base at Akyab (now Sittwe), 130 miles west on the Burma coast, where they were completely wiped out on March 22. This, and severe damage done to the runways, essentially marked the end of the RAF in Burma for the foreseeable future.

Two men of the AVG, pilot Frank Swartz and crew chief Johnny Fauth, were fatally wounded. Fauth died at Magwe, but Swartz was medevaced to India, where he recuperated in a hospital for six weeks before unexpectedly developing a fatal case of acute encephalitis.

Only three AVG P-40s survived the Magwe massacre, and these were flown three hundred miles northeast to the CAMCO facility at Lei Yun, where Bill Pawley had once promised to maintain Chennault's air force.

"We're going to make them pay," the Old Man announced from his sickbed in Kunming, where he was dealing with another bout of bronchitis. The venue for this transaction was to be the IJAAF field at Chiang Mai (also called Chiengmai) in northern Thailand, which is still a Royal Thai Air Force Base today. It is 370 miles south of Lei Yun, but only 160 miles east of the former home of the Flying Tigers at Toungoo. Chiang Mai has often been erroneously identified as the IJAAF headquarters, but it *was* an air base of growing importance because of its proximity to northern Burma and China's Yunnan Province, and it had been used by the IJAAF as a staging base for the attacks against Magwe and Akyab.

At noon on March 22, as the IJAAF was finishing off the RAF at Akyab, the contingent of Tigers who would attack Chiang Mai flew down to Lei Yun from Kunming. They included Bill Bartling, Charlie Bond, Greg Boyington, William "Black Mac" McGarry, and Ed Rector of the Adam and Eves, with Bob Neale in command. Also en route were Pandas Hank Geselbracht, Robert "Buster" Keeton, and Frank Lawlor, with Jack Newkirk in the lead of the Panda contingent.

Boyington recalled in his memoirs that the Hell's Angels of the 3rd Pursuit Squadron "were anything but warm to us" when they learned that the newcomers from Kunming were going on the Chiang Mai mission, insinuating that they thought such a mission belonged to them. He soon discovered that the Hell's Angels were billeted in quarters near a "crummy Chinese village," while the men from Kunming were invited to stay at the comfortable hilltop hostel that had been built to house the CAMCO staff. This was at least part of the source of the animosity.

While in Lei Yun, Boyington toured the CAMCO operation, reporting that the "farce called a Lend-Lease factory . . . didn't impress me at all, even though I [have a bachelor of science degree in aeronautical engineering]. I never found out whether the factory ever completed aircraft one, but that was not important, I believe. The main idea was that they lived like kings in this hostel, which, for but few differences, might have been a swanky country club back home. The view was ideal, also, as large plate-glass windows overlooked the mountainous valley and winding river below."

The place was run by a woman called "Ma Davidson," who had previously managed the dining room of the swanky American Club in Hong Kong. When that British colony was swallowed by the Japanese at Christmas, she had escaped and was hired by Pawley to run the Lei Yun hostelry. When she visited, Olga Greenlaw was impressed, noting that the place had the feel of a fine Hong Kong luxury hotel, with thick carpets and eiderdown quilts on the beds.

Chennault in his own memoirs effused about this "country club-house." Like Boyington and Olga Greenlaw, among others, he remembered its "tremendous plate-glass window offering a magnificent view of the valley, and a giant juke box."

He contrasted the CAMCO clubhouse with "the flimsy bamboo operations shack where the Third Squadron headquartered." Over the door of the Hell's Angels' shack there hung a sign that read "Olson & Co. Exterminators; 24 hr. Service," implying that Oley Olson's men were prepared to exterminate Japanese planes and that they were always on duty.

That evening at the clubhouse, Boyington found the Pandas' squadron leader in a peculiarly dark mood. "Jack Newkirk was not the same smiling Jack I had attended a few shore leaves with off the USS *Yorktown* prior to the war. Nor was he the same as he was when I had flown with him in Rangoon. Previously always an affable gent, but this night he just didn't want to talk at all—about anything."

Leaving Scarsdale Jack to brood on his own, Boyington sat down with Black Mac McGarry and two bottles of scotch they had brought from Kunming.

"We were very much alone, and as the evening wore on Mac became loquacious for a change," Boyington wrote. "He reminisced, at the time, about how his family would be shocked if it were possible for them to see him enjoying a bottle of whisky."

The Hell's Angels from Magwe flew in the following morning with the surviving P-40s. John Croft, Fred Hodges, Moose Moss, and Fritz Wolf were full of stories of the havoc wrought by the Japanese bombing.

That afternoon, the pilots who would attack Chiang Mai flew down to an RAF field at Namseng, halfway to the target, to be refueled and ready for a predawn launch on March 24. They timed their arrival at Namseng for dusk because the only early warning system at the field was a Burmese bugler manning an observation post on a nearby hilltop.

The wake-up call came at 4:05 a.m., according to Charlie Bond's diary, when an RAF officer entered their quarters to shout, "All right, you curly-headed fellows, it's time!"

About an hour and twenty minutes later, they began their takeoff roll in the darkness of an unlighted field, with only the headlights of an old truck used as a reference point to show them the end of the runway. "I couldn't see a thing," Bond confided to his diary. "I went on instruments. My basic reference was my rate of climb indicator. As long as it showed 'up,' I felt reasonably assured." Shortly after 6:00 a.m., they were all airborne without a mishap, had climbed to ten thousand feet, and had formed up, using their navigation lights and heading south to "make them pay."

Bond was flying on the wing of Bob Neale, who led because he had been over Chiang Mai previously, and Bond had not. Boyington and Bartling followed, with Rector and McGarry flying top cover. The Pandas, meanwhile, flew separately and were tasked with striking a Chiang Mai auxiliary field at nearby Nakhon Lampang. Newkirk led, with Geselbracht on his wing, followed by Keeton and Lawlor.

As Boyington recalled, "the plan was to arrive over the Chiang Mai airstrip in the morning at the exact instant—and it lasts for only a minute or so—when one can see the ground from the air and they cannot see you."

Using a mountain near Chiang Mai as a landmark, they picked out the enemy base in the mist below.

"As the haze thinned, I saw the field and outlines of the hangars," Bond wrote. "I flipped on my gun switch, and another thousand feet lower I fired my guns in a short burst to check them and let the other guys know this was it."

At 7:12 a.m., the Flying Tigers struck.

"Our lead planes turned sharp left like they were going to run into a mountain," Boyington remembered, watching Bond and Neale. "They started to dive. I wheeled my plane and dove after them, although I couldn't make out any target as yet. Even before I saw the field I saw tracers from the guns of my mates preceding me. Then the field seemed to take shape in the semi-darkness. I sighted in on the same place where the previous tracers had gone, some of these tracers were visible ricocheting as if being fired from the opposite direction."

Relishing the realization that "we had caught them flat-footed without any warning," Bond lined up to cross the airfield on its longest dimension and set his sights on a line of parked I-97s. Remaining low, he poured gunfire into the fighters, turned sharply to the left, and strafed another line of parked aircraft that were "sitting practically wingtip to wingtip."

"Hell, I hadn't seen this many aircraft in years," he thought. "Seemed like the whole Japanese Air Force had tried to crowd into this one little field. I couldn't miss. . . . I steadied my aim and strafed the entire line of ships. I was so low that it seemed as though my prop tips would clip the heads of Jap pilots who by now were trying to get into their cockpits. Other men, evidently maintenance people, were lying flat on the ground nearby. Props were turning on some of the fighters, but not a single aircraft was taxiing. . . . Tracer bullets flew all around; it was obvious they were meant for me. The antiaircraft defenses had come to life, but they still were frantic and disorganized. . . . I craned my neck searching for enemy aircraft in the air. None!"

Boyington noted that his first pass "got three transports ablaze, which, owing to their size, were the easiest to pick out that time of the morning. In turn the burning transports helped to light up our target area as we wheeled around for a pass in the opposite direction. I don't see how any of us knew which one of us was which."

Like Bond, Boyington noted that the strike force had achieved total surprise. As he stared down a line of planes parked so close together it reminded him of the US Navy training center in NAS Pensacola before the war.

"With more time and better light I could do a better job," Bond said of his third pass. "A large Jap plane stood out from the others; perhaps it was a reconnaissance ship. I settled on it as my primary and let go. As I bore on it, firing, it seemed to shake itself to pieces. With only inches to spare, I pulled off and raked other aircraft with my fire. God only knows how many planes were damaged or destroyed in that pass."

Boyington recalled that "radio silence was broken finally when someone yelled: 'Let's get the hell out of here.'"

Looking back at Chiang Mai, Charlie Bond observed that the entire airfield seemed to be in flames.

"What satisfaction!" he declared. "The resulting destruction of the successive passes in that ten to twelve minutes of aerial attack is too much to describe. . . . We apparently caught them as they were preparing a major concentration of aircraft for a big strike against us in China. It was a mission accomplished exactly according to Chennault's plan. How proud he would be. Hell, I was!"

Bond linked up with Bartling, McGarry, and Rector and started toward Namsang, where they would top off their tanks before returning north to Lei Yun. As they traveled, the others started to notice that McGarry was lagging behind and gradually losing altitude. He had nearly stalled out when they pulled alongside and noticed smoke pouring from his V-1710 engine. In the distance, they could see the Salween River, which delineates the border between Thailand and Burma in these parts, and tried to will him to reach it. It was not to be.

"Suddenly his aircraft rolled over, and Mac bailed out about a thousand feet above the treetops," Bond wrote. "His plane nosed down sharply and crashed in a ball of fire. Mac's chute blossomed open and he drifted downward. He hit in a small glade on a large plateau some three hundred yards from his burning plane. He was okay—up on his feet and waving at us. We circled him. In an effort to help him in some way, I drew a circle on the map indicating where I thought he was and wrote 7:41 a.m. near the circle. Buzzing him the last time, I dropped the map right on him and then headed northwest towards Namsang."

Rector flew to Lashio to report McGarry to the British headquarters there, while the others made their way to Lei Yun, where they made a formation victory pass.

Eight of the ten P-40s that had started out two days before made it back. In addition to McGarry, Jack Newkirk was not coming home that night.

His four-ship flight had found no Japanese aircraft at the Nakhon Lampang airfield, so they diverted to targets of opportunity, including the rail station at the town of Chiang Mai, a truck convoy, and what appeared to be a tank or armored vehicle. As Newkirk attacked the latter, the others noted that he did not pull up. They were unsure whether he had been hit by antiaircraft fire, or had just failed to pull out of his dive until it was too late. He was seen to impact the ground at high speed, tumbling nose over tail as the P-40 disintegrated. Boyington recalled the night when Newkirk had seemed so morose, as though he had a premonition of tragedy.

Newkirk could not have survived, but the Tigers were optimistic about McGarry, hoping—unrealistically—that he could hike thirty miles through the jungle and somehow make it across the Salween River without being nabbed by a Japanese patrol.

As it turned out, he never made it—but nor was he apprehended by the Japanese. He was picked up by the Thai constabulary after evading capture for nearly a month, and spent the remainder of the war in their custody. It was not a happy experience, but mercifully, they never turned him over to the Japanese.

Chennault would soon name Tex Hill, an ace plus one in the battles over Rangoon, to succeed Newkirk as commander of the 2nd Pursuit Squadron. On April 17, the Associated Press would erroneously report that the job had gone to Jim Howard.

The survivors of Chiang Mai, despite the loss, convened at the CAMCO villa on the hill for lunch that day and wound up in the bar, celebrating their success while ignoring their misfortune.

"It's surprising how quickly one gets over the horrible loss of his buddies in wartime and revels in the successes of the day," Bond reflected in his diary entry for this long day. "Everyone was laughing and enjoying the moment. Yet Jack was gone and we weren't sure of Black Mac. It makes one wonder about the nature of human beings."

In his memoirs, Chennault wrote that while the Chiang Mai raid had "cost us the services of two outstanding pilots, it was more than justified from the tactical results obtained. Later reports revealed that we had destroyed the effective strength of an entire air regiment. The survivors were withdrawn and returned to Japan for replacement of personnel and aircraft. Other Japanese air units, which had been pounding Magwe, were placed on the strict defensive at their air-

BILL YENNE

dromes, and the British were able to resume the evacuation of British and Indian nationals by air from the field."

Air Vice Marshal Stevenson wired Chennault to tell him "Many thanks for the breathing spell furnished us by your magnificent attack at Chiang Mai."

"Although everyone realized we were fighting a losing battle and would inevitably be chased out of Burma, nobody talked about it much," Olga Greenlaw reflected in her memoirs. "The pilots kept knocking down Japs, and the ground crews threw away the clock and worked heroically to 'keep 'em flying.' The only thing the AVG had more than enough of was a sense of humor and an inexhaustible supply of guts."

EIGHTEEN

To the Gold Coast and Beyond

On about Friday the thirteenth in February 1942, as the battle over Rangoon was at its most intense, there was a rumor circulating in Kunming that some of the men of the American Volunteer Group would be sent away to the outside world to bring back new aircraft to refresh the badly battered inventory of P-40Bs, all of which had been shot at, ground-looped, crash-landed, or all of the above. The rumor held that the USAAF was arranging to supply the "outlaw" air force with new and better aircraft. Time would tell.

On that very Sunday, though, George "Mac" McMillan of the 3rd Hell's Angels Squadron announced that he had been asked to leave the following day with five others to pick up a half dozen new Curtiss Model 87, series A3 (H87-A3) Warhawks. An advanced variant of the P-40, they were the same type that the USAAF was buying for itself under the designation P-40E, and which was being Lend-Leased to the RAF as the Kittyhawk. The Hell's Angels he picked for this adventure were Paul Greene, Tom Haywood, C. H. "Link" Laughlin, Chuck Older, and R. T. Smith.

Smith wrote in his diary that he and his fellow pilots were "liable to go all the way to the Gold Coast of Africa [now Ghana] for our new ships. . . . Don't know how long it will take but it should be ten days at least—we hope." This adventure would indeed take them across Africa, but it would take them nearly ten days just to reach Africa, and they would not see Kunming again for nearly a month and a half.

Why Africa?

With the Japanese so completely in control of the Far East, the only air link between the United States and China ran across Africa, and with the Germans occupying so much of Africa's Mediterranean coast—from Morocco to the Western Desert of Egypt—it was necessary for those making this flight to cross the continent closer to its midsection, between Sudan and the Gold Coast.

The Flying Tigers flew out of Kunming the following morning as passengers aboard a CNAC flight, reaching Calcutta after seven hours in the air. The following morning, they awoke after seven hours in Calcutta nightclubs and scant time in bed. Trouble with the Pegasus engine of the British Overseas Airways Empire flying boat that was to take them on the next leg of their trip delayed their departure for another twenty-four hours, but the nightclubs were still there. Smith wrote diligently in his diary that they "had to be back to the hotel by 4:30 [a.m.]" to catch their predawn flight on February 18.

That day's eleven hours in the air with one stop got them thirteen hundred miles farther west across the breadth of British India to Karachi. Upon their arrival in the future capital of Pakistan, the "CAMCO employees" learned that they were not priority passengers and, if they were going to stay together as a group, they would have to "hurry up and wait," meaning stand by for an indeterminate several days to catch a flight that could offer them six seats. Having met some other American pilots, they were directed to the nightlife and private clubs. "Admittedly," Smith wrote many years later in the annotations to his published diary, "we had more dollars than sense."

They finally reached Cairo late on the afternoon of February 23, but a worsening cold sent Smith to bed early on his twenty-fourth birthday as the others made the usual rounds of clubs catering to the growing Allied military presence in this ancient metropolis.

With the German Afrika Korps still advancing slowly toward Cairo, the Flying Tigers found themselves once again only 150 miles from an active battlefront and a determined enemy. Circumnavigating the German hold on the breadth of North Africa, they traveled a thousand miles due south to Khartoum, and turned west toward the Atlantic coast. It was still early in the war, and the USAAF had yet to build its Air Transport Command into the globe-circling intercontinental scheduled "airline" it would soon become, so Pan American Airways flight crews ran a regular service under contract.

"The Pan Am men had warned us that the native traders tried to charge outrageous prices for their artifacts, so we haggled and argued just as we'd learned to do in Burma and China," Smith recalled of a shopping trip for curios during an overnight stop in Kano, Nigeria. "When I had finally agreed to a price of $40.00 in US money for my purchase and dug out my billfold I discovered that I also had some Chinese twenty-dollar bills. Just for the hell of it I handed two of these to the trader."

The man studied the bank notes, whose value was a pittance compared to American bills, pointed out the picture of Sun Yat-sen, and wanted to know who it was. When Smith told him it was President Roosevelt, he was very pleased.

Because there were now so many Americans in the area, Smith's diary is filled with chance encounters with old friends he had met in flight school. At the same time, as they bar-hopped from club to club across Southwest Asia and into Africa, and interacted with flight crews and ground crews on flight lines, the AVG men stood apart from the average American serviceman overseas. They were Americans but not servicemen. They were the Flying Tigers, the outlaw soldiers of fortune whom an American media in search of heroes had embraced and made legendary.

It was shortly after noon on February 27, two weeks out of Kunming, that their C-53 finally touched down at Takoradi Airport in Accra, now the capital of Ghana. The airport, built before the war by British Imperial Airways, was rapidly becoming an important hub on the air route across the South Atlantic and central Africa. It had also become an analogue to Mingaladon as a place where aircraft that were shipped in from the United States in crates, especially Lend-Lease equipment for the British in North Africa, were unpacked and assembled. It is still a military air base today.

If the Flying Tigers found themselves hurrying up to wait across South Asia, this would not be the case here. Waiting for them here were the first six of a promised thirty Curtiss P-40Es. Compared to the P-40B that the AVG had been using, the P-40E had a higher gross weight, a longer range, greater armament, underwing bomb racks, and a more powerful V-1710-39 engine. Also part of the package were new, American-made parachutes, which pleased the men greatly.

After two days to finish fitting the new aircraft with external fuel tanks, the Flying Tigers departed on their return flight on the morning of March 2, following an RAF Blenheim whose pilot knew the route over the otherwise trackless wilderness. Only four of the six reached Kano on the first night, with both Haywood and Older having to stop for repairs to mechanical issues. The others pressed on, hoping that Haywood and Older would catch up to them in Cairo. As Smith noted, "Murphy's law seemed to be working overtime."

On March 6, the same day that the British abandoned Rangoon to the oncoming Imperial Japanese Fifteenth Army, McMillan, Greene, Laughlin, and Smith had passed through Khartoum and had arrived at a desolate landing strip on the Nile River at Atbara in Sudan that was called Station Number Six. Four days out of Accra, they were still nearly nine hundred miles south of Cairo.

They were short of fuel, and Smith was now having trouble with his electrical system. Reports from every direction told of an immense sandstorm blowing across the landscape, reducing visibility and fouling any machine with moving parts. The storm hit Atbara after dark and blew ferociously well into the next day. When the weather finally cleared, the other three left Smith in Atbara with a promise from the RAF that they would send a mechanic, and flew on to Cairo.

Growing impatient waiting for the RAF mechanic, Smith finally phoned the Pan Am office in Khartoum. They responded promptly, sending mechanics and parts to fix his electrical system. However, his hydraulic system was now acting up, and he found he could not retract his landing gear. He managed to limp 250 miles to Port Sudan on the Red Sea, where there was a depot at which the RAF did maintenance on its Kittyhawks.

At about noon on March 11, Smith finally reached the Heliopolis airfield at Cairo, where he was reunited with McMillan, Greene, Laughlin, and Older at the Grand Hotel. Haywood did not reach Cairo until March 13, which was 1942's second Friday the thirteenth. By now, Smith's diary was betraying a rising level of tedium when it came to nightlife. Recalling a visit to one of Cairo's many nightclubs featuring belly dancers, Mac McMillan observed that having seen one, "you've seen 'em all."

The P-40Es, which the Tigers had flown to the maintenance facility at nearby Ismailia to be all checked out and prepared for a continuation of the ferry flight back to Kunming, were supposed to have been ready to be flown out by March 15, but only four were deemed flyable.

McMillan decided that he, Greene, Laughlin, and Smith would continue on, while the others waited for nagging problems with the engines to be fixed. By late morning that day, the four had reached Lydda in Palestine, but had to stop overnight for a leak in Laughlin's reserve fuel tank to be patched.

Two days later, after a number of stops through the Middle East and along the western shore of the Persian Gulf, they finally reached Karachi. Here, they discovered that the USAAF had a growing depot operation that included assembling P-40Es for the use of new USAAF units that were being formed. The availability of parts proved useful, as the P-40Es were still experiencing minor problems.

The Flying Tigers also started to meet people who had been evacuated from Burma, and learned for the first time that the AVG had relocated from Mingaladon to Magwe. This made the men especially anxious, or in Smith's words, "rarin' to go," to get back into the action.

Indeed, the action was waiting for them. Smith reached Kunming with McMillan, Greene, and Laughlin on March 22, even as the huge IJAAF maximum effort was laying waste to Magwe, and as preparations were under way for the attack on Chiang Mai. Older and Haywood finally pulled in two days later. Smith called their epic sixteen-thousand-mile ferry flight—possibly the longest yet attempted by Americans with fighter planes—"the sort of thing you wouldn't trade for a million dollars, but wouldn't do again if *paid* a million."

———

While McMillan and his crew were living it up in Karachi and Cairo, Jim Howard had the opportunity to spend a few weeks in the world outside the combat theater where he had been for half a year, albeit only four hundred air miles to the north.

"With the approach of the monsoon season in the south, all flying comes to a standstill," Chennault explained. Howard had yet to experience a monsoon season as a pilot. "We will be moving north to the central China bases in a matter of weeks."

Chennault decided that he wanted Howard to make an extensive inspection tour of airfields the Chinese were building or upgrading in and around Chongqing. Howard complained that he did not want to be excused from combat, but Chennault countercomplained that he had no staff officers. He then buttered the bitter toast by explaining that he felt Howard, who had been born in Guangzhou and who was conversant in Chinese, to be the best man for the job. That was that.

In Chongqing, Howard was greeted by General Chou Chih-jou, the commander of the Chinese Air Force, who introduced himself as C. J. Chow. The general also shared the role of director of China's Aeronautical Affairs Commission with Madame Chiang Kai-shek.

As part of his "official" duties, Howard was invited to represent Chennault and the American Volunteer Group at a lavish afternoon reception at the home of the millionaire banker, Shanghai exile, and Chiang Kai-shek brother-in-law H. H. Kung. In Chiang Kai-shek's government the millionaire financier now held the portfolios of both minister of finance and governor of the Central Bank of China. The event brought together about two hundred dignitaries, from the Chinese government and from the foreign diplomatic corps.

"I had never seen such an exhibit of flashy military uniforms and civilians in cutaways and top hats," he wrote. He also recalled meeting several people who had known his father during his missionary years in Guangzhou.

There was no doubt, however, that Madame Chiang, who was unaccompanied by her husband, was unquestionably the star of the show. A big part of that show included her extolling the virtues of the American Volunteer Group, and presenting a painting by Hsu Shih-chi of eagles, representing the American pilots, flying over a raging sea, representing China in turmoil. Howard, as the representative of Chennault and the AVG, was expected to speak in response.

"You men of the AVG have crossed the Pacific in China's gravest hour," she spoke from the podium, nodding to Jim Howard. "For this reason the entire Chinese nation welcomes you with outstretched arms. I am proud of the title given me by Colonel Chennault as honorary commander of the AVG because you are my boys who are fighting with your hearts. You are little angels with or without wings so I am going to din into your ears the necessity for discipline. The Chinese nation has taken you into its heart so I want you to conduct yourselves in a manner worthy of the great traditions you have built up. Remember that you are China's guests and that everything you do will reflect credit upon the country which I love next to my own."

It was not lost on Howard that her remark about moderating the behavior of the "little angels" was a reference to the barracks humor racism that was not uncommon among the Flying Tigers. In his memoirs, he does not mention whether he noted this in his own remarks that day.

He was complimented for his short talk by an unexpected group of guests at the reception. Howard had to have been startled to see a cluster of men dripping with Nazi and German military regalia in the crowd, but Germany and China still maintained diplomatic relations—despite China being at war with Hitler's Axis partner, and the United States being at war with Germany. The German military attaché told him in English that he had liked Howard's speech.

NINETEEN

From Tedium to Rat Race

In late March, a few days after they returned from Africa, the men who had flown the "million dollar" mission were back in the familiar cockpits of their P-40Bs and flying patrols out of Lei Yun as the American stars on the wings of the P-40Es were being painted out and the Chinese sun being painted on.

Coming back from the Gold Coast, the belly dancers, and the curio sellers, the Flying Tigers found themselves in a completely different tactical reality than the one they had left. The operations out of Mingaladon, where the AVG had earned worldwide fame, were over. It was a Japanese base now. The short-lived interlude at Magwe ended dramatically and violently, and this had caused the RAF to pull most of its effective force back to India, though a few RAF aircraft later joined the AVG at their forward operating base in Lei Yun.

On the ground, Rangoon had gone the way of Singapore, and the Japanese were moving north with the same deliberate pace that had brought them this far. On March 11, Chiang Kai-shek had given Joe

Stilwell overall command of the 1st Route Expeditionary Forces (aka the Chinese Expeditionary Army), which was led by Lieutenant General Luo Zhuoying (then spelled Lo Cho-ying), who was already moving into Burma. This organization consisted of the Fifth, Sixth, and Sixty-sixth Armies, each about the size of a corps, or about a third the size of an American field army.

As it turned out, Toungoo, the former home of the AVG, was the place where the Expeditionary Army first made contact with the advancing Japanese. The shooting had started on March 18, with the main Japanese assault coming on March 24, the same day as the Chiang Mai raid and two days after the IJAAF had chased the Allied airmen out of Magwe. Over the next several days, the two sides traded heavy losses as the Japanese captured the western side of the town. Toungoo was turning into the biggest battle in Burma thus far. Late on March 29, as the Japanese poured more reinforcements into the fight, the Chinese began to withdraw across the Sittang to more defensible positions about fifty miles to the north.

With this, Chiang Kai-shek had asked Chennault to ask the pilots at Lei Yun to fly ground support missions over the Toungoo battlefield—strafing missions against targets less concentrated than at Chiang Mai. As Chennault pointed out at the time, and reiterated in his memoirs, "without excellent air-to-ground communications, trained air-liaison officers with ground troops, and a constant flow of reliable intelligence on the ground situation, close air support for ground troops is impractical."

He did not have to mention that the AVG had too few aircraft, none of which could carry bombs, and the Japanese now had air superiority over Burma, making it seem like a suicide mission that could bring little tactical gain. The AVG could do little more than simply show up so that the Chinese troops could see the Chinese suns on the wings of planes overhead. Gradually, it dawned on Chennault and his men that *this*, the showing of the Chinese flag, was the real purpose of the flights. The Chinese called them "morale missions."

Chennault's old friend P. T. Mao had promised to send some of his Soviet-made Tupolev bombers into action alongside the sharks of the AVG, but these never appeared.

"We're all against it," R. T. Smith wrote in his diary on March 28 about a mission over Toungoo planned for the following day. "It seems senseless, with a good possibility of nobody coming back."

This dissention was a symptom of a growing irritation in the ranks that would only increase in the coming weeks. Another factor that ruffled the ranks was the loss of Jack Newkirk and Mac McGarry over Chiang Mai on March 24. Losing two men in a "down and dirty" strafing mission seemed harder to take than losses in air-to-air combat, and it cast a shadow of aversion over the down and dirty nature of the morale missions.

Meanwhile, air-to-air combat was rare in the weeks after Chiang Mai, and the tension of waiting for the enemy, the monotonous patrols, the tedious alert missions, and the heart-stopping false alarms wore on the morale of the pilots. As March came to a close, Japanese air raids against the border towns of Lashio on the Burma side and Lei Yun, 120 road miles away on the Chinese side, were anticipated, but did not materialize. The Imperial Japanese Army Air Force seemed for a time to be preoccupied with their own strafing attacks on the ground troops of Luo Zhuoying and Joe Stilwell.

A Japanese payback attack for Chiang Mai had been expected as early as the next day or so, but after two weeks of watching, waiting, scrambling for shadows, and mounting lengthy patrols, the Flying Tigers of Lei Yun could be excused for thinking they had dodged a bullet. Dawn patrols, instituted to guard against precisely the kind of attack that the Flying Tigers had sprung on the Japanese at Chiang Mai, were gradually phased out because of the weather, the smoke from massive forest fires that were smoldering unchecked across the region, and the chance for accidents while doing takeoffs and landings in the silvery half-light at the cusp of daybreak.

In the meantime, the CAMCO facility into which they had fallen as a default after the Magwe disaster was taking on the trappings of a new Toungoo, complete with the kind of early warning system that had been installed down at the original Toungoo. It had also become the stopover point for the P-40Es that were still trickling in, flown by AVG men and contract ferry pilots, from the west.

Part of the changing face of Lei Yun were the changing faces. Most of the CAMCO employees who were not part of the AVG had pulled out, following William Pawley to India. Back at the end of 1940, entrepreneur Pawley had helped start a new company, the Hindustan Aircraft Company, in Bangalore. Gradually, inspired by the Chinese government having become an equity partner in CAMCO, Pawley brought investment from the Indian government into Hindustan, as he was bringing machine tools and know-how from the United States. It was the same business model as CAMCO. By 1941, Hindustan had become Pawley's exit strategy in his own career strategy to abandon his dealings inside China. Now, with the Japanese moving north through Burma, and the British government eager for aviation engineering expertise, Hindustan allowed Pawley to put CAMCO's troubles behind him and land firmly on his feet.

April 8 promised to be another average day, although the air, which was usually hazy, was sparklingly clear of the usual smog. After breakfast, the men at Lei Yun noticed that the IJAAF had sent a lone reconnaissance aircraft overhead for some high-altitude snooping, but that was not unusual. The Flying Tigers knew that the Japanese had eyes on their comings and goings.

Chuck Older and Ed Overend of the Hell's Angels scrambled to chase the Mitsubishi Ki-46 back toward its home base at Chiang Mai, but they never caught it.

Shortly after noon the Lei Yun early warning system came alive with the news that a substantial number of enemy aircraft were headed north out of Thailand. The Ki-46 had obviously been sent to gather last-minute details about the strength of the Allied forces at the airfield.

This was it. This was the long-awaited retaliation for Chiang Mai, and a symmetrical one at that—a strafing attack involving roughly the same number of fighters as the AVG had used on March 22. There were roughly a dozen Nakajima Ki-43 Hayabusas. The Flying Tigers had encountered the state-of-the-art Hayabusas only a few times. Because their appearance was similar to that of the well-known IJNAF Mitsubishi A6M Zeros, the Ki-43s continued to be routinely reported as such throughout Southeast Asia, and that was the case with the AVG pilots on April 8.

The Hayabusas crossed the border at twenty thousand feet, then dropped to strafing altitude and raced toward Lei Yun.

The symmetry stopped with the early warning system. Of the sixteen AVG and RAF airplanes observed on the ground by the Ki-46, only three were still on the ground when the strafing attack began. These, a Blenheim and two P-40Es, were swallowed in a hail of 12.7mm gunfire, but this was only the opening act.

The second act played differently. Diving from above, Oley Olson picked out a Hayabusa as it climbed out from its attack and made it his first aerial victory. Fred Hodges and Cliff Groh also each claimed his first victory over Lei Yun that day, but Fritz Wolf and John Donovan came close to being someone else's kill when they were jumped by two

Hayabusas flying top cover for the strike force. In both cases, they managed to turn the situation around to their advantage.

"We went down and into them," Smith wrote in his diary. "Then for about 15 minutes we really mixed it up . . . it was the most thrilling experience I've ever had."

In his memoirs, he described the scene as "the damndest rat race imaginable . . . dogfighting right on the deck, no way to escape by diving away this time. But what made the situation truly unique was that we had everything going for us for a change; speed, altitude, and surprise. Better still, we blasted four or five of them out of the picture on that initial attack, and suddenly we actually outnumbered them. I picked a Zero that was just completing a strafing run, apparently unaware that I was behind him. I opened fire at about three hundred yards as he began to pull up, closing rapidly, all six guns working beautifully. I couldn't miss, and the Zero flipped over on its side and dove for the ground, crashing in a ball of flame."

He reached another Japanese fighter as it climbed out of a strafing run and was about to open fire when the Japanese pilot started rolling to the left.

"I did the same, thinking he was about to pull around in a sharp turn, but instead he kept right on rolling, still straight ahead," Smith continued. "By then I was already committed and had to follow his maneuver, nearly inverted when I opened fire and thinking, 'This crazy bastard's doing a victory roll.' Mine was more of a sloppy barrel-roll, and I could see my tracers flying wildly all around him . . . until I kicked rudder and saw them finding their mark; smoke and flame poured from his engine, and that was that. Sayonara!"

In the melee, the Flying Tigers lost track of how many Japanese aircraft were shot down, with estimates running as high as a dozen, though in the "rat race," as Smith characterized it, more than one pilot might have fired on the same Japanese fighter and claimed it as his own.

The only Allied aircraft lost were the three that were on the ground when the attack began, and two RAF Hurricanes that were shot down.

Once again, the Flying Tigers had given the American home front something about which they could reap the pleasure of knowing that American pilots—even if they were mercenaries—were able to hand a decisive defeat to the Japanese. Lost on no one was that this news began filtering back to the United States on the same day that the people back home learned that the last American troops in the Philippines, who had held out against monumental odds since January, had finally been defeated.

Jimmy Doolittle's miraculous attack on Tokyo, which nobody— from Tokyo to Tallahassee could have predicted, and which would electrify American morale—was still ten days in the future.

———

Two days after R. T. Smith's "most thrilling experience," the IJAAF aircraft out of Chiang Mai tried it again. This time they mustered a strike force of only five Hayabusas, but they achieved the element of surprise.

As Chennault explained it, "on some days atmospheric conditions caused a temporary radio blackout during the hours just before dawn. On April 10 five Zeros slipped in through this radio silence, hitting the field just after dawn, a flattering attempt to duplicate our raid at Chiang Mai. They came in at treetop height to shoot up the field hastily and depart without doing a very thorough job."

The pilots were on their way to the field when they heard the engines of the Japanese fighters. They listened helplessly to the sound of Japanese gunfire. By the time they were at the flight line, their ground crews, who had been on duty when the attack happened, were already patching up what turned out to be minor harm. Most of the damage would be undone by noon. The American Volunteer Group had taken a few pretty nasty hits but had dodged a very large metaphorical bullet.

Meanwhile, the IJAAF had made a serious tactical flub, which they proceeded to compound. They had chosen to make a dawn attack with just five aircraft, while holding a substantial force in reserve for two later attacks, then launching these attacks after the Americans had been alerted, and in the afternoon. They should have observed by now that there is a buildup of cumulus clouds in the afternoons at this time of year in this part of the world, and clouds obscure ground targets.

Had the IJAAF concentrated all their available resources in their first strike, a surprise attack, it would have been devastating. One had only to look at what the AVG had done to *them* at dawn on March 24—with only ten aircraft, and with the element of surprise.

Chennault noted in his memoirs that "27 bombers came back to finish the job. The bombers milled around on top of a heavy overcast while our fighters, expecting more strafers, stayed below the clouds. The bombers left without contact." In turn, the strafers who were, by now, expected, did return, but not until almost three o'clock in the afternoon. There were nine Hayabusas this time, but the Flying Tigers were ready.

The AVG launched eight P-40s. Three went south on another detested but obligatory "show the flag" morale mission to Burma, but Bob Brouk, Duke Hedman, Buster Keeton, Chuck Older, and R. T. Smith were patrolling Lei Yun airspace when the Japanese arrived.

"There were many scattered cumulus clouds in the area, and the fight turned into another rat race around, between, and sometimes through the big puffy white clouds," Smith noted in his diary. "At one point I had to dive into one to shake a Zero that was about to get on my tail, and when I came out on the other side there was another Zero in front of me. I got a good burst into him but only drew a thin trail of gray smoke from his engine before he disappeared into another cloud."

After playing "hide-and-seek with a couple of others" in the clouds, Smith spotted a trio of Hayabusas flying toward Thailand and accelerated to catch up. He lined up the tail-end aircraft so easily that it almost felt like a trap, but he determined that there was no other Japanese aircraft behind him.

He gave the Hayabusa a long burst, and it flipped into a half roll and started down, observing that "there was no fire or smoke so I had no choice but to follow and keep shooting. He dove straight into the mountain below, no doubt dead from the moment I'd opened fire."

The other two continued south, apparently unaware of what had just happened, but by this time they were too far away for him to catch.

In his diary, Smith estimated that the AVG had downed "four or five" more enemy fighters, while the RAF lost two Hurricanes shot down. Duke Hedman and Chuck Older had closed in on a single Japanese fighter that had downed one of the Hurricanes and had engaged him for a half hour in a running gun battle. They both thought they got him, but they weren't sure. They had not. In fact, the AVG records confirm only two Japanese fighters shot down on April 10, one of these credited to Smith.

TWENTY

Turning Points

Despite their abundant moments of glory, and their still being able to control any aerial battlefield in which they found themselves, the American Volunteer Group was wearing thin. Though combat losses of AVG aircraft were few, and pilot losses even fewer, maintenance issues and operational losses due to malfunctioning equipment were taking a toll on the fleet. Fewer than forty of the original ninety-nine P-40Bs were operational at any given moment, and fewer than half of the promised P-40Es ever made it from Takoradi to Kunming. Some crashed, but most had been poached en route by the USAAF Ninth Air Force in Egypt or by the Tenth Air Force in India.

Chennault was making it clear in repeated wires sent to the War Department in Washington that his AVG was not only shouldering the American share of the heavy lifting in the air war over the Asian continent, but also that they were accomplishing a great deal with very little. As he pointed out in his memoirs, during the spring of 1942, "the only spare parts we received after war began were 2,000 pounds of solenoids, spark plugs, carburetors, magnetos, etc., sent out by Dr. Soong via Pan American Clipper to Calcutta . . . almost every part put a P-40 back into action."

In a rambling March 17 wire to T. V. Soong in Washington, Chennault complained despondently that he was "completely discouraged [by the] War Department failure [to] take advantage of China opportunities for air offensive against enemy. After three and half months. If airplanes promised for December delivery (including bombers) had arrived enemy would have been seriously damaged now. . . . No workable program has been drawn up, no plan for replacements, reinforcements for air units [in the] Far East has been approved and no decision made as to immediate future operations here. Numerous army and air officers constantly visiting us each with hastily conceived plans but no authority to make effective. My recommendations unsought or disapproved by all."

Chennault's obsessive sense of abandonment, which was shared by his men, did have a basis in fact. At the high-level Arcadia Conference in Washington, convened at the end of December 1941, Franklin Roosevelt, Winston Churchill, and the combined Anglo-American chiefs of staff had agreed to a "Germany first" strategic policy. This meant that the limited resources of the Allies would be devoted first to the defeat of the Third Reich. A secondary priority would be given to simply *holding the line* against the Japanese in the South and Southwest Pacific. China was even farther from the head of the list.

Meanwhile, Chennault's feelings should also be taken in context and from a perspective that he entirely ignored. As much as he complained about his own situation, he overlooked the fact that the USAAF of March and April 1942 was still very much a work in progress itself. The USAAF leadership had high hopes, but these hopes were far from being realized. Those leaders and their staffs were developing an elaborate command structure for an organization that would evolve, within two years, into the largest air force ever seen, but in the first part of

1942, the USAAF was barely ready for sustained combat missions anywhere in the world.

While the AVG was routinely in combat, the Ninth and Tenth Air Forces were still just administrative shells with small handfuls of mismatched aircraft. The Eighth Air Force, which had been tasked with the responsibility of carrying out the strategic air campaign against Germany—perceived by the USAAF as its most important mission—would consist of nothing more than just Colonel Ira Eaker and a half dozen staff officers until May. Even then, it would be incapable of any offensive missions with its own aircraft until August. The Fifth Air Force (formerly the Far East Air Force, FEAF) *was* engaging the enemy, and they were doing so on the same shoestring budget as the AVG.

At least the USAAF was on an ascending trajectory. As the AVG was wearing thin logistically and materially, so too was the morale of the individuals starting to fray.

There simmered beneath the surface of affairs at Lei Yun and Kunming the gnawing uncertainty of the ultimate fate of the American Volunteer Group as an organization and of the Flying Tigers as individuals. The men knew that Chennault himself had agreed to rejoin the USAAF and to become part of Stilwell's chain of command, and that the mission of the AVG would probably be absorbed into the USAAF command structure, but nobody within that command structure seemed to know when or how any of this would happen.

Nor did the Flying Tigers know what would happen to each of them. Would some or all of them be inducted into the USAAF—or not? Nobody knew. As late as the end of March, nothing had been decided at any level. The hardest part was not knowing what choices, if any, would be offered.

"Rumors about the future of our little group abounded," R. T. Smith recalled of the mood in February. "One had it that we would be disbanded and sent home within a matter of weeks. Another said that the Army Air Corps would soon take over and all of us would be inducted whether we wanted to or not. Nobody seemed to quite know what would happen, and the rumors were to continue for months. Meanwhile, all we wanted was to be left alone and allowed to continue the fight under the terms of our original agreement, though we knew that this could not continue indefinitely."

Some of the men had grown to prefer the informality of life in the AVG and wanted it to continue. Others would have been glad to join the USAAF or to go back to the US Navy or Marine Corps if the circumstances were right. Still others waited on the expiration of their AVG contracts on July 4, 1942, planning to be done with combat flying forever. Many of these were already sounding out Pan American Airways, who ran CNAC operations as well as its own operations, for future civilian jobs.

On the evening of March 26, Chennault called a meeting at the hostel in Kunming where the AVG was billeted and formally addressed the question.

Charlie Bond noted in his diary that "the consensus is that most want to resign from the AVG and go back to the States immediately or stay in the AVG and go home at the expiration of their contracts. . . . There was no doubt that the Old Man's first and foremost desire is to keep us together as his AVG."

"What's our chance of getting a regular commission if we are inducted right here in Kunming?" Bond asked.

"Charlie," Chennault replied, "there has been nothing said or done about that."

Chennault couldn't tell them because he didn't know. Nobody had figured it out yet.

Three days later, the future started to come into focus as Chennault was summoned to Chongqing for a parley of several days that would cover just this subject. He was still a civilian employed by the Chinese, but everyone knew those days were numbered. Chiang Kai-shek and Madame Chiang, who hosted the meeting, had made it known that they were hesitant to lose either Chennault or the AVG from their own command structure, but they were beholden to the largesse of American Lend-Lease and strings that were attached. Said strings were now being pulled by Joe Stilwell, and he saw Chennault and the AVG as loose ends that he needed to tie up. He had been promised by the War Department that they would become part of his growing administrative apparatus and subject to his chain of command, and he wanted this to happen sooner rather than later. From Washington, Secretary of War Henry Stimson and US Army chief of staff, George Marshall, had told Stilwell that *now* was finally time to bring the maverick ex-captain in from the cold.

For Chennault, the icy metaphor applied equally to his reaction upon greeting the man seated next to Stilwell at the conference table. Chennault knew that Colonel Clayton Bissell, his old antagonist from a decade earlier at the Air Corps Tactical School, would be there and he knew why.

Bissell had been posted to the Tenth Air Force in India, and its commander, General Lewis Brereton, had assigned Bissell to act as the Tenth's liaison with the Chinese. In this role, he also functioned as Stilwell's USAAF air adviser for the CBI. By all logic—and the naïve assumption that bureaucratic decisions are rooted in logic—such a job should have been reserved for Chennault. However, his renegade reputation had earned him few supporters in the halls of power in distant Washington, where such decisions were made. He was not yet wearing an American uniform, so technically, there was an easy excuse for passing him over.

The bitter animosity between Bissell and Chennault, kindled during heated disagreements at the ACTS back in the early 1930s, quickly moved to the front burner. Bissell personally resented Chennault for both his autonomy and for his international renown, and wanted to curb his independence. For example, Bissell had insisted that preparations for the Doolittle mission against Tokyo, scheduled for mid-April, be kept secret from Chennault.

While Bissell perceived Chennault as a man with a flagrant disregard for all standards of military order and discipline, Chennault candidly described Bissell in his memoirs as "a cold, meticulous man with a filing cabinet mind, who sought to cover his inability to cope with people by refuge in strict adherence to Army regulations. He carried his military fetish for parade-ground discipline and the spit and polish of garrison life into a situation where combat results were the only real measure of success. I always felt that Bissell prized a snappy salute from a perfectly uniformed staff officer more than a Japanese plane shot down in flames."

Though he had already agreed to being part of the USAAF himself, Chennault made it clear at the Chongqing conclave that he was still anxious to maintain the independence of the American Volunteer Group.

"With the Generalissimo's support, I vigorously opposed induction of the AVG," Chennault wrote. He told the Chiangs, Bissell, and Stilwell that "the AVG had a combat record that was never equaled by a Regular Army or Navy fighter group of similar size. I felt it was criminal to sacrifice the spirit and experience of the group for a mere change in uniform. The AVG was a unique organization, specially trained for a task it had performed with unbelievable success. The combat record had proved the soundness of my theories to the satisfaction of everybody except some of my Air Corps colleagues."

Chennault recalled that the reaction from both Bissell and Stilwell was to threaten that "the AVG would be shut off from further supplies if Chennault refused to allow it to be merged into the USAAF. Unless the AVG fought in Army uniforms, they were to be denied the privilege of fighting at all." The same, they told Chennault, applied to him.

As for himself, Chennault dreaded being sidelined more than induction. Of course, he had already committed to the latter for himself. As he reflected, "I was personally unwilling to withdraw from the war under any circumstances and agreed to accept a return to active duty."

Curiously, in his March 17 missive to T. V. Soong, Chennault seems to have expressed exactly the opposite inclination, admitting that he was "convinced [that] my usefulness and AVG [will be] finished April 15 unless immediate action taken. Request permission to demobilize and discharge group this date or appoint new commander. My patriotic duty [is] to return [to the] States and reveal to American public War Department program of indecision, obstructions, nonsupport, and passive inactivity [in the] Far East."

Perhaps he had just been down in the dumps that day.

As the Chongqing discussions evolved, the concept moved from a direct transfer of the AVG to the USAAF to a dissolve-and-replace scheme. It started to seem like this was what Stilwell had in mind all along. Stilwell and Bissell were both anxious that the AVG go out of business. They wanted no loose ends in the command structure they were assembling. Much to Chennault's chagrin, administrative issues trumped the tactical value of a seasoned organization in carrying out operations against a dangerous enemy.

Chennault recalled, to his dismay, that they "seemed to be concerned primarily with dissolving the AVG and not unduly interested in how they would obtain replacements or fight the war in China without it. In this, as in other conferences on the same subject, combat efficiency quickly became a secondary consideration where Army prestige was at stake. They were almost pathetically insistent upon discharging the AVG on April 30, but knowing War Department 'inertia' so well, I proposed July 4 as 'Dissolve Day.'"

This date coincided with the termination date of the one-year employment contracts signed by the personnel who had been hired by CAMCO for the American Volunteer Group, so it seemed to make sense—administratively if not tactically.

The Chongqing conferees all finally agreed that the American Volunteer Group would go out of business and be replaced by an all-new USAAF organization called the China Air Task Force (CATF), which was to inherit the winged tiger insignia of its predecessor. It would supersede the AVG and it would be under Chennault's command after he rejoined the USAAF—though it would be under the Tenth Air Force chain of command. The CATF would be comprised of various units as they became available, beginning with a fighter group that would take the place of the American Volunteer Group.

As Chennault recalled, Chiang Kai-shek finally agreed to order the demobilization of the AVG, still and always a component of the Chinese Air Force, only after Stilwell "solemnly promised to replace it with a *complete* American fighter group in China."

This unit, the USAAF 23rd Fighter Group, had been constituted in December 1941, but it had yet to be activated and it still existed only on paper with no personnel assigned.

In the meantime, Chennault had been in communication with Lieutenant Colonel Homer LeRoy "Tex" Sanders, who commanded the 51st Fighter Group, which was being moved from Hamilton Field near San Francisco to Karachi, where it would be assigned to the Tenth Air Force. According to Charlie Bond, who crossed paths with Sanders in Calcutta in early April, Sanders was anxious to get into the war, but he had only four P-40Es at the time.

Though it was underequipped, the 51st had upside potential. Being a USAAF unit, the 51st had a higher priority for new equipment than the AVG. With this in mind, Chennault and Harvey Greenlaw are believed to have been in discussions with Sanders over the idea of his taking command of the 23rd Fighter Group under Chennault *if* he would be able to bring one of the three squadrons within the 51st with him.

On April 9, a week after the Chongqing conference and two months to the day after Stilwell's meetings with Marshall in Washington, Chennault rejoined the service from which he had retired five years earlier. The man who had gone overseas as an aviation adviser masquerading as a farmer was now officially a military airman again. The man who left as a captain rejoined as a colonel. On April 22, he was promoted to the rank of brigadier general.

Charlie Bond observed in a notation in his published diaries that "it is significant that most AVG personnel involved in daily combat were not aware either of the high level bickering or that Chennault was now in the USAAF and had to take orders from Stilwell." In his diary, he noted that he was unaware of the Old Man's induction until the end of April.

Unfortunately, Chennault's promotion to brigadier general came one day after Colonel Clayton Bissell was given his own promotion to that rank, making him the senior officer by *one day*. This was thanks to Joe Stilwell. In his diary, Stilwell wrote that in that meeting with George Marshall and the top brass, "I spoke for Bissell, and insisted that he [out]rank Chennault."

Chennault's immediate future and the eventual disposition of the American Volunteer Group had been set in stone, but the future of the Flying Tigers themselves was still yet to be determined.

TWENTY-ONE

Unrest in the Ranks

There was more to the morale problem during that spring of 1942 than the uncertainty over the induction issue. AVG unit cohesion, which had once been inviolate, had begun to fray around the edges. The fissures in the airframes of war-weary P-40s were not the only cracks that were becoming a serious dilemma for the Flying Tigers.

Operationally, nothing was more dispiriting than the much-detested morale missions, the aggravating insistence by the Chinese that the AVG continue to show up over the battlefields in Burma and show the Chinese flag to the Chinese armies that were engaged and losing. The only practical value of these operations was observation, which the AVG pilots resented because they had signed on to fight the enemy in the air.

As Chennault explained, visual reconnaissance of Japanese front-line positions "could not be done in high-speed P-40s from low altitudes, without making the planes clay pigeons in a shooting gallery of Japanese flak gunners and fighter pilots. . . . Several of our morale missions had close calls after being jumped from above. Lack of reliable intelligence from the ground forces sent other missions into Japanese flak traps where supposedly friendly forces were reported. . . . Even at an altitude of 1,000 feet ground troops could hardly distinguish a fighter's insignia in the smoke haze, and visual reconnaissance of jungle-screened troops was useless. . . . Personally I agreed with the pilots' views. . . . The missions were unnecessarily dangerous and, with the exception of strafing enemy airdromes, offered no compensating results. . . . However, as long as these orders came down from my immediate superiors, the Generalissimo and Stilwell, I was obliged to execute them regardless of my personal feelings."

When he reflected cynically that "there is nothing that can take the joy out of flying faster than hours and hours of strafing just above the jungle treetops in the face of heavy ground fire," he precisely summarized the feelings of his men, feelings that were closely intertwined with their emotions around the losses of Jack Newkirk and Mac McGarry during the Chiang Mai strafing mission in March.

Because Chennault dutifully carried out the mandate issued by Chiang Kai-shek and Joe Stilwell for continuing the unproductive "morale missions," the feelings of the men, which he shared, were turning against him. Chennault was starting to earn the annoyance of the pilots who had once idolized him. This whole matter finally came to a head on April 20, when orders were posted at Lei Yun for a return to the infamous Chiang Mai. The mission called for escorting slow-flying RAF Blenheim bombers into what was now well known to be a flak trap—where the Japanese remembered March 24 as clearly as the AVG did.

At Lei Yun, someone had even started circulating a mass resignation petition.

When it reached Tex Hill, Newkirk's successor as commander of the 2nd Pursuit Squadron, he took exception. "I'm not going to sign this damn thing," Hill exclaimed. According to his biographer Reagan Schaupp, the alert shack quieted immediately as everyone looked at Hill. "Look, I don't like these missions any more than y'all do. Hell, I know they're dangerous. But this thing at Chiang Mai wasn't going to be any 'morale mission.' There were legitimate targets down there. There were Japs on the road we were going to strafe. How many of you fellows really think the Old Man would send us down there to get killed on some useless deal? We came over here as mercenaries—there are no bones about that. We all know it. But our country is at war now, and if you're part of the country, then you're at war too—uniform or not. These missions are the orders we've got, and the Old Man is giving 'em. I think we ought to follow them. I'm going to fly where I'm told, when I'm told. I'd say with that guy, we're in pretty good hands."

When Hill announced that he was going, and *leading* the mission, Ed Rector stood up and confirmed that he too would go to Chiang Mai. One by one, there were others, including Duke Hedman, Frank Schiel, and R. J. "Catfish" Raine. When word of the "revolt" reached Kunming, Bob Neale, commander of the 1st Pursuit Squadron, contacted Hill, telling him "if those bastards won't fly for you, I'll bring my boys down to take over."

Mission day, however, proved anticlimactic. Hill and his volunteers took off to fly the mission as briefed, but after the Blenheims failed to show up at the staging base, they returned to Lei Yun. Yet another Chiang Mai operation a few days later was aborted because of bad weather, again without contact with the enemy.

The resignation petition, with more than twenty signatures, did reach Chennault's desk, but he took no action whatsoever. He simply let it lie in his desk drawer, a symbol of the state of his organization. Back in the fall of 1941, Chennault had seen resignations as a useful means of weeding out men who were not up to the task at hand. However, after combat began, the Old Man came to look upon resignations with a great deal of disdain. As Charlie Bond wrote later in his diary, "he feels that anyone leaving now that we are at war and in actual contact with the enemy waxes of dishonor!"

There was probably no one in whom the festering infection of discontent and near-insurrection took a deeper hold than Greg Boyington. "I became so anxious to get out of Kunming, and all that it meant to me, that I damn nearly would have volunteered to walk back to the United States," he wrote in his memoirs.

Long the hard-drinking baddest bad boy of the AVG, Boyington had become the poster boy for the discord that had been rippling through the ranks. His combat career with the group seemed headed for a spectacular cataclysm, but instead it circled the drain and dribbled into an ignoble demise. When he cracked up his P-40 taking off from Lei Yun on an alert mission, he blamed engine trouble, but there were rumors that he had been hungover or drunk.

"I didn't even have the opportunity of getting the wheels retracted before my plane slammed into the ground, wheels and all," he recalled of the crash. "The impact was so great that my safety belt had broken and I was flung forward in the cockpit. My instrument panel tore into my knees and I damn nearly gargled the gun sight. Fortunately it didn't get my teeth, but the gun sight split my head open near my temple. . . . I was completely dazed as I struggled out of the cockpit, but I knew almost by instinct to get away from possible fire and to try to take cover before the Japs came. While half crawling and staggering in a torn and bloody condition I asked some nearby Chinese farmers to lend me a hand. They apparently didn't want any part of me."

He was patched up by Dr. Lewis Richards, one of the well-liked AVG flight surgeons, who bandaged his battered head and his injured knees. Without access to X-ray equipment there was no way of knowing whether the latter were broken. That night, however, Boyington got drunk at the wedding of Hell's Angels pilot Fred Hodges and his British-Burmese girlfriend, Helen Anderson. On the way home, Boyington fell in a ditch and his bandages became undone.

"Greg, will you do me a favor?" Richards said as he repaired the damage for a second time. "I wish you would stop drinking, because if you don't, I'm afraid you'll end up dead."

"Don't worry, Doc," Boyington replied. "I promise, I've had enough." Despite what may have been his best intentions or merely self-delusion, it would be a very long time before he fell down drunk for the last time.

One could almost leap to the conclusion that Boyington was suffering from post-traumatic stress disorder—except that at the time, there was nothing "post" about his stress and his disorder. "I was an emotionally immature person of the first order, which does not help peace of mind or make happiness. Frankly, this is what makes screwballs, and I'm afraid that I was one. Regardless of any of my self-manufactured troubles, or any troubles a mature person may have that he solves by himself, there was one thing that dwelled in my mind. If I were forced to continue my occupation for any length of time, I might not survive, for this war had all the earmarks of being a lengthy affair."

In the meantime, the last letter he had received since mail deliveries ended in December had been from his mother, who had to rescue his three youngest children after a juvenile court in Seattle had taken them away from his ex-wife. It was enough to drive a man to drink.

Boyington never flew another AVG combat mission, but when recuperating in Kunming grew too much—or too *little*—for him, he spent a week or so test flying overhauled aircraft while he waited for confirmation of the number of Japanese aircraft he had shot down so that he could apply for his bonus money. As he explained in his memoirs, "the only reason I had hung around this long was that one of

Chennault's stooges in my squadron claimed that some of our Rangoon combat reports had been lost, but they would straighten it out for pay purposes later [but] that never did fully happen."

He had claimed that he shot down six Japanese aircraft, but the AVG officially credited him with 3.5, of which only two were in air-to-air combat.

Charlie Bond noted in his diary that he saw Boyington "completely looped and staggering" at dinner on the night of April 21. Bob Neale observed that Boyington had been "that way for six days and nights."

The next day or shortly thereafter, Boyington did start walking out of Kunming—with a briefcase full of currency, most of it Chinese. He went into the CNAC terminal, where he bought a ticket to Calcutta.

When the list of individuals receiving honorable discharges from the AVG was eventually published, Boyington was conspicuously absent, but the worst of his troubles still lay ahead. Tex Hill's biographer Reagan Schaupp later observed that "if the AVG were a military outfit, Boyington would be shot as a deserter."

Soon the AVG would be, but by that time, Boyington would be long gone and destined for notoriety beyond the imagination of anyone in Kunming, including Boyington himself.

On April 23, the day after his promotion to brigadier general and three days after the pilots' revolt hit the fan in Lei Yun, Chennault received an answer to a personal letter he had written to Madame Chiang pointing out the practical futility of the morale missions and the damage that was being done, ironically, to the morale of the men who flew them. She wasted no time in replying. She wired back, telling Chennault "Generalissimo consents use of AVG for fighting Jap planes fighting our troops and not for low-altitude recon."

That night, when the Old Man again spoke to the men at Lei Yun on the subject of induction of the individual pilots, the rancor of the pilots' revolt still hung in the air like the odor of spoiled meat. Chennault was candid with the men, telling them that there would be few regular US Army commissions available and that anyone wanting one should decide for himself whether he wanted to apply. By now, the enthusiasm for being part of the USAAF was rapidly evaporating.

As R. T. Smith put it so succinctly, "not many of us were terribly interested in regular army commissions at this point, although we knew that soon we'd have to decide what to do. . . . Our main concern those days was simply survival from day to day, each of us hoping his number wouldn't come up before it was time to head back for the good old US of A."

———

C oincidentally, it was also on April 23 that the civilian who had *created* the AVG wrote to Chennault from the White House, telling him that "the outstanding gallantry and conspicuous daring that the American Volunteer Group combined with their unbelievable efficiency is a source of tremendous pride throughout the whole of America. The fact that they have labored under the shortages and difficulties is keenly appreciated."

Franklin D. Roosevelt continued by promising that "there are reinforcements on the way, both ground and flying personnel, and more are to come. The United States is making a tremendous effort to get the necessary material into hands of the men overseas. Unfortunately we have lost planes by sinkings in the Indian Ocean and west of Australia which has delayed us at a critical moment, but now planes are going forward rapidly. Leaves of absence should be given to AVG veterans just as soon as replacements have absorbed your experience, training and tradition for rest and recuperation. It is planned that when replacements are adequately trained selected AVG veterans will be recalled to the States or other theaters of operations to impart their combat experience and training to personnel in newly formed units.

"Your President is greatly concerned that the 23rd Group be fully supplied and kept in operation during the critical phase of the operations now pending. He has taken great pride in the worldwide acclaim given the Group and places great hope in its future fighting as rapidly as it is re-equipped."

Time would tell.

TWENTY-TWO

The Last Days of Lei Yun

Though the mission over Burma had morphed from ground support and flag-showing back into "fighting Jap planes fighting our troops," the men of the American Volunteer Group were taking advantage of the bomb racks on their few P-40Es to attack the Japanese columns that were closing in on Lashio, 120 miles away at the start of the Burma Road. Though attacking well-armed troop concentrations or heavily fortified positions like Chiang Mai remained objectionable, shooting up strings of trucks along a highway was okay with the Tigers.

On April 24, one month after Chiang Mai and one day after Roosevelt's message and the official end of the morale missions, the Pandas of the 2nd Pursuit Squadron ran their first bombing mission over the Burma Road. A half dozen P-40Es took part, with Tex Hill leading four others flying top cover in their P-40Bs. The only interference, aside from ground fire, came from a lone Japanese Ki-15 reconnaissance aircraft that not so much intervened as got in the way. Four pilots, including Hill, had a low-level cinematic moment, dramatically chasing the Japanese aircraft into a box canyon, where they destroyed it. They shared the victory four ways.

Four days later, on the eve of Emperor Hirohito's birthday, the Japanese mounted their long-awaited major follow-up to the April 9–10 attacks on Lei Yun. It was coordinated with their final ground push against Lashio, and designed to wipe out at least some substantial portion of the AVG contingent at their forward operating location. The Japanese knew that the Americans would be expecting something "special" from them for the emperor's birthday, but by attacking a day early, they hoped to catch the Flying Tigers off guard—and also to be able to present their success as a birthday gift to Hirohito.

Chennault had anticipated such a trick and cautiously ordered his men to beware of an attack the day before. As he recalled, "I thought a great deal about what kind of a birthday gift his air force in Burma would offer. From the knowledge gained from my previous experiences with the Emperor's birthday celebrations, I reasoned that the Japs would expect me to be ready for them on April 29, and I suspected they might try to catch us a day early."

The AVG contingent operated in three layers. The base of their aerial pyramid was comprised of ten Hell's Angels P-40Bs commanded by Oley Olson. Hill led a top cover flight of four Pandas in P-40Es, while R. T. Smith and Paul Greene of the Hell's Angels were higher still as "weavers," weaving back and forth and keeping lookout. Much of the previous week had been clouded by dense overcast and heavy rain, and there were still towers of cumulus clouds in the area that could easily block the view of the various groups of aircraft on both sides.

They were patrolling south of Lei Yun toward Lashio when they first encountered the Imperial Japanese Army Air Force strike force.

There were at least two dozen Mitsubishi Ki-21 heavy bombers escorted by about twenty Nakajima Ki-43 Hayabusas.

R. T. Smith spotted the escort first. Having alerted Hill, he and Greene dove into the nearest Hayabusas, trading their higher altitude for speed. They opened fire, failed to connect, then pulled up while still well above the Japanese. As they made their second diving pass, they saw two of the Hayabusas starting to burn.

Hill, meanwhile, also led his men into a fast pass against the Japanese fighters. He picked his target, which attempted to use his superior maneuverability to sidestep the Texan. However, Hill stayed with him just long enough to pour a stream of tracers into the cockpit.

The engagement became a tumbling dogfight in which Hill soon found himself with the tables turned as he looked up at a Hayabusa hurtling down at him. Instead of dodging, he allowed a head-on pass. Both pilots opened fire, but fired low. Hill pulled back on the stick, risking a collision. As they passed one another, several of his .50-caliber rounds ripped into the Hayabusa's belly. He banked, looked back, and saw the enemy fighter trailing fire and smoke.

At one point in the melee an enemy fighter nearly claimed Tex Hill, but fortunately Lew Bishop was in a position to help and successfully attacked the attacker.

The Flying Tigers scored heavily against the Japanese that day, with Smith mentioning thirteen enemy fighters shot down, and Hill estimating sixteen. However, in one sense, the IJAAF won the battle. By sacrificing themselves to the Flying Tigers, the Hayabusa pilots had distracted the Americans long enough for the heavy bombers to reach Lei Yun unmolested and lay waste to the field.

It could have been worse. The AVG fighters were out battling the Japanese fighters so were untouched by bombs, and the alert system forewarned the base of the incoming bombers, so several American transports that had just flown in from India en route to Kunming were able to get airborne and avoid being hit.

———————

Though no Americans were lost in the aerial battle, R. T. Smith almost became a statistic. He and Paul Greene had lost contact with the others during the battle and found themselves some distance northeast of Lei Yun and short of fuel because of having burned so much while on the weaving mission. They decided to make their way to the small auxiliary field at Mangshi (then called Meng Shih, and now the Dehong Mangshi Airport, one of China's busiest).

With much of the terrain obscured by clouds, they tried to locate Mangshi village. Though they finally found a village, no runway was visible, so they contacted the controller at Mangshi to ask for directions. He replied that he could see two P-40s several miles away. As they prepared to land, they realized that they were in a valley parallel to the one containing Mangshi, and that the controller was watching two *other* P-40s.

"I knew there wasn't enough fuel to climb back up and fly another twenty or thirty miles over the next mountain range, so I called Paul and told him I was going to try to land on a pasture-like area," Smith recalled. "I was naive enough to think I could save the airplane, and that later it could be flown out.

"Paul circled as I landed; I set her down as slowly as possible and was rolling nicely, but then ahead appeared a swale and I was momentarily airborne again before smashing down on the other side. The gear was wiped out immediately, the plane began to spin around, and suddenly all my guns were firing; I'd forgotten to turn off the switches, and squeezed the trigger on the stick. Dust and rocks and pieces of airplane were flying all over, but finally we came to a stop. I was relatively unhurt, climbed out and waved at Paul, and he headed out toward Mangshi. I stumbled down to the road, hailed a Chinese army truck full of wounded soldiers headed north, and a couple of hours later arrived in Mangshi and joined the rest of the gang. Lucky? You know it, friends."

Throughout April, with and without AVG morale missions, the Imperial Japanese Army tightened the noose on the British and the Chinese armies in Burma. They made steady progress, pushing north toward Mandalay, Burma's second-largest city. They moved against the British up the valley of the Irrawaddy River, and against the Chinese on a parallel track up the valley of the Sittang River. From the beginning of April, the Allied objective had been to organize the defense of central Burma with the hope of stopping the Japanese south of the city of Mandalay in the center of the country. It seemed for a time that with the support of the Chinese, the British might have the critical mass to finally thwart the unstoppable momentum of Shojiro Iida's Fifteenth Army.

Like Chennault, Stilwell felt abandoned. No wonder he had asked for the AVG morale flights. In her biography of him, Barbara Tuchman wrote that Stilwell had concluded that "no one really cared about Burma. It was the end of the line. The main effort of London and Washington was directed elsewhere [against the Germans]. With no reinforcements or help coming in, there was a sense of isolation in CBI."

As all sides knew, abandonment was not just a feeling, but a reality for Stilwell and the Allied effort in Burma. If the Burma Road was severed, the strategic importance of Burma in the eyes of Allied leadership in London and Washington was greatly diminished.

When the British retreated from Prome in the Irrawaddy Valley, exposing the Chinese flank, Stilwell felt abandoned by his allies. When the Chinese commanders—who reported to him—went around him to Chiang, refused to obey his orders, and withdrew from Toungoo, Stilwell felt abandoned by the Chinese armies of which he was the nominal commander.

"Through stupidity, fear, and the defensive attitude we have lost a grand chance to slap the Japs back at Toungoo," Stilwell confided in his diary. "The basic reason is Chiang Kai-shek's meddling. Had he let me concentrate at Pyinmana [north of Toungoo], we would have been set to attack. Had he not stopped the 22nd Division when I ordered it in, we would have had plenty of force to cut off the Japs when they first went around Toungoo. Had he not gone behind my back to Tu [Li-ming, commanding the Chinese Fifth Army] and Lin Wei [of the Chinese general staff], they might have obeyed my orders. He can't keep his hands off: 1,600 miles from the front, he writes endless instructions to do this and that, based on fragmentary information and a cockeyed conception of tactics. He thinks he knows psychology; in fact, he thinks he knows everything, and he wobbles this way and that, changing his mind at every change in the action."

Stilwell was outspoken in his disdain for the Generalissimo. Stilwell wrote in his diary that "Chiang Kai-shek has been boss so long and has so many yes-men around him that he has the idea he is infallible on any subject. . . . He is not mentally stable, and he will say many things to your face that he doesn't mean fully or exactly. My only concern is to tell him the truth and go about my business. If I can't get by that way, the hell with it: it is patently impossible for me to compete with the swarms of parasites and sycophants that surround him."

When writing about him in his diary and elsewhere, Stilwell routinely referred to Chiang by his code name, the unflattering term "Peanut." Under the American system of code names, Stilwell was

"Quarterback," while Madame Chiang was "Snow White." Various Chinese generals were named for Snow White's dwarfs.

Of Snow White herself, Stilwell wrote that she was "a clever, brainy woman . . . she can appreciate the mental reactions of a foreigner to the twisting, indirect, and undercover methods of Chinese politics and warmaking. . . . No concessions to the Western viewpoint in all China's foreign relations. The Chinese were always right: the foreigners were always wrong. . . . Can turn on charm at will. And knows it."

Her having intervened to overrule Stilwell and curtail the AVG morale flights may have been her siding with Chennault, for whom she had a great deal of fondness, or it was because the Chiangs had simply given up on Burma.

On April 28, the same day that the AVG was intercepting Hayabusas over Lei Yun, Chiang Kai-shek had sent a message demanding that Stilwell *hold* Mandalay. The following morning, as heavy rains lashed central Burma, he amended the order, telling the Quarterback that he need *not* hold Mandalay after all.

Stilwell decided that he would take General Luo Zhuoying (Lo Cho-ying), the overall commander of the 1st Route Expeditionary Forces and Stilwell's nominal executive officer, and withdraw toward Lei Yun by way of Lashio, the "Milepost One" of the Burma Road.

However, on the first of May, Stilwell awoke at his headquarters on a tea plantation near Shwebo, 50 miles north of Mandalay, to learn that the Japanese had reached Mandalay and had captured Lashio—*and* that Luo had stolen an entire train, loaded it with his troops, and was racing toward Myitkyina, 250 miles north of Mandalay.

"Lo's train collided last night with another," Stilwell wrote in his diary. "Unfortunately, he was not killed."

Stilwell phoned the AVG at Lei Yun, but there was no one to answer the telephone. The Old Man had issued orders on April 30 for everyone

BILL YENNE

to abandon the base. P. T. Mao had sent a convoy of trucks to haul out whatever could be moved, and Chennault ordered Harvey Greenlaw to destroy twenty-two P-40s that were undergoing repair work and could not be evacuated. The last shark departed for Kunming at 2:00 p.m. the following day. The unanswered phone was probably ringing in the operations shack even as the Allison engines were winding up on the flight line.

TWENTY-THREE

Last Exits

G et those transports off the field!" Chennault shouted to Colonel Caleb Haynes on April 28, the day before Emperor Hirohito's birthday. "We're going to have an air raid here!"

Haynes looked up to watch the signal being hoisted on the air raid warning mast that loomed above the American Volunteer Group base at Lei Yun.

"One ball alert," Chennault explained hurriedly. "That means the bombers have been sighted on their way north."

The bombers in question were the two dozen Mitsubishi Ki-21 heavy bombers that slipped through while Tex Hill, Oley Olson, and the others were clearing the sky of Hayabusas.

When Haynes and his copilot said that the C-47 they had just flown in from India was overloaded by a ton and could not possibly take off from the Lei Yun runway without being unloaded, Chennault ordered it towed aside and camouflaged with bamboo.

Haynes was the man who had come to India six weeks earlier with a dozen B-17 Flying Fortresses, a collection of C-47 transport aircraft, and the mission to bomb Tokyo that was never realized. Before the war, he had been a pilot with the 2nd Bomb Group at Langley Field in Virginia, the first operational B-17 unit. In this role, he had participated in a number of very-long-range demonstration flights, usually with Curtis LeMay aboard as navigator, to show off the capabilities of the Flying Fortress. Among these was a 1939 humanitarian relief flight to Chile for which Haynes and his crew received the Mackay Trophy for "most meritorious flight of the year."

When the mission to attack Tokyo from China was scrubbed, Haynes and his armada of aircraft were taken over by Major General Lewis Brereton, the commander of the Tenth Air Force, who was short of both aircraft and good operational leaders. He put Haynes in charge of the newly formed Assam-Burma-China Ferry Command (ABC Ferry Command), which was created in the middle of April using the C-47s that Haynes had brought, and was tasked with becoming the aerial analogue of the Burma Road. With the Japanese having severed this last land route into China, supplying Chiang Kai-shek, his army, and his government would have to be done by air, a task then being handled almost exclusively by the American civilian pilots working for CNAC and Pan American.

As the name suggests, the function of the ABC Ferry Command would be to fly personnel and supplies from the northeastern Indian state of Assam to Kunming and Chongqing by way of Burma on a route then being used by CNAC and Pan Am. When—no longer "if"—Burma fell to the Japanese, the ABC Command would effectively be an "AC" Command.

The key stopover and refueling point on the route was the airport at Dinjan, on the Brahmaputra River in Assam. Dinjan was 550 air miles northeast of Calcutta and 500 air miles west of Kunming. Between Dinjan and Kunming, the route crossed over a stretch of the

Himalayas that the pilots came to know as the "Hump." This section proved to be one of the most challenging and dangerous air routes in the world—studded with fifteen-thousand-foot mountain peaks and towering "hard-centered" cumulus clouds filled with two-hundred-mile-per-hour turbulence.

As his executive officer and operations man, Haynes picked one of the pilots who had been with him on the flight from the United States, piloting one of Haynes's gaggle of B-17s—Colonel Robert Lee Scott Jr. "Scotty," as his friends knew him, had been one of the many pilots who had tried, only to be turned down, to join the American Volunteer Group back in the summer of 1941. Now, flying into Lei Yun as Haynes's copilot, he found himself literally dropping in on the AVG forward operating base at the moment it came under attack by the Japanese. He had arrived in the midst of the AVG in fulfillment of his fondest dream, though he came not as a fighter pilot, but in the right seat of a transport aircraft of the type that the men of the USAAF called a "Gooney Bird."

Haynes and Scott, the top brass of the Assam-Burma-China Ferry Command, had flown into Lei Yun personally tasked with a mission of utmost importance. With the Allied forces on the Burma front going through the convulsions of total collapse, USAAF commanding general Hap Arnold had wired an order to Haynes—bypassing Brereton—to *find Joe Stilwell* and evacuate him safely to India.

When it was determined that Stilwell was still at the plantation in Shwebo, north of Mandalay, Haynes and Scott took off from Lei Yun to pick him up. Battling their way through a blinding downpour using instruments, they arrived at the landing strip at the plantation on the afternoon of May 1, the same day that Stilwell learned of the fall of Mandalay and of his having been abandoned by his Chinese armies. He was a shell of a man in charge of a shell of a command, surrounded not by organized regiments but by about four dozen military people, mostly staff officers, along with some Burmese nurses, Indian cooks, and random civilian hangers-on.

As they emerged from the C-47, Haynes and Scott were greeted by the British plantation superintendent, who begged them to take him with them when they departed. They ignored his pleas and asked to be taken to Stilwell, who remained seated, engrossed in thought, as they came into his room.

"General Arnold sent us to rescue you, sir," Haynes told Stilwell as Scott pointed to the C-47. "We couldn't taxi any closer. Have the transport down there."

"The Air Force didn't bring me in here . . . and it doesn't have to fly me out either," Stilwell finally replied as his staff grimaced and glanced uncomfortably at one another. "I'll walk."

"But General Stilwell," Scott began, glancing at Haynes, who was shaking his head with incredulity. The nearest British fortified position in India, at Imphal in the state of Manipur, was *three hundred miles* away. "General, we saw the enemy patrols just south of here, on this side of the river. They'll be here before night."

As Scott recalled in his memoirs, "Vinegar Joe sat there in that peaked campaign hat and glared at me through his rimless glasses."

Haynes muttered, "Let's knock the old fool in the head and take him anyway."

Scott described his boss's comment not as a threat, but as a "reflexive statement . . . merely his observation of a three-star general who was off his rocker and plainly not responsible."

After an awkward silence in which neither Stilwell nor Haynes moved, Scott finally turned to Stilwell's chief of staff, Major General Thomas "Long Tom" Hearn, and told him, "We're going back to the plane. I'd advise you to get General Stilwell and all yourselves aboard, for we haven't much time. I have seen enemy fighters all the way south from Lashio, and we saw their advance patrols a few miles south."

When Haynes, Scott, and the C-47 were wheels-up out of Shwebo ten minutes later, most of Stilwell's staff, though not Stilwell himself, were aboard. As they climbed to cruising altitude, Scott turned and asked Hearn whether he thought they should go back for another try at getting Stilwell aboard. Hearn shrugged and said this would be a pointless exercise. Vinegar Joe Stilwell, as though to underscore his professional roots as an infantryman, was stubbornly determined to walk all the way to Imphal.

He did, and he made it without losing any of the people who hiked with him, but it took him three weeks, during which time he was completely out of touch with the outside world. As Barbara Tuchman wrote in her biography of Stilwell, "many of those who walked out under his command did hate his guts [when it was over] but all 114 knew they owed him their lives."

"I have never been able to understand why Stilwell refused to fly with Haynes," Chennault wrote after the war. "By [air] he was only a few hours from India and less than six hours from Chungking. At either point he would have been in a position to direct the reorganization of Chinese resistance wherever the need was most acute. In the jungle he was of no use to anybody except his immediate party . . . it was a startling exhibition of his ignorance or disregard for these larger responsibilities. . . . While Stilwell was trudging through the Burma jungle, China faced its darkest hour since the fall of Nanking [five years before]."

———

Within twenty-four hours of the last flights out of Shwebo and Lei Yun, the Japanese rolled in. At the former, they knew that they had just missed Stilwell, but they assumed he had left by air. They did not realize that he was just a few miles away and on foot.

At the former CAMCO base of operations in Lei Yun, the Japanese stood among the still-smoldering ruins of CAMCO facilities, the burned-out shell of the "magnificent country clubhouse," and the twenty-two AVG P-40s that Harvey Greenlaw had torched. They gloated, of course, at the sooty remnants of the hated sharks. Perhaps many of the infantry-men imagined that this damage had been wrought by Japanese bombs and that it marked the final demise of the hated Flying Tigers.

TWENTY-FOUR

Saving China
While the Quarterback Hiked

By May 1942, the war across the whole landscape of Burma and southern China was no longer a fight between the Japanese and the Allies, but one between the Japanese and time and terrain. The British Army had withdrawn and the Chinese Army was either in retreat and capable of only an occasional skirmish that could hardly be called a holding action.

Within days of the last exits from Shwebo and Lei Yun, virtually all of Burma was under Japanese control, and they were invading China from the south. On the Burma Road, the Imperial Japanese Army's 56th Division, spearheaded by mechanized units, rolled through Lei Yun and deeper into Yunnan Province. Here they were slowed only by the masses of refugees who clogged the route, trying to make their way to Baoshan (then Paoshan), about 150 miles from Lei Yun and the Burmese border.

Halfway between Baoshan and Kunming, at an airfield near Yunnanyi, Chennault had established a flying school for the Chinese Air

Force back in 1938. He had installed a radio station and a servicing detachment there, as well as a substantial stockpile of aviation fuel so the field could be used as a refueling point for AVG missions into northern Burma.

On May 2, the Old Man ordered Bob Neale, commander of the 1st Squadron Adam and Eves, to take an eight-man AVG contingent from Kunming to operate out of the primitive grass landing field at Baoshan to protect Yunnanyi. From Mingaladon, to Magwe, to Lei Yun, and now to Baoshan, the advance base of the Flying Tigers had been pushed back, and back, and back, but it was some consolation that they had still not yet been defeated in an aerial battle.

On their first day at Yunnanyi, the Adam and Eves escorted nine Chinese bombers that were supposed to have attacked a bridge on the Burma Road at Kutkai, fifty miles north of Lashio, which would have halted the Japanese advance at least temporarily. However, much to the disbelief of the Americans, they ignored it and hit the railyard in Lashio instead.

Baoshan had no paved runway, nor did it have the early warning net that had served the AVG so well at Lei Yun. The sight of two early morning reconnaissance aircraft should have provided that warning on May 4, but apparently there was an air of complacency at the grassy strip. Bob Little and Charlie Bond were cleaning their pistols when an armada of the Imperial Japanese Army Air Force came overhead.

At the sound of engines, Bond and Little looked up, saw about twenty-five bombers in a "vee" formation at about eighteen thousand feet, and ran for their sharks. Bond had been in such a hurry that he didn't even finish strapping on his parachute until he was climbing into the sky. The controls felt a little sluggish, and he realized that he had forgotten to retract his landing gear. Bob Neale and Mickey Mickelson were on the field but they had just flown in from Kunming and were therefore short of fuel.

By the time Bond and Little reached their altitude, the Mitsubishi Ki-21s were targeting the city of Baoshan with deadly precision. The only good news was that they were ignoring the airfield. Bond and Little climbed to nineteen thousand feet to make a diving attack. They saw no fighter escort in the area, but did not realize that the IJAAF fighters were holding back to catch the AVG after the battle, when they were low on fuel and ammunition.

"I closed in on the outside bomber and squeezed the trigger," Bond recalled in his diary. "My bursts completely enveloped the fuselage, but I saw no smoke or fire. The two adjacent bombers immediately started streaming a bluish white smoke to attract me to them as 'wounded' aircraft. We had been briefed about this trick, but this was the first time I had seen it. I wasn't about to take that bait. The bomber on the extreme flank end, pulled away a bit, and this made it even more obvious. I continued my rear right quarter attacks. On my third attack I saw his right engine disintegrate and ignite into a flaming torch. He went down and through the overcast. I turned on the bomber at the tail of the vee, but suddenly my guns quit firing. I had become too engrossed and had been firing long bursts, by far too long. Recharging the guns produced no results. Hell, I was out of ammunition!"

Passing over the burning city, he headed for the airfield. Lining up on the runway, he lowered the flaps and was rotating his landing gear.

"Suddenly I heard several loud explosions," he recalled. "The noise stunned me. I immediately concluded that my landing gear hydraulic system had blown up."

As he reached down to cycle the gear lever, he discovered that his cockpit was on fire all around him.

He looked around to see three Japanese fighters on his tail pumping 12.7mm rounds into his P-40 from their Ho-103 machine guns at a rate of nearly five rounds each second. Bond's fuselage tank had exploded. Rounds were slamming into the armor plate behind him, saving his life but pounding the back of his head in the process. Indeed, his head was grazed by several slugs that would have killed him if not for the armor.

"For a split second I considered giving up, but something wouldn't let me," Bond recalled, having considered a final surrender to desperate, impossible circumstances.

Instead, he cranked open the canopy, unbuckled his seat belt, and stood up. The slipstream grabbed him and sucked him out of the cockpit. As he cartwheeled through the air, one second of blue sky was followed by the terrifying sight of the ground rushing up at him as the parachute snapped open.

Bond crashed to earth in a cemetery, his flight suit still in flames. Fortunately, the Chinese civilians who came to beat him to death realized that he was an American, and by the end of the day, AVG flight surgeon Lewis "Doc" Richards was treating the throbbing agony of third-degree burns over much of his body. It would be thirty-three days before he again had a throttle in his hands.

Bob Little survived unscathed but was killed two weeks later.

It turned out that the May 4 raid was only the beginning of a sustained campaign by the IJAAF. A second wave of bombers came over Baoshan later in the day, and they returned on May 5. A radio intercept told Chennault that they were coming, so he forward-deployed Tex Hill to take nine Pandas to Yunnanyi at dawn that day to refuel and be ready. At 9:45 a.m., the Old Man learned that the IJAAF had launched one formation of bombers each from Mingaladon and from Chiang Mai. Picking up escort fighters at smaller fields along the way, they had an estimated arrival time over Baoshan of approximately 12:30 p.m. Chennault told Hill to take off to greet them.

At 12:45, Ralph Sasser, the AVG radio man on the ground at Paoshan, confirmed, "They're strafing the field—bombers too."

Engine trouble on takeoff had delayed Hill as the others took off to intercept the Japanese strike force, and he was separated from the others. Reaching Baoshan on his own, he spotted a gaggle of seven Ki-43 Hayabusas and decided on a fast diving attack. He picked out one and claimed him almost effortlessly in a three-second burst of .50-caliber lead.

Suddenly, the sky was filled with a dogfight, as other Pandas materialized and began going after the remaining Hayabusas. Hill picked another, and opened up with his six Brownings, but this time the Japanese pilot used his superior maneuverability to roll out of the line of fire.

"Wow! They're dropping like flies," Sasser told Chennault over the radio link.

"Who?" Chennault asked.

"Don't know. Just went outside again. Must be Japs—they're burning. Three burning in the air right now."

In turn, the Pandas waded into the second bomber formation and forced them to retreat without dropping their ordnance.

When the dust had settled, the Flying Tigers claimed eight aircraft with no losses and returned to Kunming rather than landing at Yunnanyi.

Chennault had already decided that Baoshan was no longer viable as a forward operating location. Yunnanyi was abandoned less than a week later. As with Magwe, they had outlived their usefulness sooner than anyone expected. With the end to the flight school at Yunnanyi, the American instructors were checked out in P-40s and promptly brought into the AVG. Chennault then ordered the final exit to Kunming. In the back of his mind, he already was worrying that time might be running out even for Kunming.

The only natural obstacle for the Japanese 56th Division was now the Salween River Gorge, just west of Baoshan and about three hundred miles west of Kunming. As the Old Man described this bottleneck in his memoirs, "the Salween River carved a mile-deep chasm through the solid rock of southwestern Yunnan's mountains before settling into the broad valleys of Burma. The Burma Road, winding northeast from Lashio, spilled over the western crest of the Salween gorge and crawled down the sheer, waterworn precipice in 35 hairpin curves, hewn by hand out of solid rock. It took 20 miles of serpentine road to traverse the vertical mile from the crest to the suspension bridge that spanned the turbulent sepia waters of the Salween. On the east bank, the road repeated its tortuous windings up the rocky cliff to the Baoshan plateau."

The retreating Chinese had blown up this bridge, but the Japanese had engineers on the scene and were preparing to construct a pontoon bridge. If they got across the Salween Gorge, there was a real probability that they would reach Baoshan and even Kunming. If so, it could very well be the beginning of the end for China, because if the Japanese armies did reach Kunming, there would be little to stop them from reaching Chongqing itself.

While the Quarterback, Joe Stilwell, the designated commander of the entire theater, was in the midst of his strange exercise in infantry nostalgia and out of touch with his command, the only force that could match and defeat the Japanese anywhere was the American Volunteer Group—and six or eight sharks at a time could do only so much.

On May 6, Chennault sent a message to Madame Chiang in Chongqing, explaining that the Japanese force, complete with tanks and artillery, was on the west bank of the Salween and meeting no opposition. He concluded his memo with a terse "Consider situation desperate and Japs may drive Kunming in trucks unless road and bridges destroyed and determined opposition developed."

She wired back that "Generalissimo instructs you send all available AVG to attack trucks boats etc. between Salween and Lungling city. . . . Tell AVG I appreciate their loyalty and redoubled efforts particularly at this critical juncture. . . . Please continue attacks especially boats and transports on Salween River."

She even made sure that General Chou Chih-jou, the commander of the Chinese Air Force, would contribute a few of his Tupolev SB bombers to the effort to attack the Japanese at the Salween bottleneck.

Fortunately, the AVG's small number of P-40Es with their factory-installed underwing bomb racks gave the Flying Tigers the capability to attack the enemy with bombs. Chennault also boasted that the two of his AVG armorers, Charley Baisden and Roy Hoffman, "improvised a belly rack that could carry 550-pound Russian high-explosive bombs, which were plentiful in China."

It was also fortunate that within AVG ranks were pilots who had trained in single-engine dive bombers while with the US Navy. Among them, according to Jim Howard, was Tom Jones, late of the USS *Yorktown*, who pushed the idea of using P-40s to dive-bomb—a technique that improved pinpoint bombing accuracy even if it made the attacking aircraft more vulnerable to antiaircraft fire.

Chennault wasted no time, planning the strike mission for the next day, May 7. Coincidentally, it would be the same day that General Jonathan Wainwright was led by his Japanese captors to radio station KZRH in Manila to formally announce the surrender of American forces in the Philippines—and the worst defeat ever suffered by the US Army, at least since the Civil War.

The AVG strike force consisted of four ex–US Navy pilots in P-40Es—Tom Jones, Frank Lawlor, and Ed Rector, led by Tex Hill—while four P-40Bs under Oley Olson flew top cover.

Though there were violent thunderstorms in the area and heavy rain lashed the planes as they stopped to refuel at Yunnanyi, the airspace above the target was clear and visibility was unobstructed.

Tex Hill led them down single file though the narrow gorge. As the Old Man described the scene, the Japanese column "lay along the serpentine road that coiled like a dusty python across the dark rock wall. During their advance through Burma, the jungle had effectively screened the Japanese against AVG strafing attacks. On the Salween escarpment they were trapped in the open like flies on flypaper—a sheer precipice on one side of the narrow road and a rock wall on the other."

The plan was not to use their mere handful of demolition bombs against specific Japanese equipment or positions, but to target the steep banks of the gorge across which snaked the road in a long series of switchbacks. As the bombs exploded at the top, a road section crumbled, slipped, and avalanched into the switchback below. In turn, a larger swath of rock and crumbling roadway crashed down onto the switchback below that, and onto those farther beneath. It was like a stack of vertically falling dominoes, each more massive than the one above. Tons of falling rock and dirt snowballed into tens of tons of sliding gorge face dropping away from the cliff face like a calving glacier. Hundreds of troops and dozens of vehicles were swept downhill along with the plunging rocks and gravel to be buried in a massive, dust-billowing heap at the bottom.

"I circled above with the rest of my formation, watching the destruction below," recalled Jim Howard, who was flying top cover over the Salween. "Then I peeled off and dived. With the rest of my formation following, I hit the bomb release lever and then pulled back on the stick in a steep climb. I could see our bombs explode on the convoy road where a stream of soldiers and vehicles stretched for more than half a mile. We then came around and dived on the pontoon bridges with our six .50-caliber guns rattling. As I passed over, I could see that our bombs had caused a terrific landslide on the exposed road, closing it to all traffic."

The sharks all descended, mercilessly strafing the bridge-building crews at the edge of the river and plastering them with the fragmentation bombs they carried beneath their wings. After standing down for bad weather on May 9—a harbinger of the fast-approaching monsoon season—the AVG continued their sustained ground attack work.

"For four more days I threw everything we had against the Salween Gorge and the Burma Road as far back as the Burma border," Chennault wrote. "The Japs sent another group of light tanks up from Burma to escort more motorized infantry. A flight led by Frank Schiel caught them just below Lungling and scattered them with bombs and machine gun fire. Every town and village along the road that could serve the Japanese as shelter or a supply depot was bombed and burned. Another flight caught a truck column loaded with gas and left behind at least fifty billowing gasoline fires. By May 11 the only military traffic along the Burma Road was moving south toward Burma."

Tex Hill's biographer Reagan Schaupp wrote that "Few historians would later understand the importance of the Japanese retreat back down the Burma Road to the southwest. During the course of the Second World War, the Allied nations won a handful of key victories on which the course of history hinged: the Americans at Midway, the British at El Alamein, the Russians at Stalingrad. The Salween Gorge attack was indisputably just such a victory for the Allies. There was no effective resistance between the 56th Division and Kunming, and little from there to Chungking."

It was more than a week later that Joe Stilwell finally showed up in

India with his Burmese nurses, Indian cooks, assorted hangers-on, and a diary filled with entries about battling insects and worrying about heat exhaustion. He had no idea what the Flying Tigers had done on the gorge, nor of the implications of their having stopped the Japanese at this point.

Chennault commented that "Stilwell's long trudge through the jungle was an amazing feat of physical endurance for a man nearing sixty [but Chiang Kai-shek] hardly expected his chief of staff to leave his Chinese armies to shift for themselves and deliberately to remain incommunicado for three weeks while the fate of China teetered precariously on the rim of the Salween Gorge."

On May 24, four days after emerging from the jungle, Stilwell was in Delhi, having consented to be taken by airplane on the last leg of the trip. The following day, the man who had been completely out of touch for three weeks faced international reporters with comments that were transmitted around the world in hours.

"I claim we got a hell of a beating," the Associated Press reported of his comments. "We got run out of Burma and it is humiliating as hell."

He made no mention of the great victory achieved by the AVG at the Salween Gorge.

"Much has been written about it, more has been said," Robert Lee Scott recalled of Stilwell's headline-capturing jungle odyssey, which became an iconic moment in the contemporary media coverage and in the popular memory of the CBI. "But honestly, I have never seen the value of such a thing. We had his staff, but for three whole weeks we didn't know where he was and the theater didn't have a commander. But he walked out. I dropped food to him for all those 21 days, dropped it to his party as well as to everybody else we saw. Stilwell never did put out an identification panel to let us know where he was. He was consistent, though. . . . He was a brave man, all right, but he was fighting the wrong war."

As Chennault recalled so poetically in his memoirs, "the final act of the 1942 Burma tragedy was played in the tremendous natural amphitheater of the Salween River Gorge."

The only American players in that final act were Flying Tigers.

TWENTY-FIVE

Scotty and the Tigers

"My tongue hung out with envy as I watched them dive across the field in their roaring P-40s, leering sharks' mouths grinning at me, those sharp teeth mocking me," Robert Lee Scott wrote of the first time he saw the aircraft of the American Volunteer Group at Lei Yun on April 28, 1942. "They landed with a flare, churning up all the dust of centuries on that bare dirt runway, and sheer envy ate my heart out."

Nine long months and a declaration of war earlier, Scott had aspired to be a Flying Tiger, and he had read jealously the tales of their exploits spun by an American media hungry for heroes. Scotty had become what is best described as a "diehard fan" of the Flying Tigers. Most of those who had tried and failed to make the cut back in the summer of 1941 had moved on, but Scott held fast to an almost childlike dream of one day *being* a Tiger himself. Though his USAAF résumé for the past few years had found him as a transport pilot and before that as a Training Command flight instructor in Santa Maria, California, Scott's earliest operational days *had* been as a fighter pilot, flying P-12 biplanes over Panama, and he wanted to get back to fighters—AVG fighters.

Sitting down for his first conversation with the real Flying Tigers at Baoshan in early May, Scott at last found himself among the men he imagined as ten feet tall, but it was a very disappointing encounter. He recalled in his memoirs that they chided him for being a regular USAAF man in a regular USAAF uniform, a mere truck driver in the seat of a cargo plane, while *they* were "a formation of extroverts . . . swaggering around in their wild and wooly uniforms . . . one was even dressed like a pirate." As he admiringly described their "Texas boots, Levi's and belted six guns," Scott's awed description begins to sound like a Willie Nelson song.

At Baoshan, when the Tigers asked the ferry pilots about their cargo and Scott said he assumed they were carrying food and ammunition, it was decided that they should look. It turned out that the airplane was filled with bales upon bales of 100-yuan Chinese currency that had been printed by the American Bank Note Company of New York. This cargo, perceived by the AVG men with some degree of validity as worthless, was being shipped to Chongqing. This discovery, and that of office supplies destined for AMMISCA, did not help Scott's case that he had been risking his life for the war effort.

Recalling the cargo and passengers of dubious tactical value that were being transported by the ABC Ferry Command, Chennault wrote in his memoirs that the "sight of the numerous American Army staff officers scuttling pompously about India and China with brief cases, taking up valuable air cargo space was infuriating to us all. The group developed a strong feeling that they had been abandoned by the United States and were being left to die one by one in a foreign land by people who really were not much concerned over the outcome of the war."

As these comments illustrate, much of the AVG's frustration over having been abandoned by a regular USAAF that was out of touch with what they were doing was vented upon pilots of the ABC Ferry Command. This, from the perspective of ferry pilots who had just flown the Hump in dangerously overloaded transports to bring supplies to the wild and woolly AVG, smacked mightily of ingratitude.

"I'll swap seats with any one of you any day in the week," Scott said, directing his attention toward Tex Hill. "I'd a hundred times rather fly an armed fighter than this overloaded goon, overloaded with stuff for you. How the devil you think you get your ammo and your fuel and even food? You all think it comes in by itself or through some secret pipeline?"

When someone muttered something about a ferry pilot flying a fighter, Caleb Haynes came to Scott's defense, angrily telling the others that Scott had a great deal of time in fighters and that "he got out this far in as tough a way as any of you. You all hit him in a sore spot. He hates that airborne truck they make him fly like poison. . . . Fights his way out of the Training Command where they want to make him a general and ends up flying this overloaded barge. Now he's mixed up and I am too. You all don't only joke about us being over here, you ridicule the job we're doing. Remember, he took this assignment just so he could get over here close to you all."

This endorsement served, if not to break the ice, at least to create some fissures in the frosty reception that Scott had received when he said he had dreamed of flying with the AVG.

Scott first met Claire Chennault, whom he adored as a hero, at Lei Yun on April 28, that day when they had scrambled to camouflage their overloaded Gooney Bird. Like a pilgrim bringing tribute to a holy man at a distant and barely accessible temple, he had presented the venerable Old Man with a bottle of scotch and a carton of Camels—his preferred brand of cigarettes.

"Thank you, son," Chennault said as he began to drive away in a well-worn jeep. "I can use these, if I ever get to."

After helping to camouflage the C-47, Scott went looking for Chennault and caught up with him at his slit trench command post between the Japanese air attacks. When he saw Scott, he gestured for him to enter.

"That fighter, sir," Scott said, nodding toward a P-40 that was parked nearby. "Can I take it?"

Chennault simply ignored him for a moment as he barked orders to the flight that was airborne over Lei Yun at that moment.

Finally Chennault turned to him, and Scott could see the Old Man's face harden.

"Why, you're in the wrong uniform, Colonel!" Chennault said, looking at the insignia on Scott's uniform. "Haven't you noticed the wings of that ship, the insignia beneath them? They're Chinese."

He then looked away and went back to work, communicating with his men. Scott recalled that "I felt put in my place all right. I'd heard about this man. I remembered his boys working me over at Baoshan. But I couldn't help remember another thing—this Chennault was a fighter. By some reflex or luck, if you'll have it that way, I automatically made the right answer."

When there was a pause in the action, the young colonel told the newly minted brigadier general, who might as well have been a field marshal for the deference Scott showed toward him: "All my life I've heard about you, sir. There's a ship out there now going to be bombed and strafed if those Japs come down. And I've been on my way here a long time. I didn't think it mattered what uniform a man wore if he wanted to fight. And that's why I came here. I want to be a fighter pilot again."

Chennault continued to scan the sky with his field glasses, appearing to be ignoring Scott. Finally, after what seemed like a very long time, he spoke.

"Go ahead, see if you can start it," Chennault said. "But hurry, or they'll get you and the ship."

Scott climbed in, and he did get it started.

He took off and flew his first fighter mission in a combat zone, but by this time the Japanese attackers were just glints above the distant horizon.

He returned to Lei Yun and helped to unload the transport, which was now carrying drums of gasoline and crates of ammunition, not bales of worthless paper money. When the work was finished, Scott sought out the Old Man once again.

"How did she fly?" Chennault asked.

"Fine, sir, once she smoothed out," Scott replied. "The engine seemed rough but maybe I've been flying transports too long. Hard as I tried, I never made contact with the enemy. I just wasted gasoline."

Chennault then told him that he had only started worrying *after* the V-1710 engine roared to life and taxied away. Others had tried, but this particular airplane would not start and was scheduled for maintenance. The Old Man explained that he had not expected Scott to get it started, and had directed him to the aircraft simply to get him out of the way.

"You must really be peeved at us regulars, sir," Scott said, hiding his incredulity.

———————

Having gotten the Old Man's attention, Scott did not let go. The next time that he had a chance for a conversation with Chennault, he proceeded to outline a proposal that was audacious to the point of absurdity. Scott told stories of transports hauling supplies across the Hump that had been attacked by Japanese fighters, and of pilots in the cumbersome transports having to defend themselves with a combination of small arms and potentially deadly evasive action. It took little imagination for Chennault to picture the difficulty of evasive action in an overloaded C-47. Having put this image in Chennault's mind, Scott asked the AVG boss to *give* him a P-40 so that he could fly as a fighter escort with the transports.

Much to Scott's surprise, Chennault agreed, as long as Scott would use it *only* for combat missions. He said that three P-40Es, then being ferried across Africa and India from Takoradi, had reached Dinjan, the ABC Ferry Command refueling stop on the west side of the Hump. Scott could have his pick.

"It was mine, and I was as proud of it as of the first bicycle my father had given me," Scott wrote in his famous memoir *God Is My Co-Pilot*. "All through the night I read the technical files and learned every little item about the Allison engine and the engine controls. I memorized the armament section of the book, and by morning I was ready to put theory into practice. That morning I found a painter. Buying red and white paint from the village, I had him paint the shark's mouth on the lower nose. . . . I remember that as I waited for the paint to dry I walked round and round my ship, admiring the graceful lines, a feeling of pride in my heart. I gloried in the slender fuselage, in the knife-like edges of the little wings. The sharp nose of the spinner looked like an arrow to me—the nose that sloped back to the leering shark's mouth. At sight of the wicked-looking blast tubes of the six fifty-caliber guns in the wings, I felt my chest expand another inch. This was shark-nosed dynamite, all right, but even then I did not quite realize what a weapon this fighter ship could be when properly handled."

During May, according to his logbook, Scott averaged seven hours a day of flight time in his P-40E, flying escort missions, and occasionally a strafing mission over Japanese-occupied Burma. On May 5, the same day as the big Japanese raid on Baoshan, he strafed and destroyed an IJAAF Ki-21 heavy bomber on the ground at Lashio. He found a target-rich environment for strafing along the Burma Road as the Japanese troops and supply trains moved toward the front. Appropriately, he named his aircraft *Old Exterminator.*

As the AVG pilots usually ignored the lone Japanese reconnaissance aircraft that appeared high in the skies overhead, the Japanese were generally ignoring this lone P-40 when the AVG presented a greater threat with their six or eight at a time.

Scott wrote that he would occasionally stay overnight with the AVG in Kunming, "drinking weak Australian gin or Chinese rice wine with them" and trying to fit in. By the second week of May, Chennault, who was evidently pleased with what Scott was able to do with his purloined P-40, invited him to fly some missions with Oley Olson and the 3rd Pursuit Squadron Hell's Angels.

In his diary for May 15, R. T. Smith recalled that he had first known Scott as his instructor back at Santa Maria, and that "as a check pilot, he was a mean s.o.b., washing out as many cadets as he passed, but now that we were on more or less equal footing he was as affable as could be."

By this time, with the Japanese invasion of southern China stalled on the Salween, much of the attention of the American Volunteer Group was directed toward Japanese air bases in French Indochina, which were being used to launch bomber missions against Kunming and Chongqing. Indeed, Smith had just returned from a mission to Hanoi on the same day that he ran into Scott for the first time since training school in California.

One Indochina target in particular was the big modern airport at Gia Lam in Hanoi, built by the French in 1936 and commandeered by the Japanese in 1940. Coincidentally, it was same air base that would be the home to the MiG interceptors that bedeviled American pilots during the Vietnam War, and remained a military facility until being turned over to civilian use in 2015.

Scott recalled that his first trip to Indochina was a ground attack mission led by Lew Bishop on May 17 against Lao Kay, 200 miles south of Kunming and 150 miles northwest of Hanoi. He wrote that he was flying as Smith's wingman as part of the strike force, though in his diary, Smith mentions that he was flying top cover with Bill Reed.

Smith remembered that he and Reed spotted a train some distance from Lao Kay, and reported this to Bishop, who ordered them to attack the train while the remainder of the force bombed the rail station at Lao Kay. Scott's recollection was that they all strafed the train before moving on to the station at Lao Kay.

"I saw Bishop's bombs hit dead center on the roundhouse," Scott wrote. "Then I dropped mine. Just at that instant Bishop's fighter belched fire and smoke, and I saw him slide his canopy open and jump. His chute opened so close in front of my ship that I pulled up for fear I'd run into it. I hung there for what seemed like hours, with my air speed indicating three hundred miles an hour, while black bursts of antiaircraft fire broke all around me. The ship just seemed to stand still, but I saw Bishop floating towards the river that was the boundary between China and Indochina."

Jim Howard, who was also on the mission, noted that "if he had waited three seconds more, he might have dropped on friendly territory across the [Red] River in China."

Bishop managed to evade capture for three days, but was picked up by the Vichy French, who turned him over to the Japanese. Charlie Bond, who was in the hospital in Kunming recovering from the burns he had suffered over Baoshan, wrote in his diary that "just the other day he was visiting me and saying how much he looked forward to going home and seeing his wife and baby."

He had yet to see his daughter, Sheila, who had been born in November 1941.

Bob Little, who was with Bond over Baoshan on May 4, was not so lucky. On May 22, he was killed when one of the bombs on his wing pylon exploded on a mission over the Salween Gorge.

"This is my closest friend yet; it gets to my innards," Bond wrote in his diary. "Bob Neale took it awfully hard, for those two were very close. What an awful business."

After the Lao Kay mission, Scott rotated back to Dinjan and resumed his one-man war on the Japanese in Burma. In his memoirs, he wrote of a day late in May when he attacked the Japanese on the Chindwin River in Burma about 180 miles south of Dinjan. He dropped out of the overcast and saw a flotilla of loaded barges putting into Homalin. He dove at forty-five degrees, leveled out, and let one of four five-hundred-pound bombs glide into the barge nearest to the dock. Having waited for the smoke to clear, he strafed two other barges and watched as one, probably loaded with gasoline, became a fireball.

He then banked over the city and put a second bomb on the largest building in town, which turned out to be the local police station, commandeered as a Japanese headquarters. Even Radio Tokyo referenced the raid, and soon Western reporters in India were mentioning his exploits, and he became grist for newspaper and magazine accounts back home.

To convey the impression to the Japanese that he was *not* just one man, and that his *Old Exterminator* was not just one airplane, he used the trick of painting his propeller spinner different colors on different days. However, it didn't work. Based probably on the reports of journalists who saw Scott operating out of Dinjan, the media had started using the phrase "one-man air force."

He was lucky. Often he came home with his P-40 riddled with holes from small-arms fire. One time, a round had pierced his cap. Another time, he scored a direct hit on a bridge, but the bomb exploded almost immediately and not with a ten-second delay. Back at Dinjan, he discovered "holes as big as footballs in the fabric flippers and in the metal stabilizers of the tail section. There was a hole in the fuselage and five holes in the wing."

The one-man air force was developing a reputation as an aggressive pilot, the kind that Chennault valued. One wonders what might have been the case if Chennault *had* picked him for the American Volunteer Group back in 1941.

"I had the experience of ten years of military flying, and I knew I was a good pilot," Scott wrote of what he had learned in his rapid education as a combat pilot during May 1942. "There is no substitute for combat. You've got to shoot at people while you're being shot at yourself. . . . I carried a Tommy gun with me in the cockpit of the ship, for at strafing altitude there would probably be no time to bail out with the chute anyway, and I knew that prisoners taken by the Japs received very harsh treatment, especially those who had been strafing the capturing troops when shot down. With that gun, after my crash landing I'd have one more crack at the Japs—I certainly didn't intend to be captured."

TWENTY-SIX

Fixated upon a Mirage

B y May 1942, the future of the American Volunteer Group in the USAAF scheme of things, which had been fodder for the rumor mill early in the year, had been confirmed. It had been known since early March that the AVG would be dissolved and replaced by the USAAF 23rd Fighter Group as part of the new entity called the China Air Task Force (CATF), but there had been no timetable for this transition. At the Chongqing conference with Chiang Kai-shek at the beginning of April, Joe Stilwell and Clayton Bissell had lobbied for this to happen by the end of that month, but Claire Chennault successfully argued otherwise.

The Old Man realized—and Bissell *should have* known—that the 23rd was still just a shimmering mirage. It existed only on paper and could not possibly be ready to supersede the AVG in less than four weeks. Chennault had proposed, and the others reluctantly accepted, that the day the Old Man himself described as "Dissolve Day" should be July 4, a date that coincided with the terminations of the one-year employment contracts that the AVG personnel had signed in 1941.

The question of what would happen to those people when their contracts expired had long been a subject of conjecture, though nothing had been decided. The rumors included a scenario under which everyone would be shipped back to the States, and there was also the idea that the USAAF would simply induct everyone in place. There were numerous speculated possibilities in between.

On March 26, when he held the group meeting in Kunming on the eve of his going to Chongqing to learn of his own induction, Chennault had been asked whether the pilots could expect a regular commission if they were inducted in Kunming, but he replied that he honestly didn't know. After a follow-up meeting on April 11, R. T. Smith wrote that Chennault "told us the deal on induction [was] we'll be able to finish out contract [on July 4] and then go back to the States and into the Army there."

Chennault now had sufficient additional information from the USAAF to be able to tell the men that they would receive their AVG paychecks through July 4. These would include compensation for accrued leave to that date, as well as a travel allowance of $500 because their CAMCO contracts stipulated a return trip to the United States. If inducted into the USAAF, they would receive a lump sum payment equal to the difference between their AVG pay grade and that of their rank in the USAAF.

As Chennault wrote in his memoirs, the men were "not enthusiastic about rejoining the services. All of them were reservists, and most of them joined the AVG as an escape from rigid discipline and discrimination by regulars against the reserve. . . . Most of the men were willing to serve out their contracts and accept induction terms if they were given a 30-day furlough before returning to combat. By the time their contracts expired in July, all of them would have served a year on foreign service and seven months of combat under the worst conditions."

When Bissell asked Chennault to resist the idea of a thirty-day leave, he refused, telling Bissell that after what they'd been through, this was the *least* that should be offered to his men. Fixated upon the mirage that was the 23rd Fighter Group, Bissell didn't care. He believed that he did not need the men and the aircraft of the only organized group of experienced American fighter pilots in the Far East.

———

The USAAF was running out of time to stand up the still nonexistent 23rd as a component of the planned CATF. Virtually nothing had been done. Of course, the USAAF was short of resources worldwide, and a full-strength fighter group in the most remote corner of its logistical network was not high on the list of priorities *or* capabilities. The USAAF, and indeed the entire American war machine, was far from ready to fight a global war. Aside from Doolittle's audacious raid, there was little to celebrate. The great victory at Midway would not occur until the first week of June, and the realization of it as the milestone we now know it to be was *many* weeks away.

Finally, when the third week of May rolled around and the 23rd Fighter Group had yet to materialize, Clayton Bissell realized that he might need the men of the despised Flying Tigers for his new CATF after all.

"Desperate because he knew the Army could not provide replacements to meet the July fourth deadline, Bissell asked for permission to make a speech to the [AVG personnel] at Kunming," Chennault recalled.

Chennault agreed, and a meeting was scheduled for the evening of May 21 in the auditorium of Yunnan University.

"I warned Bissell that he might get a rough reception, but he was confident," Chennault wrote. "He outlined all the reasons why he thought the group should stay on in China."

The men, who felt they had been jerked around by a distant and indifferent establishment, had reached the point where their overarching concern was their own futures. Charlie Bond wrote in his diary that Bissell "spoke pessimistically about our chances of getting a job in the States that would prevent us from being drafted back into the service. He painted a dark picture for us if we did not stay here and accept induction. All the fellows feel that Bissell is jamming the Army down our throats."

When Buster Keeton asked about their chances for getting a regular commission, Bissell shrugged that this was beyond his power.

R. T. Smith wrote that Bissell had "all the charm of a cobra." When his remarks required a soft touch, Bissell counterintuitively turned to intimidation. Indeed, when he most needed to coat his words with honey, he chose vinegar. Bissell threatened them that if they remained in China, they would be prevented from taking jobs with airlines such as Pan Am or CNAC, which had let it be known that they would readily hire AVG alumni at sizable salaries.

In his memoirs, Chennault noted that Bissell, growing more aggravated by the grumbling, spat out a menacing threat that would have been ridiculous if he had not been serious. "For any of you who don't join the Army," he threatened, "I can guarantee to have your draft boards waiting for you when you step down a gangplank onto United States soil."

Jim Howard recalled this comment, adding that "the acerbity of Bissell's message turned most of the men away from any mass voluntary induction. Bissell's foot-in-mouth speech had achieved just the opposite from what he wanted and hurt Chennault even more."

As Bissell flew off to Chongqing, and with Dissolve Day less than six weeks away, the 23rd Fighter Group and the CATF remained little more than a figment of his imagination.

B y that time, with Bob Scott still in the Tenth Air Force chain of command, Chennault had one—and only one—uniformed member of the USAAF under his direct command. Captain Albert "Ajax" Baumler, the veteran of the Spanish Civil War who had attempted to join the American Volunteer Group nearly a year earlier, and whose second effort had been stymied at Wake Island on Pearl Harbor Day, had finally reached the end of his rainbow. He had flown into Kunming on a P-40E delivery flight from Takoradi by way of Karachi and had stayed on in Kunming.

Chennault, who had long complained of a lack of staff officers, put Baumler into a desk chair instead of a cockpit. It had been apparent to the Old Man that Baumler, like Greg Boyington, was an excellent, naturally skilled pilot who became a different person, erratic and violent, when he drank too much. This may have contributed to Chennault's decision to keep him close to headquarters until he got to understand him. In his memoirs, Chennault said only that Baumler's "notions of military discipline were vague, but in the air he was a cool combat pilot with rare ability in shepherding green pilots through their first fights."

Sidelined by pushing paper, Baumler would not resume his combat career until the end of June.

Soon, other USAAF fighter pilots, men who were earmarked for the 23rd, finally started to arrive, though they trickled in two or three at a time, and many were not deemed fighter pilot material. As Claire Chennault recalled in his memoirs, "with few exceptions the first Army pilots to reach China matched the quality of the planes. They were ample proof that combat pilots can't be turned out like quick-lunch hamburgers, no matter how urgent the emergency. Most of these pilots were graduates of war-shortened training programs. Many of them paid for this shoddy instruction with their lives. They had little air gunnery practice, no navigation experience, only a smattering of formation fly-ing, and most of them had never flown a P-40. Five of the early arrivals frankly confessed they were afraid to fly combat and were sent back to the Air Transport Command."

Though technically assigned to the 23rd, those who passed muster with the Old Man were gradually integrated into AVG operations, where they flew under the command and control of the three AVG squadrons.

———

Ironically, the first aircraft that would come directly from the USAAF to serve with the China Air Task Force would not be fighters, but bombers. The Old Man had been trying to get bombers under his com-mand since he had gone to Washington with P. T. Mao back in the fall of 1940. Indeed, from the beginning, his original idea for operations in China had included using bases there to attack Tokyo. When the 1st American Volunteer Group had been given Roosevelt's green light, Chennault had been promised a 2nd American Volunteer Group com-prised of A-20 bombers—and if it had not been for Pearl Harbor, he might have gotten these by the end of 1941. Then, in early 1942, Lauch-lin Currie had managed to secure a promise of obsolescent Lockheed A-29 Hudsons from the USAAF, but those Hudsons that were sent across the Atlantic were diverted to the Mediterranean Theater as soon as they reached North Africa.

If it had been up to the citizens of Chennault's home state of Loui-siana, he would have had his bombers—or at least *a bomber*. Earlier in 1942, the popular "Buy a Bomber for Chennault" campaign spear-headed by former governor James Albert Noe raised $15,109.36, but that was not nearly enough, and Noe gave the cash to Madame Chiang Kai-shek's war orphan fund.

With the creation—at least on paper—of the CATF, the idea of bombers for Chennault, long a pipe dream, evolved into a commitment. Now a USAAF general, he had been promised the services of the USAAF 11th Bombardment Squadron. One of the first squadrons to see service in World War II, it had been dispatched to Australia with its B-17 heavy bombers in December 1941, and had experienced its baptism of fire in the Dutch East Indies earlier in 1942. It was among those that escaped to India with Lewis Brereton, but it had returned Stateside to refit and reorganize. Now the 11th was back, operating North American Aviation B-25s, the same type of aircraft used by Doolittle in his famous Tokyo raid in April. Classed by the USAAF as a "medium" bomber, the B-25 was actually in the same size and weight class as the Japanese Mitsubishi Ki-21 "heavy" bomber.

American bomber operations in China might have begun with Harry Halverson, had he not been waylaid by the Ninth Air Force, or with Caleb Haynes, if he had not been intercepted by the Tenth—but they finally did begin with the arrival in Dinjan on June 2 of the first six B-25s of the 11th Bombardment Group. Led by Major Gordon Leland, these six aircraft were to be foundation stones of the permanent USAAF operational presence in China.

However, this event, which might have been celebrated as a landmark accomplishment, was overshadowed by the type of bureaucratic inefficiency that Chennault despised in the standard operating procedures of the regular USAAF. As USAAF historian Herbert Weaver described, "it was planned that on [June 3] the flight would be completed to Kunming after a bombing of Lashio en route. . . . In the face of an unfavorable weather report and against the advice of Colonel Haynes, the six planes took off early the next morning. They unloaded their bombs on the Lashio airfield, but subsequently three planes—including that of Major Leland—crashed into a mountainside while flying through an overcast at 10,000 feet, and another plane was abandoned when it gave out of gas near Chanyi. Only two of the aircraft landed at Kunming, one with its radio operator who had been killed in a brush with enemy fighters."

It was an exercise in planning that begged the question "*What were they thinking?*"

The diversion to Lashio was a naïve idea that apparently originated in Washington and didn't even look good on paper. It added more than two hundred miles to the difficult crossing of the Hump, and the bombs added additional weight. Apparently the B-25 crews were not even given the frequencies of the AVG radios in Kunming.

"When Chennault heard the bad news, he hit the roof," Jim Howard recalled. "Instead of just allowing the planes to be ferried and escorted by an experienced AVG pilot over the unfamiliar terrain, the generals had laid on a mission that ended in disaster. He complained that this sort of rash stubbornness was typical of the attitude of the newly arrived Army brass. They felt the AVG had nothing to teach them and wouldn't stoop to ask for guidance and assistance from that awful organization of undisciplined mercenaries."

Howard was at Kunming when the two bombers arrived, and spoke to the pilot of one of the surviving B-25s as he climbed out of his aircraft. Major William Bayse was a veteran of the difficult combat actions flown by the 11th Bomb Group in the Dutch East Indies.

"We approached Lashio from the northwest at three thousand feet," he told Howard. "We could see Jap fighters taking off. We opened our bomb bay doors and made an excellent pass over the field and released our bombs simultaneously on an execution signal from the lead plane. The Japs must have had some advanced warning. Several [IJAAF Hayabusas] were climbing to meet us. We got out of there with full throttle. For protection against our pursuers, we entered some thick clouds and started climbing in tight formation. Our heading was on a direct course for Kunming. We were still climbing in the soup at eight thousand feet when I suddenly noticed below and out the window, bushes and trees rushing by. I hauled back on the yoke and as I did so, I saw blinding flashes and felt thundering reverberations. The rest of the formation must have all crashed into a mountain top."

Weaver mentions that over the next two weeks, Bayse returned to India and led six more B-25s across the Hump without mishap. The official records of the 11th Bomb Squadron note that eight B-25s were in Kunming on June 10, though in his diary, R. T. Smith counted only seven after two arrived on June 16. The 11th was the first, and would remain for some time as the only operational component of the CATF.

In the meantime, as the USAAF was sending in B-25s, bombers new to the theater, Chennault had his eyes on a new type of fighter aircraft. Nearly two hundred of these new airplanes had been earmarked for the Chinese Air Force, and a few had actually reached India. Since the AVG was *still* part of the Chinese Air Force, Chennault decided to get his hands on some before they were requisitioned by the Tenth Air Force. The aircraft was the P-43 Lancer, developed by Republic Aviation as a private venture and loosely based on the company's P-35. It was known to have some shortcomings, and the USAAF had been lukewarm about its capabilities, but Charlie Bond, who had flown one in Karachi when he was there in April to pick up a P-40E, wrote in his diary that it "climbs like a scared angel and easily outruns a P-40E, particularly at higher altitudes."

The USAAF had decided to wait for the much more promising Republic P-47 Thunderbolt, which was evolving from the Lancer but only just beginning to enter production. For this reason, the USAAF decided to Lend-Lease most of their Lancers to China. Chennault felt that the AVG did not have the luxury of waiting. The Lancer *now* was better than the Thunderbolt *later*, and given his track record of getting things from the USAAF, there was no way of knowing *if* he would ever be offered Thunderbolts.

The P-40s could barely function above 20,000 feet and could not intercept Japanese high-altitude reconnaissance aircraft, while the Lancers, with their turbosupercharged Pratt & Whitney R-1830 engines, could operate at 36,000 feet. In fact, a Lancer had been the aircraft that Bob Scott had used when he made his flight, that same month, two miles over the 29,029-foot peak of Mount Everest, an event memorialized in one of the most often-cited passages in his best-selling 1943 autobiography *God Is My Co-Pilot*.

On the same April ferry mission that Bond first flew the aircraft, Ed Goyette had flown a P-43 back to Kunming. When Chennault saw it, he knew he wanted more.

Tex Hill and Duke Hedman, along with ten Chinese pilots, took a CNAC flight west to Karachi to meet the Lancers. The idea was that they would all learn to fly the new birds and then fly back together. Given that none of the Chinese pilots could speak English, their week of familiarization flights was a comedy of errors, though none of the slapstick landings cost any lives or aircraft.

What was to be a very long return trip began on May 28, but ran into trouble east of their refueling stop at Jodhpur, when they were overtaken by a sandstorm. Hill, who was leading, decided to fly low because of the poor visibility and to use the old navigational trick of following the railroad to get them into Delhi. Here they made contact with Tenth Air Force headquarters.

While they waited for the weather to clear and for the sand to be cleaned out of the moving parts of the Lancers, they enjoyed the pleasures and distractions of the British colonial city that were a far cry from life at Lei Yun, or even reasonably comfortable Kunming.

They also crossed paths with Harvey and Olga Greenlaw, who had left Kunming for the last time on May 8, and who had arrived in Delhi a week later by way of Calcutta. The Greenlaws were staying in the best suite at the Cecil Hotel. When the clerk had told them it was always reserved for Bill Pawley, Olga had told him that Pawley would not mind, adding, "if he comes, we'll let you put a cot in there for him."

Pawley, who was in Bangalore at the Hindustan Aircraft facility, never showed up and probably never knew they were there, but when Hill and Hedman did, Olga called for cots to be brought in for them. The weather was unbearably hot, but the Cecil had a swimming pool, which was a welcome treat after many long months in the field.

"I saw a lot of Tex Hill," Olga wrote in her memoirs. "When we were not out shopping or looking around town, we were at the swimming pool, surrounded by war correspondents talking about the war or playing bridge. . . . I had seen him once when he was very angry, lips turned into a thin line and his eyes narrow, blazing slits. But at the swimming pool he was smiling and his eyes were open wide and very blue."

"I wish I had known you better in Kunming," he said as they chatted, sharing stories about their lives back home.

"Your fault," she said, flirting back. "Why didn't you come around? All the others did."

"I was waiting for an invitation," he said with a smile. "You never asked me."

"No, nor did I ever ask the others," she replied. "But didn't you once tell Moose Moss that I must be a cold-blooded woman?"

"Yes, I did," he said, smiling. "But I didn't know you then."

"If and when we fold up, will you join the Tenth Air Force here?" Olga asked, changing the subject.

"There's no reason why I shouldn't," he said after a long pause. "Our country is at war, and I have to fight, whether it is here, Australia, or

Africa. It doesn't make any difference. As long as I'm fighting, I'll be doing my duty."

"But don't you want to go home and rest up a bit?"

"Hell no, I'm in stride now. Why stop? I might lose my technique."

Tex Hill and the first of the Lancers departed Delhi on June 5, but were delayed in Dinjan because of the monsoons and did not reach Kunming until June 13, three days after the B-25s of the 11th Bomber Squadron. During the coming weeks, more and more P-43s reached Kunming, though many were lost over the Hump by Chinese pilots, who flew the majority of the ferry missions. There would never be enough Lancers available to make a difference, and operationally, the aircraft never lived up to expectations.

Because of the lack of armor for their cockpits, Chennault decided not to use them for air-to-air combat, though Caleb Haynes reportedly commandeered a couple in Dinjan to use as fighter escorts for the transports flying the Hump.

As summer arrived in China, it was business as usual for the American Volunteer Group, with operations still dependent upon the tried and tested P-40s, and with the 23rd Fighter Group still little more than a figment of Clayton Bissell's imagination.

TWENTY-SEVEN

Bombing Season

The severing of the Burma Road at the Salween Gorge had changed the complexion of the war in Southeast Asia. With the successful conquest of Burma and the establishment of a defensible front line on the Salween, the mission of the Imperial Japanese Army on that front moved from offensive action to occupation. Meanwhile, the arrival of the 1942 monsoon season in Southeast Asia brought a refocusing of the air war north into China and a shift of IJAAF assets to air bases near Hankou and Guangzhou (then called Hankow and Canton) in eastern China. This would bring an intensification of air attacks on Nationalist-controlled cities such as Chongqing, as had been the case each summer since the beginning of the war in 1937.

To meet the threat to Chiang Kai-shek's capital in exile, Claire Chennault took steps to relocate two of the three American Volunteer Group squadrons, as well as the headquarters, from Kunming to Baishiyi (then called Peishiyi) airfield, about twenty miles northwest of the center of Chongqing. As Chennault put it in his memoirs, "the

Generalissimo's main concern for the summer was the air defense of Chungking, where the bombing season was about to begin."

The field at Baishiyi, which expanded considerably under Chennault's management during World War II, remains a major base for the Chinese People's Liberation Army Air Force to this day.

With his immediate concern being the air defense of Chinese cities, Chennault opened his new headquarters in Baishiyi on June 5 and was preparing to implement his new strategy. As he recalled, "I gambled on bluffing the Japanese away from Chungking and catching them by surprise in East China, where they were showing signs of renewing their annual terror-bombing campaign against undefended cities."

Chennault's "bluff" involved flying numerous low-level missions over the Chongqing metropolitan area to impress upon the Japanese agents in the city—as well as the citizenry—that the AVG was preparing to provide a robust air defense for Chiang's capital.

As he recalled, "a Japanese photo plane could record most of CATF strength on Kunming Airfield one afternoon, and 24 hours later the enemy in Canton, 700 miles away, would be heads down in slit trenches, listening to our bombs exploding. By the time a raid was organized to catch us, we were in the north pounding Hankou or back in Kunming. For over a year, when our forces were so small that ordinary defensive tactics would have doomed us to extinction, we kept the Japanese guessing with this aerial shell game all the way from Burma to the Yangtze."

With this illusion having been established, all but four real P-40s and dozens of painted bamboo dummy P-40s were relocated to provide air defense for the population centers in southeastern China. The key to these tactics, as Chennault saw it, was forward-deploying his Flying Tigers on a rotating basis to a chain of fighter bases in a 250-mile line along the Xiang River (then the Siang), from Hengyang in the north, through Yongzhou (known then as Lingling) in the middle, to Guilin (then called Kweilin) in the south.

Chennault ordered the Panda Bears of Tex Hill's 2nd Pursuit Squadron to relocate to Hengyang. Six years earlier, Hengyang had briefly been the headquarters of Bill Pawley's CAMCO's operations after he withdrew from Hankow in the face of the Japanese ground assault in southeastern China.

On June 11, Bob Neale and Charlie Bond led the Adam and Eves of the 1st Pursuit Squadron into Guilin, where they were greeted by the Old Man himself, who had come in the day before on a CNAC flight. They were surprised to find what Bond described as the biggest air base that he had yet seen in China, with a hard-surface runway more than a mile long and "revetments that can take a B-17." Of course, heavy bombers for operations in China were still a long way off.

Guilin, the anchor in the line, whose name means "Forest of Sweet Osmanthus," was a once quiet city about 375 miles southeast of Chongqing and 474 miles east of Kunming. The operations room had been set up inside Qixingyan, or Seven Star Cave, one of many extensive caverns that punctuate the steep rock pinnacles surrounding the city.

As Chennault observed, "the water-worn caves in these mountains gave us a bombproof operations office, headquarters, air-raid shelters, and a welcome refuge from the steamy summer heat. . . . What these fields lacked in facilities they made up in durability. It was impossible to bomb them out."

He recalled that "no matter how many holes Japanese bombardiers punched in the runways," Chinese laborers repaired the damage in a few hours. The only way the Japanese could destroy the effectiveness of these fields was to catch the AVG aircraft on the ground—and Chennault's famous early warning network made this virtually impossible.

There had been a Japanese attack against Guilin on June 10, and Chennault expected a follow-up raid. He did not have to wait long. Two days later, three flights scrambled after a Japanese reconnaissance aircraft was spotted at 4:00 a.m. To be ready for anything, George Burgard took a flight of three to twenty thousand feet, while Bob Neale took four to eighteen thousand feet, and Charlie Bond took four to fifteen thousand feet.

The Japanese strike force arrived two hours later, consisting of five Kawasaki Ki-48 twin-engine bombers. They were escorted by Nakajima Ki-27/Model I-97 fighters, with which the Flying Tigers were familiar from having fought them over Rangoon. Also in the mix were several Kawasaki Ki-45 twin-engine fighters with which the Americans were less familiar, and which they often mistook for bombers because of their multiple engines. The Japanese had named this fighter type "Toryu," meaning "Dragon Slayer." They hoped that it could double as a "tiger slayer."

Joe Rosbert, Charlie Bond's wingman, spotted the bombers as they were approaching from slightly below. Bond led his flight into the attack, making three passes. Bond lined up behind a Ki-48 and tried to open fire, but five of his six guns had jammed. As he pulled away to recharge his guns, he discovered that his cooling system was overheating, probably from having been hit by defensive fire from the bomber, and this compromised the hydraulic system that ran his guns.

As he was working on his guns, Bond saw a half dozen Ki-27 fighters above and to his right, and watched as two peeled off and lined up behind him. He nosed over and went into a dive, partly to escape and partly to relieve stress on his overheating engine.

One of the two Ki-27s followed him down until Bond pulled out with less than a thousand feet to spare. He looked at his instruments. His airspeed was 315 miles per hour and his oil pressure was zero.

As he put it, with calm understatement, "I was beginning to feel that my number was up this time."

This was a reasonable assumption, but fortunately, he was wrong.

With the enemy on his tail, Bond hunched behind his armor plate, "listening for the pings of the Jap's guns while trying to make a decision about bailing out or belly landing. Luckily, the Jap must have thought I was a goner, for he turned his fighter away and climbed back to the battle area."

One second later, his propeller stopped and he "stared at one of the three blades straight up in front of the nose of my ship. I was dropping fast toward an area of rice paddies located at the base of a mountain. I was too low to bail out, so I decided to risk a wheels-up landing. I picked out a field and glided in. . . . I tried the flap levers. Hell, they wouldn't work! I was going to overshoot the field. I wasn't over a hundred feet above it, and my speed was giving out fast. I risked a drastic bank and turn, trying to hit the slope of the rice paddy."

As he flattened out the wings, the P-40 slid into the ground, bounced out of one muddy rice paddy, sailed over a dike, and smashed down into another paddy with a jolt that slammed his head into his gunsight.

He climbed out onto the wing to find that much of his P-40 had disintegrated into a mass of scrap metal that stretched for some distance across the paddies through which he had bounced. There was neither sight nor sound of other aircraft in the sky, so he started walking. Several farmhands who were nearby ignored him. He decided they thought he was Japanese, so he ignored them back and continued walking through the swampy terrain toward a line of shacks in the distance. Reaching these, the blood-spattered American airman tried to ask for a telephone using sign language and finally found a man who understood. He dialed the phone and handed the receiver to Bond, who found himself speaking with Father Herbert Elliot, a Catholic missionary.

Hiking for more than three hours, Bond and one of the Chinese men reached Father Elliot's mission, where Bond was rewarded with a drink of fresh water while the priest cleaned the gash on his face. He then took Bond to the local mayor and explained to the still suspicious Chinese that Bond was not Japanese, but American. With this understood by all, everyone relaxed and the priest took Bond back to the mission.

After a warm bath, a good lunch, and clean dressings for Bond's wounds, the mayor arrived at the mission to take the American to the nearby rail station.

"We were joined by four Chinese soldiers, and along the way we picked up groups of curious people," Bond wrote in his diary. "It turned out to be a parade down the main street. Many little children tugged at my hands, and the soldiers began lighting strings of firecrackers and throwing them in our path. . . . The reverend told me that this was the greatest moment in the life of the village. The Flying Tigers are heroes to them, and now they had seen one. I must admit that in spite of all my misery I felt very proud and honored."

An hour later, he was in downtown Guilin, where a car picked him up and took him to the airfield. Here, the Old Man greeted him and told him that he hoped that Bond's bad luck, this being his second nearly fatal crash landing in the space of five weeks, was over. Bond said he hoped so too.

In the debriefing that night, they counted up the stats. In his memoirs, Chennault wrote that the "11 P-40s knocked down 12 out of 18 Jap raiders," though the official tally was actually nine. George Burgard claimed two, one Ki-27 and one of the twin-engine Ki-45 fighters, whose rear gunner survived the crash and was captured. Two P-40s were lost in crash landings, but the pilots, Bond and Allen Wright, both walked away.

"With the appearance of the AVG in East China, Jap terror bombing of cities stopped," Chennault claimed in his memoirs. "Henceforth Jap targets were airfields not cities."

TWENTY-EIGHT

Countdown to Dissolve Day

The June 12 action, in defense of a major city much larger than Kunming, reminded the Flying Tigers of their glory days over Rangoon. Perhaps it was easy to feel nostalgic when they knew the ends of their tours of duty were now in sight. Harder to fathom is that morale remained intact now that they understood the circumstances under which the American Volunteer Group would go out of business on Dissolve Day.

On June 17, preparations were made for the AVG to escort the long-awaited first bombing mission against the Japanese by the still underequipped 11th Bomber Squadron, but this was scrubbed because of heavy rainstorms. Three days later, four B-25s of the 11th *attempted* a bombing mission, with the AVG 3rd Squadron Hell's Angels flying escort. It was a tentative effort, with the bombers getting separated from their escorts and never finding the target in the heavy cloud cover.

According to Kit Carter and Robert Mueller in the official USAAF *Combat Chronology*, the 11th finally completed its first mission, the first mission credited to the CATF, on July 1, three days before the official CATF activation. In it, Ed Rector led five Pandas, escorting four B-25s, from Hengyang to bomb the Yangtze River port of Hankou. Carter and Mueller report that "the effects of the raid are inconsequential."

Charlie Bond elaborated further, writing that "the bombers got lost, and Ed had to take over and direct them to the target twice. They finally released their bombs on some little village on the Yangtze. Immediately after the bomb run they passed directly over the designated target—the Jap field at Hankou. The field was covered with planes, and there was no Jap opposition in the air. Everyone was either disgusted or just downright embarrassed about the fiasco."

One is reminded of the axiom that one must start somewhere.

As the CATF was starting, the AVG was nearing the end. Dissolve Day was on the minds of the Flying Tigers, and it was no secret from the Japanese. Indeed, at home and abroad, the USAAF had issued press releases, widely publicizing the fact that it would be taking over from the American Volunteer Group on the Fourth of July. In her sarcastic broadcasts from Japan, Tokyo Rose had promised that Japanese airmen would not let the Flying Tigers go away peacefully on the American Independence Day, and that the Japanese would then sweep the incoming 23rd Fighter Group from China skies.

———

On June 21, with just a little more than a week left, Chennault arrived in Guilin, accompanied by Colonel Caleb Haynes, who had come to China to run all the bomber operations for Chennault's CATF. Within Haynes's entourage was Lieutenant Colonel Tex Sanders. Though he still commanded the 51st Fighter Group of the Tenth Air Force, Sanders had been assigned to head the AVG induction board. He was making the rounds, conducting exit interviews and trying to convince the Flying Tigers to remain in China as part of the USAAF. He still considered himself in line to assume command of the 23rd Fighter Group when it was activated on July 4.

Sanders set up shop in Seven Star Cave, not far from the AVG operations center, and interviewed each man individually as the Old Man sat nearby, Camel cigarette in hand, listening.

"What are you going to do?" Charlie Bond recalled him asking. "I'm sure you're going to stay with us, aren't you?"

"Colonel Sanders," Bond replied slowly, "I'd stay here without a moment's delay if I were given a regular commission in the Air Corps."

Sanders told him that his hands were tied when it came to authorizing regular, rather than reserve, commissions. Bond knew that only with a regular commission could he realize his dream of a military career. He noted that Sanders then "continued to try to talk me into staying anyhow and said something about high chances of getting torpedoed aboard ship on the way home [and] that riled me."

"Colonel, I assure you, that thought doesn't bother me after all I've been through in the last several months!"

When Sanders saw Chennault nod and chuckle, he laughed nervously.

When all was said and done, only five AVG pilots chose to stay on to join the USAAF and to make the transition to the 23rd Fighter Group. From the 1st Squadron, there were Chuck Sawyer and Frank Schiel, and from the 2nd, Gil Bright, Tex Hill, and Ed Rector. Nobody from among the roster of the 3rd Squadron opted to join the USAAF in China. In addition, about two dozen ground and support personnel also committed to join the USAAF.

Thanks in no small part to Clayton Bissell's antagonistic approach to the men he perceived as scarcely more than desperadoes, the AVG as an organization would just fade away. Had Bissell handled it differently—or if Chennault had been allowed to handle the matter without interference—things might have been different. The pilots were exhausted by half a year of combat under primitive conditions, and many would have opted out of remaining as part of the 23rd Fighter Group anyway, but enough would probably have remained to assure a reasonably seamless transition.

C harlie Bond recalled that at first, his conscience bothered him for not staying, but a later conversation with George Burgard assuaged his guilt. Burgard, who had been Bond's roommate at the home of the Danish oilman named Jensen during the long-ago battles over Rangoon, had spoken with Chennault, who admitted that, under the circumstances, he did not blame the men for wanting to leave.

"My respect for the Old Man soared higher than ever tonight," Bond told his diary. "Maybe I can sleep now."

Sleep came for Charlie Bond that night, but there was still another week on the American Volunteer Group contracts, and as Tokyo Rose foretold, it would not be restful.

For the most part, though, the restlessness of the last week was that of false alarms, a sort of calm before the storm that the Japanese seemed to have in store when the 23rd took over from the AVG. Each day, there seemed to be something cropping up on the radar screens, but it was usually a lone enemy reconnaissance plane that turned tail when the Flying Tigers took off to pursue it. Sometimes, cautiously patrolling empty skies can be as stressful as knowing that there is a foe on your tail. At least in the latter case, there is a chance to shoot back.

There were exceptions. On June 22, out of Hengyang, the Pandas had that chance. Ed Rector was flying lead because Tex Hill was out of town on another ferry mission across the Hump. The mission was significant for being the first live combat mission for Ajax Baumler since July 15, 1937, when he flew his last one in the skies over the Spanish province of Aragon in the wake of an ill-fated Republican offensive. Finally freed from desk duty, Baumler was now officially a member of the growing cadre of USAAF men who would be assigned to fly with the 23rd Fighter Group.

This was despite the fact that Baumler's drinking problem and his aggressive behavior when drunk had by now become well known around the AVG. Only four days earlier, he had gotten into a brawl with a ground crewman that Charlie Bond had to break up and that ended with Baumler "lying in the middle of the floor on a crying jag." Tex Hill recalled him pulling a gun on another man. When he was first assigned to Tex Hill's 2nd Squadron, Chennault warned Tex, saying that Baumler was "a good pilot, but he gets in a lot of trouble when he drinks." When Hill called Baumler on his behavior, he promised he would stop drinking. For a while, he did.

The activities for June 22 began with a strafing attack against a Japanese gunboat patrolling the Yangtze River, which elicited a counterstrike by the Imperial Japanese Army Air Force, who sent more than a dozen Nakajima Ki-27s to exact revenge. Picked up by defensive radar, the Japanese were intercepted by the Flying Tigers over Hengyang. In the ensuing battle, the Americans lost none and claimed two—including the first for Baumler since 1937, when he had downed his third Italian CR.32 fighter over Spain. Baumler's was also the first aerial victory for a USAAF pilot over China. Because he had earlier downed a German Heinkel He-51, as well as the CR.32s, over Spain, Baumler was now the first American with victories over aircraft of all three Axis powers.

As Dissolve Day neared, there was growing nervousness within the Tenth Air Force command structure and within Chennault's own headquarters at Baishiyi. The 23rd Fighter Group, which was little more than a mirage a month earlier, when Clayton Bissell was insulting the Flying Tigers at Kunming, was now an organization that was barely at squadron strength, and it was comprised largely of pilots whose only combat experience had been flying patrols with the Flying Tigers. Most had yet to see a Japanese aircraft, much less *fight* one.

The situation was so bad that on June 28, Caleb Haynes radioed General Joe Stilwell, the Allied theater commander for the China-Burma-India Theater, telling him that "from present observations I deem it imperative that AVG induction be deferred until October first and present contracts be continued otherwise our operations are in serious jeopardy. Induction board strongly concurs above recommendation."

When he was looped into Haynes's conversation with Stilwell, Chennault probably reveled in the irony of the situation. He noted that "Haynes' warning was ignored. Induction of the AVG had already been publicized as part of a world-wide Air Forces public relations splurge [for] July 4. The Chinese were not unique in their efforts to save face."

Haynes and Stilwell turned to Chennault. Though he was reluctant to go against the promise to his men that they could go home, he also had the responsibility for the CATF and the 23rd, and he could not abide the impending disaster that was about to strike his command. In the middle of June, he had already started to ask for volunteers willing to postpone their departure for two weeks, until July 18.

Apparently the first man with whom he shared this idea was Tex Hill, the commander of the 1st Squadron Pandas. Returning from across the Hump on his latest ferry flight, Hill reported to Chennault's office at Baishiyi.

"Tex, I'm sure you've heard about the boys' meeting with General Bissell by now," Chennault said, referring to the ongoing efforts by the disliked Bissell and men such as Homer Sanders to recruit AVG men into the USAAF.

"Yes, sir, I did," Tex said with a nod.

"Hell, I think the boys are all planning to go home in two weeks," Chennault said, his dark eyes drilling into the tall Korea-born Texan. "Bissell poisoned them. They all deserve a rest. I'm going to be left holding the bag here with a handful of green Army pilots that are going to get themselves killed. Tex, I haven't talked to you yet about your plans, but if you leave, I don't know what I'm going to do."

"General," Tex told him, reiterating what he had confided to Olga Greenlaw in Calcutta, "I'll stay around as long as you need me."

"That's what I hoped to hear. I think we can get by if some of the boys just stay on for another two weeks—extend their contracts—to get the Army pilots up to speed on how we operate over here. I wonder if you'd be willing to talk to some of them, to see if they wouldn't stay. I know they'd listen to you."

"Sure," Tex told him. "I'll do that."

As he walked out of Chennault's office, the first man Hill passed was Pete Petach, a flight leader who served under him in the 2nd Squadron. He was carrying his overloaded duffel bag and looking like he was headed for the exit. And who could blame him? He had married attractive, red-haired AVG nurse Emma Jane "Red" Foster in February and they were ready to go home and start a family. In fact, Red was already pregnant, though few people knew this at the time.

"You look about ready to pull chocks, there, John," Hill observed, eying the duffel bag.

"Sure, isn't everybody?" Petach asked rhetorically. "I was just going to say good-bye to the Old Man."

"Right," Hill said thoughtfully. "Listen, he's mighty concerned right now about losing all the guys with experience at one time. Any chance you'd be willing to stay on for two weeks?"

"Sure, Tex, I'll stay," he replied hesitantly. "I guess two weeks won't make much difference. I don't think Red will mind, either."

"Man, I know he'll appreciate it," Tex said.

Next, Hill approached his old friend Ed Rector, with whom he had flown SB2U Vindicators off the USS *Ranger* long ago and who was the first man to stand with him during the pilots' revolt.

"I suppose you're staying?" Rector asked, though he need not have. When Hill nodded, Rector said "well then, count me in."

Chennault took the idea to the Adam and Eves in Hengyang on July 30, briefing Bob Neale, the squadron commander, who then took it, long-faced, to his men.

"How many of you are willing to stay two more weeks beyond the Fourth to permit the USAAF to arrive here and get in shape to replace us?" Neale asked.

Charlie Bond, who had sensed something was wrong when he saw Neale's face, wrote in his diary, "There it was; I knew it. . . . I was mad as hell. I knew my conscience wouldn't let me do anything about it but say yes. I blame it all on the US Army. They knew we were supposed to be disbanded on the Fourth. Why the hell didn't they lay their plans accordingly and get their replacements in here? How can I say no under the circumstances? The Japs have threatened to wipe out the USAAF after the AVG leaves. We picked it up on all their radio frequencies; the Old Man is using this crutch. Now he can tell the Japs: We dare you to try it. Perhaps he is right."

Among the Adam and Eves, Neale had agreed to stay on, and so did Charlie Bond.

As Bond blamed the US Army as an institution, Tex Hill later blamed Bissell for the exodus of AVG men, calling his May 21 speech "an unmitigated disaster" that added insult to injury by "downplaying the AVG's accomplishments as negligible—adding that the Western press had fabricated and enhanced their stories to 'make them look good.' He continued by intimating that the Flying Tigers were a bunch of screw-ups who would have been kicked out of US military service eventually, had they not signed up for the AVG."

As Tokyo Rose had promised, during the final seventy-two hours before the end of Dissolve Day, the aerial battlefield over southeastern China suddenly came alive with a series of strikes. In turn, the counterstrikes began on July 2, as the 11th Bomber Squadron, now based at Hengyang along with the AVG Pandas, returned to attack Hankou to redeem itself after its sloppy mission on the previous day. According to the official recollection by Carter and Mueller, this raid, "more successful than the first, causes considerable damage."

As Chennault wrote in his memoirs, "air fighting broke out all along the East China front. We dive-bombed enemy airfields and shipping at Hankow and Guangzhou, supported the Chinese counteroffensive in Jiangxi, and fought off counterattacks over our fields. . . . For three days we kept the squadron buzzing ostentatiously over [Chongqing] at low altitude. By that time I estimated the Japanese would have word that the AVG was ready to defend [Chongqing]."

In the wake of the July 2 mission to Hankou, the Japanese retaliated with a nighttime attack against the AVG at Hengyang. Charlie Bond noted in his diary that the men were awakened at 2:10 a.m. and had reached the flight line as five enemy bombers came overhead, visible in the night sky by the eerie blue-white glow of their exhausts. The bombs fell, missing the field by several hundred yards. Later on July 3, the 11th sent its B-25s, escorted by four AVG P-40s, to attack the Japanese field at Nanchang, about 230 miles northeast of Hengyang, from which the bombers had originated.

In turn, the Japanese hit back with an attempted fighter sweep of the AVG base. Bond was among those who scrambled to meet them. Another was Ernest "Bus" Loane, who had originally come to China as a flight instructor for the Chinese Air Force and who had later begun flying with the AVG.

"One came in on Bus Loane's tail," Bond recalled of his first sighting of a Japanese fighter that day. "I turned into it and it broke off. I shot at it, but my bursts were low. It went up into a climb, a turn, and then a shallow dive. I looked back and found myself alone. . . . I scanned the skies for aircraft and finally picked up one in the distance. It was too far away to identify until it got closer. . . . We passed each other at about 17,000 feet, and both of us immediately went into a violent bank to get around behind the other. In no time he was getting the advantage, so I began a vertical dive to the lower cloud level. He followed me at first. I hit 410 mph when my radio antenna tore off, but I lost the [enemy fighter] in the clouds."

Determining that he was low on fuel and deciding that he did not want to lose the third P-40 of his career to a crash landing, he touched down at a small auxiliary field "rather than risk getting strafed while landing at Hengyang."

When he finally reconnected with Bob Neale and the rest of his squadron, Bond told him, "I ought to quit at the rate I am going."

Neale grinned and offered him another drink from the bottle of bourbon he was passing around.

Saturday, July 4, 1942, Independence Day at home and Dissolve Day in China, was observed in a variety of ways. It was the first Independence Day since Pearl Harbor, and as a show of solidarity, nearly every national magazine on the newsstands in the United States put the Stars and Stripes on its cover that week. Those were difficult days when national resolve was crucial to morale. They were difficult days when an Allied victory was just a goal, not a foregone conclusion.

The IJAAF celebrated the wee hours of July 4 with air attacks on the AVG airfields in and around Hengyang. "I could see the bomb flashes through my window," Bond wrote in his diary. "I presume they meant to hit the field with the first drop and the second salvo was meant for our barracks. They had it figured out just about right. The second salvo hit just short of my barracks and shook me out of my bunk. My heart almost beat out of my body. That was close."

Bond and Dick Rossi spent the day on alert at Guilin, while Ed Rector, Jim Howard, and the Pandas intercepted another raid on Hengyang and claimed seven Nakajima Ki-27 fighters. The Japanese, under the impression that the AVG was already out of business, had intended to deliver a message that the IJAAF was once again in charge of the airspace over southeastern China. The enemy pilots got the surprise of their lives, and in a few cases the *last* surprise of their lives.

That day found Claire Chennault in his office in Baishiyi. In his memoirs, he wrote that he was doing paperwork, but if that was true, it was only in an attempt to keep his mind off the momentous turning point that was upon him. That evening, he and the Flying Tigers who were in the Chongqing area at the time were invited to a party that was hosted, not by Chiang Kai-shek, but by seventy-four-year-old Lin Sen, the enigmatic figurehead chairman of the Chinese government who remained behind the throne in Chiang's shadow. The Old Man recalled that it was supposed to have been a barbecue, but it was moved inside because of a rainstorm.

He wrote that Madame Chiang Kai-shek's two sisters, Soong Ai-ling, the wife of financier H. H. Kung, and Soong Ching-ling, the widow of Sun Yat-sen, were both present at the party. They presented Chennault with a group portrait in oils of himself, along with Madame and Chiang Kai-shek. The Old Man made no mention of whether either of the Chiangs attended the party, though Tex Hill's biographer Reagan Schaupp wrote that they were there, and so too was H. H. Kung himself.

It was a strange affair. Chennault noted that "we played musical chairs, drank nonalcoholic punch," hardly amusements befitting the circumstances or the participants, and that the party broke up by 11:00 p.m.

Chennault concluded his reminiscences of the evening by writing that "at midnight the American Volunteer Group passed into history."

But that is not exactly true. With contracts for some of the men having been extended for two weeks, there was still more history to be written by the Flying Tigers.

TWENTY-NINE

Coming out of the Cold
on a Shoestring

Dissolve Day plus one dawned like any other muggy monsoon season morning in southeastern China. Five pilots had committed to futures with the USAAF, but fifty-five AVG pilots and ground crewmen—to use the figures from the memoirs of both Chennault and Jim Howard, who were there—would continue to operate for two weeks as though Dissolve Day had never happened.

Tex Hill flew into Hengyang from Kunming on the morning of July 5, leading the nine serviceable P-40s that had still been left at the AVG's original China home. Though he was not formally sworn into the USAAF until July 19, he now wore the uniform of a major in the USAAF. It was an indication of the shoestring nature of operations at the end of the line logistically that he was wearing hand-me-down khakis given him by R. T. Smith, who had brought a regulation uniform all the way from San Francisco in 1941 and had hardly worn it.

It was also indicative of the shoestring nature of the new 23rd Fighter Group that it officially came into being with all of its aircraft being hand-me-down P-40s from the American Volunteer Group. By Chennault's reckoning the group possessed fifty-one fighter aircraft, of which thirty-one were survivors of the original consignment of ninety-nine P-40Bs, with the rest being the newer P-40Es and P-40Ks that had been flown in across the Hump.

Of the total, only twenty-nine were flyable, and as Chennault noted, "at training fields in the States these planes would have been rushed to a scrap heap. In China they had to do for combat. Not until December 1943 did the last P-40B of AVG vintage reach the Kunming salvage dump. . . . Army replacements for China—when they finally arrived—were P-40Ks that had already flown hundreds of hours in training schools and combat. Some P-40s sent to China from North Africa had swastikas painted on their cockpits testifying to their previous combat service against the Luftwaffe."

Also courtesy of the AVG was the entire command staff of the 23rd, which was still being led by an outlaw. Until his contract extension expired at midnight on July 18, Bob Neale—a civilian—was the operational leader of a USAAF fighter group. He did not do so by military rank, as he had none, but by the fact that he was the senior AVG squadron leader, having led the 1st Squadron Adam and Eves since Sandy Sandell was killed in early February. As always with this band of American warriors in China, tactical realities trumped administrative regulations. It did not hurt matters that Neale was the highest-scoring ace among the Flying Tigers.

The 23rd's three squadrons would each be commanded by a newly inducted USAAF man who had been a mercenary on July 3. Tex Hill commanded the new 75th Fighter Squadron, with Gil Bright as his second in command, while the group's 74th and 76th Fighter Squadrons would be led, respectively, by AVG alums Frank Schiel and Ed Rector. Each of them now also wore the gold oak leaves of USAAF majors. Chuck Sawyer also joined the USAAF as Rector's deputy.

To command the 23rd—on paper as of July 4 and in the air after Neale's departure—Chennault needed a USAAF colonel. The colonel he picked was not Horace LeRoy Sanders, who had eagerly auditioned for the job, but Robert Lee Scott, the zealous pilot from the Ferry Command who had turned himself into a one-man air force with the P-40E nicknamed *Old Exterminator* that Chennault had given him. Perhaps this had been Chennault's long-term goal two months earlier when he had let Scott "borrow" that aircraft.

Scott had learned of his appointment only eight days before Dissolve Day. As late as June 20, when Sanders and the official induction board had passed through Dinjan, where Scott was based, he had no inkling that Chennault was considering him.

As Scott wrote in his memoirs, when Sanders and his team went into China on that trip, "my hopes faded of ever getting over to work under General Chennault. I knew that out of those Colonels, the powers that be had surely picked some lucky one to get the greatest job in the world. This was of course that of commanding the AVG after it came into the Army. . . . If the Scotch hadn't given out, I would have got drunk that night. But instead I went on another strafing raid in the late afternoon, and had to land after dark."

Over the ensuing days, to keep his mind off the opportunity that he saw slipping away, he took *Old Exterminator* to attack targets across Japanese-occupied Burma. On June 26, when he returned from another one-man fighter sweep that took him almost to Mandalay, a radiogram was waiting that ordered him to Kunming the following day to meet with Chennault, who was considering him for the leadership of the 23rd Fighter Group.

The next day, en route to Kunming for the job interview of a lifetime, Scott strafed Homalin on the Chindwin River, bombed the railyards at Mogaung, and strafed the former RAF airfield at Myitkyina that was now being used by the Japanese.

At Kunming, Scott recalled being met not only by Chennault, but by Chiang Kai-shek as well. When Chiang asked him how long it would take him to relocate from Dinjan to Kunming, Scott replied, "I am already here. I do not have to go back to Dinjan."

Farther to the east, in the Hengyang-Yongzhou-Guilin salient, the Japanese probed the American defenses. They had figured out—after the beating they took on July 4—that the Flying Tigers were still in the sky. Meanwhile, the AVG pilots had finally received external fuel tanks to extend the range of their P-40s and were now able to join the 11th Bomber Squadron in taking the war to the Japanese in Guangzhou.

On July 6, as the B-25s took their first run at that city to target a petroleum refinery, Tex Hill and the six escorting P-40s found themselves in a ferocious fight with Japanese fighters. The enemy reacted unfavorably to the arrival of the Americans, launching a dozen Ki-27s to sweep the raiders from the skies over the city. Outnumbered two to one, the erstwhile Flying Tigers rolled into the fight.

Hill picked out a Japanese fighter and shot off its wing. Pete Petach, meanwhile, claimed another Ki-27 to take his own score to 3.98, bringing him almost within striking distance of becoming an ace before he went home. As so often before, the P-40s returned to their field without a loss.

On July 9, another bomber mission went out to Hankou, but compared to the Guangzhou mission, this proved to be a milk run for the fighters, with no IJAAF interceptors to be seen. On the way back, they entertained themselves with strafing runs against the Japanese gunboats that plied the Yangtze harassing Chinese cargo sampans.

With the next day, there came a request from the Chinese Army for a routine ground attack mission against a local Japanese headquarters building in a small town that appeared lightly defended and that was a long distance from any Japanese air base. Tex Hill considered it an easy mission and tasked Petach with leading a four-ship strike force. His team included a new USAAF man, Lieutenant Leonard Butsch, Panda Bear veteran Arnold "Red" Shamblin, and Ajax Baumler.

As so often happens in life when something is predicted to be easy and perfunctory, the opposite is true. The place veritably bristled with antiaircraft artillery that put up a wall of flak unlike anything the men had seen in recent weeks. Nevertheless, Petach led them in and personally put a five-hundred-pound high-explosive bomb directly on the target.

Then, as the others watched in horror, flak ripped the left wing from Petach's P-40, which tumbled into the Chinese countryside in a ball of fire from which no one could have escaped.

Seeing this, Shamblin attacked the antiaircraft gun emplacement that seemed to have been responsible for nailing Petach. The guns now turned on Shamblin, tearing his P-40 apart. The others watched him bail out, but he was never seen again. He was presumed to have been captured and killed. It was only the second time since December 1941 that two men were lost on the same day, and it was the first time since Jack Newkirk was killed and Mac McGarry was captured on March 24—the event that had been the catalyst for the pilots' revolt, the nadir of Flying Tiger morale.

When he heard the news about Pete Petach, whom he had convinced to stay in China—when he should have been on his way home with his pregnant bride—Tex Hill had the difficult task of conveying the news to the newly widowed Red Foster Petach.

In a footnote to the incident, Jim Howard wrote in his memoirs that "unknown to those of us who had volunteered for the two weeks of additional duty, we had been inducted into the Army Air Force for that period. The paperwork had been done without our knowledge. My first inkling of this came years later when Pete Petach was cited for the Distinguished Flying Cross posthumously. The medal was awarded to his family by the Army in a ceremony in 1984."

———————

The end of the American Volunteer Group as an active organization finally became official at midnight on July 18. Only a few of the Flying Tigers were still around Guilin for a big send-off party given for the AVG vets by the newly arrived USAAF pilots.

The final transition of Claire Chennault's command from American Volunteer Group to China Air Task Force on July 19, 1942, was anti-climactic. As his last act as head of the induction board that inducted a grand total of five pilots, Colonel Homer Sanders flew in from India to conduct the official swearing-in ceremonies that day. When he congratulated Tex Hill, the only thing the commander of the new 75th Fighter Squadron could think to say in reply was "Great." Chennault had sent word to Bob Scott on July 17 to head up from Kunming to Guilin to take over fighter operations. Clayton Bissell was nowhere to be seen.

THIRTY

From Flying Tigers
into Hungry Mastiffs

A s the era of the outlaw Flying Tigers gradually faded into the new era of the legitimized China Air Task Force and its 23rd Fighter Group, Chennault still found himself on a logistical shoestring. He wrote with abundant hyperbole that "the CATF lived off the land like a pack of hungry mastiffs. China was completely cut off from the rest of the world—sealed in a military vacuum between the Japanese, the Gobi Desert, and the frozen Himalayan peaks. Only an occasional Army plane crossed the Hump from India. The idea of an aerial supply line was still fantastic to orthodox military minds although DC-3s of CNAC were showing what could be done with a small but steady trickle of airborne supplies into China."

The feelings were even shared by Joe Stilwell, the man whom Marshall had handpicked to run the theater. Even two years later he would still be complaining to his diary that "we are the step-children of World War II."

Indeed, though the tonnage hauled across the Hump by the heroic transport pilots of CNAC and the USAAF would continue to increase greatly in the coming years, both Chennault and Stilwell would remain at the very end of the Allied logistical line for the rest of their time in China.

———

As replacements for the men of the most successful American fighter group in the world, Chennault got some excellent pilots and good leaders, men such as Bob Scott, but most of the rank-and-file lieutenants who showed up were barely fit for the task at hand. In his memoirs, he cited an incident in which Scott greeted a group of twenty-one fighter pilot replacements who had arrived to serve with the 23rd. When he asked for a show of hands from those who had more than three hundred hours of flight time, nobody raised his hand.

"Sorry, boys, but we can't use you here," Scotty told them, ordering them back across the Hump.

As Chennault pointed out, "green pilots were a double liability. We had neither the time, gas, nor planes to spend on training them in China. When they were sent into combat immediately, they jeopardized lives of our veterans by failure to hold formation and lack of flying ability. Combination of old planes and new pilots proved more deadly than the Japanese. A dozen planes were lost in accidents for every one destroyed by the enemy."

At the 74th Fighter Squadron, which became known as the "school squadron," Frank Schiel took those who came closest to passing muster, and turned them into the kind of pilots that were needed by the 23rd if it was to prove itself a worthy successor to the AVG.

Scott, who was already known back home as a "one-man air force," became, in the absence of the Flying Tigers as an organization, the media's iconic man in the shark-faced P-40. In the August 10 issue of

Life magazine, Jack Belsen—who had interviewed him while on assignment in China—called Scott "the most romantic American in China today . . . likely to become the D'Artagnan of the air in the Far East. He gives a damn for neither man nor beast, weather nor Japs, and is a regular hell on wheels."

He had finally scored his first aerial victory on July 31, on a routine flight between Kunming and Guilin. He was north of Guilin and low on fuel when he got word by radio that the early warning net had detected incoming Japanese aircraft. Picking his way through the clouds, he spotted a Japanese bomber, attacked head on, dodged the two Japanese fighters that were escorting it, and returned to finish it off. He lost the two enemy fighters and landed at Hengyang with his fuel gauge reading "empty."

On September 25, when Scott scored his fifth, to become an ace, that fact was reported in the *New York Times*. It was over Hanoi while Scott and two flights of P-40s were escorting bombers on a strike mission against the big Japanese fighter field at Gia Lam, which would be notorious during the Vietnam War a generation later.

Scott wrote in his memoirs that "I had just had my twelfth little Japanese flag painted on the fuselage of my P-40K" as the Christmas season approached. When he scored his thirteenth and last on Christmas, Tokyo Rose called him a war criminal.

Among the best of the first round of replacements was Major John Richardson "Johnny" Alison, who arrived in Guilin on July 10 with nine P-40s and eight other pilots who technically belonged to the 16th Fighter Squadron, a component of Sanders's 51st Fighter Group in India. The idea was that they were coming in "temporarily" and for "training," but the 16th would not be sent back to the 51st until 1943.

Sanders had not gotten the coveted 23rd Fighter Group command job, but Chennault *had* gotten a handful of P-40s from him.

Alison had more experience with the P-40 than most, going back to when the USAAF was still the Air Corps. He and Hubert "Hub" Zemke had been two of the first Army pilots to fly the aircraft. In the spring of 1941, they had gone to the United Kingdom with a batch of Lend-Lease Tomahawks for the RAF. On June 22, 1941, two days after the Air Corps became the USAAF, they were still in England when the news came in that the Germans had launched Operation Barbarossa, their massive invasion of the Soviet Union. A month later, the two men were mysteriously summoned to the US embassy in London, where they met with Harry Hopkins, Franklin Roosevelt's closest adviser, and Averell Harriman, Roosevelt's roving ambassador and Lend-Lease manager. They were told that more than a hundred Tomahawks were being rerouted from Britain to the Soviet Union, which was now, by virtue of its being at war with Germany, a British ally and an American Lend-Lease recipient. Zemke and Alison were being sent to Russia "on assignment to the American Embassy in Moscow as assistant air attachés." In other words, they were to coordinate the assembly and deployment of the Tomahawks.

On December 7, when the bombs started falling on Pearl Harbor, Alison and Zemke were in Kuybyshev (now Samara), a city of half a million people that was serving as the temporary seat of government of the Soviet Union. At that moment, 550 miles to the northwest, German armies were encircling Moscow and preparing for their final assault on the Soviet capital. The two Americans were then faced with the challenge of getting back to the United States in order to go overseas again.

Zemke would be assigned to the Eighth Air Force in England, where he became an ace and commanded the 56th Fighter Group, which became legendary as "Zemke's Wolf Pack." Alison helped pioneer the route through Alaska for delivery of Lend-Lease aircraft to the Soviet Union, and now he was about to become part of the immediate successor to the Flying Tigers.

Jim Howard, who was among the AVG men who remained in China for the extra two weeks and was assigned to Alison's contingent to familiarize them with Japanese tactics, recalled "how charged up and eager for combat they all were."

Later in the month, Alison managed to accomplish something the AVG never had: he intercepted and shot down *three* Japanese bombers by moonlight. However, as he was silhouetted against the moon, Alison was also shot down himself. He defied all odds with a belly landing in the Siang River and managed to swim ashore. Alison was presumed dead until he finally hitched his way back to Guilin a few days later. As he was a USAAF officer and not a civilian soldier of fortune, he was eligible for—and eventually awarded—the Distinguished Service Cross.

Chennault recalled witnessing a dogfight over the field the following morning as the Japanese mounted an attack during which Tex Hill sought to exact revenge for Alison, still thought to be deceased. He watched as Hill "singled out the Japanese formation leader and then ensued one of the strangest sights ever seen in air combat. Tex headed for the Jap leader in a head-on pass with both of them shooting and closing the range at better than 600 miles an hour. It was like a pair of old-fashioned Western gunmen shooting it out on the main street of some cow town. Watching from the ground, a collision seemed certain. Neither would give an inch. At the last split second before a crash, the Jap pushed over into a steep dive. Tex barely brushed over his cockpit. The Jap trailed a thin plume of smoke. He must have been badly hit, for he circled over the field and then deliberately pushed over into a vertical dive, holding it until he crashed into a row of bamboo dummy P-40s parked on the field."

When he departed the 23rd Fighter Group for the last time on January 9, 1943, Scott turned over command to Lieutenant Colonel Bruce Holloway, another new man who had proven himself. As Chennault recalled, Holloway had been "selected by Bissell to be CATF operations officer [but] since Bruce had had no combat experience, I transferred him to a fighter squadron. He had a dead-pan face, and I never could tell whether my lectures on tactics ever made any impression on Bruce. A few weeks of fighting showed he had learned all I could teach and added a few wrinkles of his own. He ran up a score of 13 Japanese planes confirmed and wore himself to a shadow during a year of combat."

First assigned to the 75th Fighter Squadron when the 23rd had been activated, Holloway had displayed an aptitude for air combat worthy of the successor organization to the Flying Tigers. He later took over command of the 75th Fighter Squadron when Ed Rector had gone Stateside on medical leave. Shot down over the remote mountains of Yunnan and presumed killed in action, Holloway was picked up by Miao tribesmen and spent more than a month making his way through the jungle to return to Kunming. His postwar career in the US Air Force is notable for its having culminated in his commanding the Strategic Air Command from 1968 to 1972 as a four-star general.

Though China did loom small amid a thinly stretched Allied strategic vision ruled by the "Germany first" dogma, a substantial portion of Joe Stilwell's problems were of his own making. Within the Allied leadership, especially among the British but also including the American chiefs of staff, there was a predisposition to write off the Chinese armed forces as an inefficient organization beset with insurmountable internal problems. In turn, these issues were only exaggerated by Stilwell's reminders of corruption and ineptitude within the Chinese leadership, especially in the person of Chiang Kai-shek himself, whom Stilwell continued to insist on referring to as "the Peanut."

In short, by his belittling Chiang, Stilwell only degraded the perceived importance of China as a theater by reinforcing Washington's predisposition to consider Chiang's government as impossibly corrupt. Meanwhile, because he had aligned himself with Chiang, whom he continued to respect, Chennault was seen by the American chiefs as suspect for backing the flawed generalissimo.

In early February 1943, as part of an inspection tour he undertook after the Allied high-level Casablanca Conference, Hap Arnold himself traveled to China to meet with Chiang Kai-shek. He was underwhelmed, writing in his diary that "the Generalissimo does not impress me as a big man; he casts aside logic and factual matters as so much trash. Apparently he believes his power can force from his subjects the impossible. He never gave any indication of thoughts of the outside world, except insofar as it gave aid to China. He gave evidence of quick thinking at times but only at times."

Arnold also had an opportunity to view firsthand the corrosive dynamics of the complex relationship between Chiang and Chennault on one side, and Stilwell and Bissell on the other. The visit was an eye-opener for Arnold.

"Logistics, air and general military progress were one thing," Arnold wrote in his memoirs. "Matters like Chiang's attitude toward Bissell, his unlimited confidence in Chennault, Chennault's own oversimplification, along Chinese lines, of various problems, and above all the personal position of Stilwell, who called Chiang Kai-shek 'Peanut Head' practically within the Generalissimo's hearing—these were complications a bit beyond the Book."

Arnold went on to add that "Bissell was an excellent staff officer who carefully worked out every operation before he undertook it, or said he could not do it. Chennault had the originality, initiative, and drive the Chinese liked; also, a knack of doing things in China that was possessed by very few other American officers. He stood in well with the Generalissimo and Madame Chiang. On the other hand, General Bissell was not particularly liked by the Generalissimo."

Again, it was the association with Chiang and his circle, perceived in Washington as a den of corruption, that hurt Chennault. An important element of this perception was the fact, uncovered by American journalists, that Chiang was hoarding supplies that could have been used against the Japanese for a later war against the Chinese Communists, and that he was doing so with Chennault's knowledge and support.

In his memoirs, Chennault addressed this, writing that "the cry of hoarding military supplies was raised. These dumps of bombs, ammunition, and 100-octane gas that existed around airfields all over Free China were cited as proof that the Chinese were not using American Lend-Lease supplies to fight the Japanese but were storing them for civil war against the Chinese Communists. I helped the Chinese 'hoard' those supplies. Most of them were paid for in cash in early 1940 long before Lend-Lease began. Some of them were smuggled from Hong Kong into small Chinese ports for the far-eastern fields in Chekiang and Kiangsi. Some of them came up the Yunnan railroad from Haiphong, and some of them were trucked up the Burma Road from Rangoon and Mandalay. The Chinese had no air force then and no allies. But they stored those gas drums, bombs and bullets near fields in Free China against the day when there might be an air force in China. They were aware that when that day came China's rickety internal-transport system might be unable to move supplies fast enough to meet emergencies, and so they cached these stores wherever they anticipated future need."

In fact, at least part of the matériel in question *would* later be used against the Communists, but with the war against Japan ongoing, the hoarding was perceived throughout the chain of command, from Marshall to Stilwell, and including Arnold, as a black mark against Chiang and Chennault.

Nevertheless, Arnold did take steps to alleviate some of Chennault's logistical woes. In his diary, Arnold wrote that upon arriving in China "I found that there were but 62 transport planes on the India-China run. Within 24 hours orders were issued to raise that number to 137. The tonnage carried in December [1942] was 1,700; I have arranged to bring it up to 4,000 by the month of April."

As Arnold left Chongqing, Chiang Kai-shek asked him to carry a personal letter to Roosevelt recommending a new USAAF numbered air force independent of the Tenth and placed under Chennault's command, adding that Chinese soldiers and airmen "have confidence in Chennault but they will not serve under Bissell."

General John Huston, who edited Arnold's wartime diaries, wrote in his annotations that "presumably ignoring or discounting any data or recommendations Arnold brought back, as well as the known opposition of Stimson, Marshall, and Arnold, FDR acceded, only two days after Hap's return [to Washington], to everything Chiang wanted in behalf of Chennault. . . . The president had indicated as early as December [1942] his inclination to give Chennault his own air force but held off in view of Marshall's opposition, the Casablanca meeting, and Arnold's trip."

Within the American leadership, Roosevelt was the one man who still had confidence in both Chiang and Chennault. He was as sympathetic to Chiang and to China's plight as he had been before the war.

It was Roosevelt who had deliberately created the American Volunteer Group and who had personally dispatched Chennault to China to help save it from the Japanese. It was now Roosevelt who favored the creation of a separate air force in China with Chennault as its commander, divorcing him from the Tenth Air Force and Clayton Bissell, an opinion that was not favored by the president's chiefs of staff.

On March 10, 1943, the USAAF Fourteenth Air Force, fully independent of the Tenth, was activated in China with Claire Chennault, now a major general, as its commander. As Chennault's position in the hierarchy was now elevated, Stilwell's was in decline. In August 1943 the Allied leadership decided to subordinate his CBI command to the newly created Allied South East Asia Command (SEAC), which was placed under the command of British admiral Lord Louis Mountbatten—though Stilwell would act as his deputy.

"Recently you have been accorded the status of independent commander of an air force," Arnold wrote in a cautionary memo to Chennault on March 3. "With this status comes, as you know, certain responsibilities that you must meet."

History tells us that he did, albeit while continuing to complain about being short of matériel, and with but a handful of the men who had been called the Flying Tigers.

In November 1943, to succeed Holloway as commander of the 23rd Fighter Group, Chennault sent for one of that handful of men: Tex Hill. Like his old friend Ed Rector, Hill had served with the 23rd through its first five months, but they both had gone Stateside in December 1942—Rector to Walter Reed Army Hospital with a nearly fatal parasitic infection, and Hill to brief the top brass at the Pentagon, which had just opened in January 1943. Like Bob Scott, who was also in Washington that month, Hill carried the message that Chennault had been trying to convey—that the CATF was short of everything it needed to do his job. If his comments did some good, it was not in the near term. During that month, the CATF was largely grounded for lack of fuel.

By the end of January 1943, Hill had returned to Texas. He reunited with his family, invested the bonus money he had earned in China in a ranch north of Kerrville, and met Mazie Sale, who became his wife on March 27. The Hills moved on to Florida, where Tex was assigned to the USAAF weapons testing facility at Eglin Field as a test pilot. It was here that he was introduced to the relatively new North American P-51 Mustang, destined soon to prove itself as the best fighter aircraft in the USAAF. Things continued in civilized fashion, with Tex going to work and coming home for dinner each night, until one night in early November, when a telegram arrived from Claire Chennault requesting Tex Hill's immediate presence in China to assume command of the 23rd Fighter Group.

Hill stepped off a transport in Kunming on November 3, 1943, and into his new job in Guilin the following day, where he was pleased to see P-51s starting to take the place of the obsolescent P-40s. On Thanksgiving Day, November 25, Hill led the first USAAF air strike on Taiwan, a major staging area for Japanese military air operations against China.

The mission was a five-hour round trip with a strike force including fourteen B-25s and a mix of P-38s to run a strafing attack and P-51s to supply top cover. As the clouds parted over the air base complex at Hsinchu, and as the bombers began their attack, Hill found himself practically on top of an enemy fighter. A split second after he opened fire, he had to bank hard to avoid the tumbling mass of wreckage. He had reentered the world of aerial combat by taking out the first of fifteen enemy aircraft to be shot down that day. The bombers claimed another forty-three on the ground, and the Americans suffered no losses.

For Tex Hill and the 23rd, operations through the spring of 1944 were a continuation of the bomber escort missions that began during the twilight of the AVG, and there was no shortage of the air-to-air combat that had been the inducement that brought those men who would be tigers to the Far East in the first place.

Among the five AVG pilots who both fulfilled their contracts and signed up for the transition into the 23rd Fighter Group, Hill added six aerial victories to those he accumulated as a Flying Tiger, while Gil Bright added three and Ed Rector one. Frank Schiel, who had taken command of the 74th Fighter Squadron, was killed when an F-4—the reconnaissance variant of the P-38 Lightning—that he was flying went down on the way back from a mission.

The date was December 5, 1942, two days short of the first anniversary of Pearl Harbor and five months after the AVG was officially disbanded after seven months in combat. This provides a useful illustration of how much the Flying Tigers had accomplished—and in how short a time.

THIRTY-ONE

Out of China

When the sun had come up on July 19, 1942, the morning after the delayed Dissolve Day, most of the Flying Tigers had already quietly slipped away from the country to which they had pledged their support for a year and two weeks. They had already sold all the accumulated personal possessions that couldn't be crammed into their duffel bags, and were at airfields from Chongqing to Kunming hoping and waiting to catch a ride on a USAAF C-47 or CNAC DC-3 across the Hump to Dinjan and home.

Bob Neale and Charlie Bond were among the last to leave. As they were waiting for a flight out of Chongqing on July 18, Skip Adair, Chennault's longtime assistant and the man who had recruited much of the AVG back in 1941, took them aside. Pete Petach's pregnant widow, nurse Emma Jane "Red" Foster Petach, was also headed home, and Adair asked if they would not mind traveling with her as her escort. They readily agreed.

Two days later, the three travelers were at the Great Eastern Hotel in Calcutta, which was filled with AVG vets waiting around for passports and visas, documents to be supplied, respectively, by the American consulate and the British at the Calcutta police department. Mired in red tape, this process proved much more complicated than expected.

Chennault had conveyed a War Department promise that those who had signed up for the two-week contract extension would be able to travel all the way home by air. However, when they contacted Tenth Air Force headquarters, the retired Flying Tigers learned that traveling by air west of Karachi was virtually impossible given the high demand that was being put on available air transport capacity. The trip from there back to the United States would have to be by sea, around the Cape of Good Hope, and through the U-boat-infested Atlantic.

"Red is down in the dumps and I can understand it," Bond wrote in his diary as they looked forward to several weeks on two oceans. "She doesn't relish the idea of going home by boat. She is pregnant but doesn't know that Skip told us. . . . We ran into one of the crew chiefs of the AVG who had come in from Karachi. The boat situation there is not good. I made up my mind to go to New Delhi and at least try to get Red air transportation home. I learned that a USAAF gooney bird at Dumdum Airport was leaving tomorrow for New Delhi, so I started checking on the crew. Luckily the pilot was an old buddy of mine from MacDill Air Base."

Through this connection, Bond managed to work his way up the chains of command, and ultimately to an audience in New Delhi with General Earl Naiden, commander of the Tenth Air Force, who remembered Bond from Langley Field before the war. When he learned their story, the AVG refugees—especially the young widow—were treated like heroes. Bond proposed that they wire Air Transport Command in Washington, but Naiden countered with a suggestion that they send their telegram to Hap Arnold directly. The reply, finally received on July 28, was "Request approved. Grant all three highest priority."

On August 7, the threesome landed in Miami aboard a Pan American Clipper. Bob Neale never returned to combat flying, later joining George Burgard, Jim Cross, and Buster Keeton among the AVG alums who went on to careers as pilots with Pan American. Eventually Neale retired to the Pacific Northwest and was running a fishing camp on Puget Sound when he passed away in 1994.

When Red and Pete's daughter was born early in 1943, Red named her Joan Claire Petach, with the middle name being a homage to Chennault. Red returned to her alma mater, and taught at the Yale School of Nursing before going on to a distinguished career as executive director of the Pennsylvania Health Council and as president of the Maryland Public Health Association. She raised her daughter alone, and did not remarry until Joan had left home. In 1964, Red married Fletcher Hanks, who had flown with CNAC in China during the war, making 347 round-trip flights across the Hump.

Hap Arnold never allowed the friction between him and Chennault to shade his opinion of, nor his actions toward, Chennault's men. On August 14, 1942, as the discharged AVG pilots started reaching the United States, he wrote to Chennault that "as a concrete example of the world-wide effect of your superior performance of most difficult duty I want you to know that I am personally directing an intense effort to enroll in the Army Air Forces all of your ex-American Volunteer Group combat personnel who are now in the States. We are after these lads in order that their skill, experience and ability which you have instilled into them shall not be lost to the Army Air Forces."

He made good on this promise. The pilots who rejoined the USAAF did so as lieutenants, but were majors within a month or less.

Jim Howard flew out of China at about the same time as Bond, Neale, and Red Petach. For Howard, who was born in Guangzhou twenty-nine years earlier, it was his second "final" exit. He made it as far as Bombay before he learned that he would have to make the trip home by sea aboard the former Matson liner SS *Mariposa*, en route to New York. As he came aboard, he was greeted by more than eighty AVG men, including Parker Dupouy, Tom Haywood, Bill Reed, and R. T. Smith.

Also aboard the *Mariposa* when it cast off from the dock at Bombay on August 6 were Harvey and Olga Greenlaw, who had been living in Bill Pawley's suite at the Cecil in Delhi since the middle of May. When they finally reached the United States, they settled in Southern California, but were divorced soon afterward. Olga did succeed in finding a publisher for her memoirs, which were published in 1943.

Early in January 1943, Robert Lee Scott, by now the most famous American fighter pilot in Asia, was summoned home by Hap Arnold to make a public relations tour. Every step that Scott took seemed guided by unfathomable luck.

While in Buffalo, New York, to speak at the Curtiss-Wright headquarters, where the P-40s flown by the AVG had been built, he met Episcopal bishop Dean Perdue, who introduced him to New York publisher Charles Scribner, who in turn asked the "D'Artagnan of the air" how soon he could write a book about his experiences. According to Scott, he dictated his tales onto about a hundred wax cylinders in record time, and turned them over to Scribner. The title, *God Is My Co-Pilot*, came from a vision he said he'd had looking into the darkness of a Chinese cave.

Shortly after being posted to Luke Field in Arizona, a routine flight to Southern California led to a chance meeting with Jack Warner of Warner Brothers, and a deal for the film adaptation of the book, a project that the USAAF embraced because of its public relations value. The book became a best seller in 1943, and the film was a successful release in 1945.

For those who had remained in China, and those newly arrived, the sense of desert island abandonment of which the Old Man had complained since 1941 still prevailed—and the Japanese knew it. The air bridge across the Hump had saved China from total collapse and it kept Chennault's Fourteenth Air Force viable, but it could not support theaterwide offensive operations. The Japanese knew this.

Often overlooked in general histories of World War II is that Japan never lost the land war in China, and ultimately this sent Joe Stilwell home without a victory. By April 1944, Allied armies throughout the world were gradually moving into an offensive posture, but in China, that "stepchild" of theaters, the situation was exactly the opposite. The Imperial Japanese Army launched Operation Ichi-Go (Number One), their biggest series of major campaigns across eastern China since 1937. As had been the case then, the Chinese were no match for such a major offensive, and they began to crumble, despite the heroic efforts of the Fourteenth Air Force to strike their supply and troop concentrations.

As the Japanese advanced in the east, Joe Stilwell, the nominal American theater commander in China, was distracted on two opposite fronts—his long-festering obsession with reversing his 1942 loss of Burma, and his increasingly bitter feud with Chiang Kai-shek. In the face of the cataclysm of Chinese defeats, he called Chiang a "crazy little bastard [with] idiotic tactical and strategic conceptions."

Stilwell insisted, in memos to Franklin Roosevelt and to anyone else who would listen, that only *he* could meet the challenge of Ichi-Go. If the supreme command of the Chinese armies was transferred from Chiang to him, the quarter million troops then being used against Mao Zedong's Communist insurgency could be thrown into the war against the Japanese, and things would be different.

With the collapse of the front in southeastern China, Roosevelt admitted that he was finally willing to have a frank talk with Chiang Kai-shek about letting Stilwell take over. However, instead of finessing a diplomatically complicated situation to his benefit, Stilwell used this moment to rub Chiang's nose in Roosevelt's impatience. On September 21, 1944, Stilwell gleefully turned to verse. "I've waited long for vengeance; At last I've had my chance," Stilwell wrote in a private letter that was reproduced in his published diaries. "I've looked the Peanut in the eye; And kicked him in the pants. . . . His face turned green and quivered. As he struggled not to screech. For all my weary battles, For all my hours of woe, At last I've had my innings, And laid the Peanut low."

Far from being laid low, Chiang Kai-shek wrote to Roosevelt, insisting that Stilwell must go. On October 19, as Guilin was falling to the Japanese onslaught, General Vinegar Joe Stilwell, sadly more engrossed in Chongqing palace intrigues than in the war, was relieved of duty and ordered back to the United States and a desk at the Pentagon. As often noted in the *I Ching*, "perseverance brings good fortune," but Chinese literature is so often filled with warnings to be alert for hidden danger. In American literature, they say that he who laughs last, laughs best, but aside from outlasting Stilwell, Chiang had little about which to chuckle. Just as often, the *I Ching*, that book of changes, reminds us that "perseverance brings *misfortune*."

O n October 15, 1944, four days before Stilwell was summoned homeward, Tex Hill departed from China and from the 23rd Fighter Group. For him and for the 23rd, Ichi-Go came as a disaster at a time when USAAF fighter groups from Germany to the Pacific were beginning to savor the sweet taste of victories. On June 20, Hill had to abandon the once-secure base complex at Hengyang, and by September, the headquarters of the 23rd had moved back to Liuzhou (then Liuchow), 260 miles southwest of Hengyang and nearly 100 miles from Guilin.

Hill turned the reins of the 23rd Fighter Group over to his deputy, Lieutenant Colonel Philip Loofbourrow, who would run the show until Ed Rector returned to China to take over the group. Headed west, Hill crossed paths with an eastbound Rector as they both passed through Cairo.

Having recovered from the infection that nearly killed him, Rector had served for a time at Eglin Field, but Chennault wanted another Flying Tiger to take over the 23rd. Rector would serve as commander of the group through the end of World War II. He scored his last aerial victory on April 2, 1945, over Shanghai.

C laire Lee Chennault remained in command of the Fourteenth Air Force until a week before World War II came to an end. When he requested on July 8, 1945, that he be relieved of duty, he did not know that nuclear weapons would be dropped on Japan a month later, nor that Emperor Hirohito would order his armies to stand down on August 15. Like most strategic planners, he believed that the final battles to subdue the Japanese homeland would last well into 1946 and that they would soak up American blood and treasure on an unprecedented level.

What he did know was that with the death of Franklin Roosevelt in April 1945, there was a declining willingness within the US government to continue to support the China that he had come to know and love. He saw "Free China"—as he called that part of the country ruled by Chiang Kai-shek and the Kuomintang—as a state on the verge of becoming a failed state, crowded between an increasingly active Communist insurgency and a Japanese occupation, neither of which could be defeated by a gradually declining Nationalist Chinese Army, one that had never recovered from Operation Ichi-Go a year earlier.

He did know that Stilwell, now in Washington, wanted him out of China and was pulling strings to make this happen. As Stilwell had seen his CBI command subordinated to the British-led SEAC two years earlier, Stilwell now wished to do the same for Chennault. He supported the consolidation of the Fourteenth Air Force with the Tenth under General George Stratemeyer's Eastern Air Command inside SEAC. This provided the final catalyst for Chennault's decision to ask to leave China.

On one point, though, Stilwell and Chennault agreed. China was strangling in corruption. Stilwell blamed Chiang Kai-shek, while Chennault blamed the American failure to vigorously support the American-educated modernists in Chiang's circle, including the Soong sisters, their surviving husbands, and their brother, T. V. Soong, whom he believed represented a solid and Western-leaning Chinese future. At home, public opinion sympathized with Chennault. The *New York Times* editorial page concurred, asserting that "no American is better qualified . . . to raise his voice for China."

When the news of Chennault's departure broke in China, it was greeted with alarm and sadness. The influential daily *Ta Kung Pao* lamented the news, calling Chennault China's "best bosom friend." When

Claire Chennault, no longer of the Fourteenth Air Force, flew out of Kunming on August 8, 1945, hundreds of Chinese civilians and military personnel were on hand to see him off. At home, two weeks later, when he was introduced in the stands at a baseball game between the Brooklyn Dodgers and the New York Giants, the *New York Times* called the applause "thunderous." When he returned home to Monroe, Louisiana, shortly after the surrender of Japan, thousands turned out to greet him.

THIRTY-TWO

And into History

Even when the AVG as an active organization was officially gone in July 1942, the AVG as a cultural archetype lived on, kept alive and robust in the hearts and minds of a press and public that would not let it go. It had been, and it would continue to be, chronicled in countless feature stories in the American and global media. Within a year, more than a half dozen books about it—including the memoirs of Olga Greenlaw and Bob Scott—had been published. The name "Flying Tigers" resonated in popular culture then, and it is still remembered today.

The Flying Tigers fought about fifty major aerial battles against hugely lopsided odds and never lost one of those contests. During their seven-month "undefeated season," from mid-December 1941 through mid-July 1942, the AVG, by Chennault's reckoning, had destroyed 299 Japanese aircraft, with another 153 probables. Including all aircraft destroyed on the ground, many estimates put the number much higher. By the records of the bonuses paid by the Chinese government under the CAMCO contracts for Japanese aircraft shot down, the number was 296. Frank Olynyk, who undertook a meticulous review of AVG records that was published in 1986, noted that the Flying Tigers had downed 229 Japanese aircraft in aerial combat alone. Considering the number of pilots and their length of service, the record of the American Volunteer Group ranks was comparable to those of the best fighter groups in the USAAF during World War II.

Of the men who flew against such odds with the AVG, sixty-seven were paid bonuses for having destroyed enemy aircraft, and of these, there were nineteen aces, meaning men who shot down five or more. Bob Neale was the highest-scoring AVG ace, credited with 15.55, the fraction being computed on the basis of victories shared with other pilots who contributed to the destruction of a specific aircraft. Frank Olynyk lists thirteen of Neale's victories as having been in aerial combat.

In second place, Tex Hill is credited with 11.25 or 10.25 by the bonus count and by Olynyk, respectively. Close behind Hill, five Flying Tigers survived the war with scores on the bonus chart between ten and eleven, including their shared victories: George Burgard, Ken Jernstedt, Mac McGarry, Chuck Older, and Bill Reed. Two others with scores in that range, Bob Little and Jack Newkirk, had been killed in action. They were two of only ten men lost in combat. Just seven were killed in accidents. Of the three who were captured, McGarry and Lew Bishop survived. Only Arnold Shamblin never came back from captivity.

Based on the unit's effectiveness from the Japanese perspective, Radio Tokyo estimated that AVG combat strength was about three hundred aircraft. In fact, the average rarely exceeded three dozen available, or a dozen in the air at any given moment. The Japanese knew that they substantially outnumbered the AVG, but they just could not comprehend that they outnumbered them by such a wide margin. A good laugh was had by the men when they tuned in to Radio Tokyo's English-language broadcasts.

Though often overlooked in the history books, the actions of the Flying Tigers at the Salween Gorge in May 1942 may well have altered the course of Chinese history by halting a Japanese offensive that could not otherwise have been stopped. As Winston Churchill said of the Battle of El Alamein, that British triumph in the North African desert half a year later, the Salween Gorge was not the beginning of the end of the great Japanese offensive through Burma to China's back door, but it was "perhaps, the end of the beginning."

The total cost to the Chinese government in 1942 dollars was about $5 million for aircraft and $3 million for salaries and personnel expenses. When Chennault admitted to T. V. Soong that this had exceeded his original estimates, the Chinese foreign minister reminded him that with less than a third of its combat strength, the AVG had saved China from final collapse on the Salween Gorge and freed Chongqing and the cities of eastern China from the fear of air attack. Soong scolded Chennault, telling him crisply, "the AVG was the soundest investment China ever made. I am ashamed that you should even consider the cost."

In the early years after Chiang Kai-shek lost the Chinese civil war in 1949, the Communist government spurned the memory of the Flying Tigers because of their association with Chiang. In recent decades, however, their role in having helped to save China was recognized, and it is now celebrated across China.

The "passing into history" of the men of the American Volunteer Group, which Claire Chennault marked in his recollections of July 4 and July 19, 1942, did not happen that month. Rather it unfolded gradually over time, as those men who were the Flying Tigers moved on to future careers and future acts of heroism.

Bill Reed and R. T. Smith both rejoined the USAAF and went their separate ways, promising to reconnect after the war. As fate would have it, they crossed paths in Southeast Asia at about the end of 1943, much sooner than expected. Reed had gone back to China, once again to serve under Chennault, and Smith was assigned to the 1st Air Commando Group, an organization created for special operations over Burma. Coincidentally, it was commanded by Johnny Alison, who had concluded his tour of duty with Chennault, had gone home, and had come back overseas.

While he was based at Hailakandit in Assam, about 260 miles southwest of the transport hub at Dinjan, Smith was visited by both Reed and their old Hell's Angels squadronmate George "Mac" McMillan. In January 1944, not long after their reunions with Smith, both Reed and McMillan were killed, a few days apart, near Hengyang. After the war, Smith had a long and varied career as a pilot with TWA, as a Hollywood scriptwriter, and as an executive with Lockheed.

Charlie Bond rejoined the USAAF as a lieutenant in October 1942, and was promoted to major within three weeks. A year later, after Hap Arnold personally selected him to serve as the pilot for Averell Harriman, the US ambassador to the Soviet Union, Bond logged a great deal of flight time over Russia. As he had with Tex Hill, Ed Rector, and Bill Reed, Chennault requested that Bond be sent back to China, but Arnold emphatically refused to send him. He did not want to see another former Flying Tiger killed in action or taken prisoner. After the war, Bond remained with the US Air Force in a variety of roles, including as deputy commander of the Thirteenth Air Force during the Vietnam War, and later as commander of the Twelfth Air Force. He retired in 1968 as a major general.

When he returned home, Jim Howard received invitations from

both the USAAF and the US Navy to enlist as an officer. He first went back to NAS North Island in San Diego, where he had served as a naval aviator before the war. He still had his old pass, so he was waved through the front gate. When he went to call on the station commandant, the heavyset captain grew red-faced and threatened to have the AVG ace with six Japanese aircraft to his credit arrested for illegal entry. Howard joined the USAAF.

He went overseas again, this time to serve with the 354th Fighter Group, flying P-51 Mustangs with the Eighth Air Force, based in England. On January 11, 1944, he single-handedly engaged about thirty Luftwaffe fighters that were attacking American bombers over snow-covered Germany. Using tricks learned over the steamy Far East, he downed three enemy aircraft that day, and continued to distract the Germans even after running out of ammunition.

Howard soon became a media star and was later awarded the Medal of Honor for this action. In February, now a colonel, he was named commander of the 354th, which ended the war as the highest-scoring USAAF fighter group in Europe. Jim Howard added a total of six victories against the Luftwaffe to the 6.33 for which he had been paid bonuses as a Flying Tiger. He left the US Air Force as a brigadier general in 1949.

Not everyone who left combat flying for the airlines left their familiar stomping grounds in China. Some, including Bob Prescott, went back overseas to fly with CNAC. An ace credited with 5.29 aerial victories, Prescott added to his résumé with more than three hundred flights across the Hump as a transport pilot.

Back in Los Angeles after the war, Prescott's résumé brought him to the attention of a group of well-heeled investors who were interested in backing an all-freight airline—and National Skyway Freight Corporation was born in June 1945. In turn, as pilots, Prescott hired a bunch of former Flying Tigers, including Bill Bartling, Cliff Groh, Link

Laughlin, Thomas Haywood, Duke Hedman, Bus Loane, Catfish Raine, Joe Rosbert, and Dick Rossi. In 1947, Prescott also appropriated the obvious name, renaming the airline as the Flying Tiger Line. Prescott remained at the helm until his death in 1978, and a decade later Flying Tiger was acquired by Federal Express.

Of the Flying Tigers, the man who would likely have been voted "least likely to succeed," defied the odds, becoming a Medal of Honor recipient and later a best-selling autobiographer. Disgruntled and determined, Greg Boyington walked out on the AVG in April 1942 after a week-long drinking jag and an acrimonious quarrel over his claim to have shot down six Japanese planes when the AVG credited him with only 3.5. He caught a CNAC flight to Calcutta and a British Imperial Airways flight to Karachi. He was hoping to fly all the way home, but spent six weeks rounding the Cape of Good Hope and plying the Atlantic aboard the SS *Brazil* in the company of a large number of would-be Chinese pilots being sent to the United States for training. At home, Boyington applied to rejoin the US Marine Corps. Finding himself broke, he spent two months working in a Seattle parking garage while he waited to hear back from the service.

In January 1943, Major Greg Boyington was once again at sea, this time heading across the expanse of the Pacific Ocean, which he had crossed in 1941, this time bound for the South Pacific and an assignment to the 1st Marine Aircraft Wing. After a series of staff assignments, during which he was "going mentally crazier by the day" trying to get into an active squadron, he became commander of Marine Fighter Squadron 214 (VMF-214) in September 1943. Because the unit had been cobbled together from a collection of pilots lacking squadron assignments, they called themselves "Boyington's Bastards," a name later softened for media consumption as the "Black Sheep Squadron." Boyington, because he was thirty-one, a decade older than most of his men, was nicknamed "Grandpappy," a name soon abridged to "Pappy."

Flying Vought F4U Corsairs against IJNAF Mitsubishi A6M Zeros, VMF-214 soon found itself in the thick of an intense air combat environment that ranged over numerous Pacific islands from the Russells to Bougainville to New Britain. On September 16, the first day of combat for the Black Sheep, Pappy Boyington fought a series of duels with Japanese aircraft, shooting down five and initiating a narrative that would make him an unlikely legend.

On October 17, two dozen Black Sheep engaged five dozen Japanese aircraft and shot down twenty. In the space of thirty-two days, Boyington himself had claimed fourteen, and he increased his score to twenty-five by the end of 1943. On January 3, 1944, he downed another Japanese aircraft to match the score of twenty-six achieved by World War I "ace of aces" Eddie Rickenbacker, but on that same day, he was shot down himself. Declared missing in action and presumed dead, Pappy Boyington became a tragic hero on the home front and was posthumously awarded the Medal of Honor.

However, unknown to anyone at home, Boyington had survived, was taken prisoner, and spent the remainder of the war as a POW. When he was repatriated at the end of the war, the Marine Corps promoted him to lieutenant colonel and sent their returning hero on a nationwide publicity tour. On the last night of the tour, he appeared in public very drunk, very incorrigible, and very much an embarrassment to the service.

Soon discharged, Boyington spent most of the next decade battling alcoholism and drifting from job to job—which included being a draft beer salesman and a referee for wrestling matches. His life turned around by the late 1950s, when he began flying for a charter airline out of Burbank, California. He also completed his best-selling 1957 autobiography *Baa Baa, Black Sheep*, which was adapted for a television series of the same name that aired in the 1970s. The book became a classic, but the series was not well received by former squadronmates and other Marine Corps pilots who derided it for its inaccuracies. The bad boy whose real life never measured up to the legend that surrounded him left a mixed legacy. A hero in popular culture, he remained a black sheep in the minds and memories of most of those, from the Flying Tigers to the Marines, with whom he had served.

<hr />

Unlike Boyington, neither of the two Flying Tigers who had survived being captured early in 1942 were still POWs when the war ended. Instead, both came home with amazing stories. Lew Bishop, who had been picked up by the Vichy French, was eventually turned over to the Japanese. His daughter, Sheila Bishop Irwin, who was born in November 1941 and who had not yet met her father when he was shot down, much later wrote in a blog for the Museum of the American Military Family that in December 1943, her mother received a letter from Lew dated November 5, 1942, that proved he had survived being shot down and this gave the family some hope.

Amazingly, Bishop later escaped from a prison train headed from Shanghai to Manchuria one night in early 1945. He was in an open-topped cattle car and had managed to work himself free of his leg restraints in the dark without anyone noticing. At an appropriate time, in open country between stations, he just stood up, hopped the side of the car, and jumped. As he rolled into a gully, shots were fired but the train did not stop. Bishop eventually made contact with an English-speaking Chinese man who was connected to the underground resistance and was smuggled back to Kunming.

Captured by the Thai police after the March 24 raid on Chiang

Mai in northern Thailand, Mac McGarry was handed over to the Japanese for interrogation, but when they were finished with him, they handed him *back*. Thai authorities then jailed him in Bangkok. According to Myrna Oliver, who wrote his 1990 obituary in the *Los Angeles Times*, his family learned in October 1942 that he was still alive.

What happened next was as improbable as it is cinematic. The global reach of the covert hand of the rapidly expanding US Office of Strategic Services (OSS), the fabled precursor to the CIA, had extended into Southeast Asia, especially Thailand. Acting on a request from Chennault to recover his pilot, the OSS enlisted the aid of a man on the inside with the Bangkok police, who forged a death certificate so that McGarry could be successfully spirited out of the prison and out of the country in a coffin. After the war, McGarry became an attorney, practicing in Southern California.

Fate had given Ajax Baumler three chances to fly with the Flying Tigers, and he had begged Tex Hill for a second chance to *stay* on when the 23rd Fighter Group was activated. He had promised Hill that he would curb his drinking and straighten out his life. Apparently he did. After Frank Schiel was killed in December 1942, Chennault went so far as to name him to succeed Schiel as commander of the 74th Fighter Squadron. This is illustrative either of his renewed confidence in a man whom he had warned Tex Hill about, or of how few experienced pilots were available to assume command responsibilities—even as late as December 1942. The former may be indicated by Baumler's being awarded the Distinguished Flying Cross and the Air Medal. Bob Scott later described him as "the best operations officer I ever saw."

Baumler remained at the head of the 74th until February 18, 1943, when he was sent Stateside to recover from malaria. When he did, he was utilized by the USAAF public affairs apparatus at war bond rallies and he served as a test pilot for the Air Matériel Command at Wright

Field in Ohio. However, his drinking problem reemerged and a promising career unraveled. Because of this, and for his having flown under Soviet command in Spain, he was denied a regular commission after the war when the Soviets became objects of distrust, and was taken off flying duty. There were no more second chances. As a sergeant, he remained in the US Air Force until 1965, working as a ground controller during the Korean War and in a series of lower-level jobs. Though he was never again on flying duty, he continued to wear his wings.

Hap Arnold sent Robert Lee Scott back to China in 1944 as part of a project to evaluate the use of high-velocity aerial rockets against ground targets, incurring his boss's displeasure for flying live combat missions against Arnold's explicit orders. After the war, he returned home to his wife, Catharine "Kitty" Rix Scott. He remained in the US Air Force as it became independent of the US Army in 1947, and served in a variety of roles, including as commander of the 36th Fighter Bomber Wing in West Germany, and retired in 1957 as a brigadier general. In the 1970s, he resumed his project to retrace the route of Marco Polo across Asia that he had abandoned in 1932. Traveling by bus, train, and even by camel, he crossed much of China. He hiked the Great Wall to Beijing and visited the Marco Polo Bridge, where the great war between Japan and China had begun in 1937. In 1996, a decade before his death, the tenacious Scott carried the torch ahead of the Olympics in Atlanta, Georgia.

When he turned the 23rd Fighter Group over to Ed Rector in the fall of 1944, Tex Hill went home to an assignment with the 412th Fighter Group, which had been designated to be the first group to receive the earliest USAAF jet fighters. These had included the Bell P-59 Airacomet, and by the time Hill arrived, the Lockheed P-80 Shooting Star. In September 1945 he took over command of the 412th, where he remained until early 1946, when he finally left the USAAF to go home to his Texas ranch. Within the year, though, Texas governor Coke

Stevenson coaxed him back into uniform as a wing commander in the Texas Air National Guard. Remaining on reserve status with the US Air Force, he finally retired as a brigadier general in 1968.

Ed Rector stayed on in China as a US Air Force officer in the postwar American Military Assistance Advisory Group. After Chiang Kai-shek and his Nationalist government abandoned mainland China to the Communists in 1949, Rector followed Chiang and company to Taiwan, continuing as an adviser to the Republic of China Air Force. He retired from the US Air Force in 1962, but remained involved in commercial air freight operations in the Far East.

Vinegar Joe Stilwell finally got the field army command for which George Marshall had always felt he was destined, but it was short-lived. When General Simon Bolivar Buckner, commander of the US Tenth Army, was killed in action toward the end of the Okinawa campaign in June 1945, Stilwell was appointed to succeed him. However, operations were already winding down, and Japan surrendered before the planned use of the Tenth in the ground invasion of Japan that had been scheduled for later in 1945.

After the war, Stilwell was given command of the Stateside Sixth Army at the Presidio of San Francisco, which is where he died in 1946 after surgery for stomach cancer.

Meanwhile, Chennault's old nemesis Clayton Bissell had been recalled to Washington in August 1943, mainly because of his ongoing feud with Chennault. He spent the remainder of the war serving mainly as a staff intelligence officer. In this role, he was the recipient of an account by Lieutenant Colonel John Van Vliet, who, as a POW, had visited the site of the 1940 Katyn Massacre, in which the Soviet secret police executed approximately six thousand Polish prisoners of war and fourteen thousand Polish civilians. Bissell classified the report as Top Secret and allowed it to disappear. When this came to light during a congressional investigation in 1952, Bissell, then retired, claimed that he had not wanted to embarrass the Soviet Union. Instead, he had embarrassed himself, and added a black mark to his own legacy. It was not until 1990, after the end of the Cold War and eighteen years after Bissell's death, when the Russians opened their files and apologized, that the world became cognizant of the staggering extent of the atrocities that Bissell had deliberately covered up.

In October 1945, eight years into his second career in the US armed forces, Claire Chennault retired for the last time. Within a year, as he had in 1937, he had left Louisiana to go back to China as a civilian to run air operations. This time it was a cargo airline called Civil Air Transport, but better known by its acronym, CAT. After passenger services were added to CAT's repertoire, advertising materials typically included pictures, not of tigers, but of cats.

In the meantime, Chennault had divorced his wife, Nell, whom he had married in 1911, when he was eighteen. In 1947, he married journalist Chen Xianmei, known as Anna Chan, who was three decades younger than he. They had first met during the war in Kunming, where her sister worked at the AVG headquarters.

As the Chinese Civil War ensued, and as the Communist warlords gradually took over more and more of China, CAT was often an aerial lifeline to surrounded Nationalist enclaves. Meanwhile, despite inquiries from hundreds of "volunteers," Chennault dodged reports that he was planning to create a new "Flying Tigers" to help save Chiang from Mao Zedong's armies. He had helped to save China from the Japanese at a critical moment during World War II, but at this juncture in history, the aging general chose not to enlist in the fight to save China from the Chinese.

When the Communists won in 1949 and Chiang Kai-shek fled with his Kuomintang government to reestablish as the Republic of China in Taiwan, CAT fled with him. In a bizarre twist of fate, when Communist China sued CAT in civil court in Hong Kong to get hold of aircraft stranded in the British colony, Chennault *lost*. He won on appeal.

During the coming years, CAT became involved as a contract cargo airline in numerous covert operations for the American CIA and other clandestine entities. In 1957 it became Air America and part of a network of CIA-owned air carriers that operated in Southeast Asia through the Vietnam War.

Chennault and his young wife returned to the United States early in 1958 so that he could seek treatment for the lung cancer that had developed after a lifetime of heavy smoking. He died in New Orleans on July 27, two weeks after receiving a final visit from Madame Chiang. He was buried in Arlington National Cemetery. Anna Chennault continued to be active as a journalist, and later as a spokesperson for various political and philanthropic causes in the United States.

Tex Hill and Ed Rector were among the Flying Tigers who attended Chennault's funeral. Bob Scott was a pallbearer. So too were a cast of US Air Force generals, including current chairman of the Joint Chiefs of Staff Nathan Twining, former Air Force chief of staff Carl "Tooey" Spaatz, former Fifth Air Force commander George Kenney, and the then-current Strategic Air Command boss Curtis LeMay.

Reflecting on this turning out of top brass for a man once treated suspiciously as an outsider and an eccentric, Scott wrote "to me it meant that Chennault, a fighting nonconformer to the bitter end, was by this tribute being recognized, after all, as having been right in his originality. I thought that this last honor might well be the judgment of his peers that he had been the greatest airman of them all."

As it is written in Hexagram Gui Mei of the *I Ching*, "the superior man understands the transitory in the light of the eternity of the end." With the passing of the Old Man, the book could finally be closed and a story left for posterity, a story written in .50-caliber lead and with the blood of a unique and incomparable cadre of young Americans.

There are perhaps no more appropriate final words, nor better tribute to Chennault and the men of the Flying Tigers, than a rhetorical question posed by R. T. Smith, who asked, "What might have happened in Burma and China if the AVG had *not* been there?"

ACRONYMS

AAF Army Air Forces [United States]

ABC Assam-Burma-China Ferry Command

ABDA American-British-Dutch-Australian Command

AMMISCA American Military Mission to China

ATFERO Atlantic Ferry Organization

AVG American Volunteer Group (the "Flying Tigers")

CAMCO Central Aircraft Manufacturing Company

CAT Civil Air Transport

CATF China Area Task Force (of the USAAF)

CBI China-Burma-India Theater

CIA Central Intelligence Agency

CNAC China National Aviation Corporation

FEAF Far East Air Forces (of the USAAF)

HMS His Majesty's Ship (United Kingdom)

IJA Imperial Japanese Army

IJAAF Imperial Japanese Army Air Force

IJN Imperial Japanese Navy

IJNAF Imperial Japanese Navy Air Force

MS Motor Ship

NAS Naval Air Station

OSS Office of Strategic Services

POW Prisoner of War

RAAF Royal Australian Air Force

RAF Royal Air Force (United Kingdom)

RCAF Royal Canadian Air Force

ROTC Reserve Officer Training Corps

SB Skorostnoi Bombardirovschik (Soviet high-speed bomber)

SEAC Southeast Asia Command

SS Steamship

TWA Transcontinental & Western Air (later Trans World Airlines)

UHF Ultra High Frequency (radio)

USAAF United States Army Air Forces

USMA United States Military Academy (at West Point)

USMC United States Marine Corps

USS United States Ship

VHF Very High Frequency (radio)

VNSM Verenigde Nederlandse Scheepvaart Maatschappij (United Netherlands Navigation Company)

BIBLIOGRAPHY

Arnold, Henry Harley. *American Airpower Comes of Age: General Henry H. "Hap" Arnold's World War II Diaries.* Edited by General John W. Huston. Collingdale, PA: Diane Publishing, 2002.

————. *Global Mission.* New York: Harper & Brothers, 1949.

Ayling, Keith. *Old Leatherface of the Flying Tigers: The Story of General Chennault.* New York: Bobbs-Merrill, 1945.

Baisden, Chuck. *Flying Tiger to Air Commando.* Atglen, PA: Schiffer Publishing, 1999.

Bishop, Lewis S., and Shiela Bishop-Irwin. *Escape from Hell: An AVG Flying Tiger's Journey.* New York: Tiger Eye Press, 2005.

Black, Conrad. *Franklin Delano Roosevelt, Champion of Freedom.* New York: Public Affairs, 2003.

Blum, John Morton. *Roosevelt and Morgenthau.* Boston: Houghton Mifflin Harcourt, 1970.

Bond, Maj. Gen. Charles, and Terry Anderson. *A Flying Tiger's Diary.* College Station: Texas A&M University Press, 1993.

Boyington, Col. Gregory, USMC, Ret. *Baa Baa Black Sheep.* New York: G. P. Putnam's Sons, 1958.

Byrd, Martha. *Chennault: Giving Wings to the Tiger.* Tuscaloosa: University of Alabama Press, 2003.

Caidin, Martin. *The Ragged, Rugged Warriors.* New York: Ballantine, 1978.

Cambridge University Press. *The Nationalist Era in China, 1927–1949.* Edited by Lloyd E. Eastman. Cambridge, UK.

Carter, Kit, and Robert Mueller. *The Army Air Forces in World War II: Combat Chronology.* Washington, DC: Office of Air Force History, 1973.

Chennault, Anna. *Chennault and the Flying Tigers.* New York: Paul S. Eriksson, 1963.

Chennault, Claire Lee. *Way of a Fighter*. New York: G. P. Putnam's Sons, 1949.

Crouch, Gregory. *China's Wings: War, Intrigue, Romance, and Adventure in the Middle Kingdom during the Golden Age of Flight*. New York: Bantam, 2012.

Dictionary of American Biography. "Claire Lee Chennault." In *Dictionary of American Biography, Supplement 6: 1956–1960*. Biography Resource Center. Farmington Hills, MI: Thomson Gale, 1980.

Ford, Daniel. *Flying Tigers: Claire Chennault and His American Volunteers, 1941–1942*. Washington, DC: HarperCollins-Smithsonian Books, 2007.

Frillmann, Paul, and Graham Peck. *China: The Remembered Life*. Boston: Houghton Mifflin, 1968.

Greenlaw, Olga S. *The Lady and the Tigers*. New York: E. P. Dutton, 1943.

Gunther, John. *Inside Asia*. New York: Harper & Brothers, 1939.

Hessen, Robert, ed. *General Claire Lee Chennault: A Guide to His Papers in the Hoover Institution Archives*. Palo Alto, CA: Hoover Institution Press, 1983.

Hill, David Lee, and Reagan Schaupp. *Tex Hill: Flying Tiger*. Spartanburg, SC: Honoribus Press, 2003.

Hotz, Robert B., et al. *With General Chennault: The Story of the Flying Tigers*. New York: Coward-McCann, 1943.

Howard, James H. *Roar of The Tiger: From Flying Tigers to Mustangs; A Fighter Ace's Memoir*. New York: Crown, 1991.

Maurer, Maurer. *Air Force Combat Units of World War II*. Maxwell AFB, AL: Office of Air Force History, 1983.

Olynyk, Frank J. *AVG & USAAF (China-Burma-India Theater) Credits for Destruction of Enemy Aircraft in Air to Air Combat, World War 2*. Aurora, OH: privately published, 1986.

Parks, M. Coble. *The Shanghai Capitalists and the Nationalist Government, 1927–1937*. Cambridge, MA: Harvard University Asia Center, 1986.

Romanus, Charles F., and Riley Sunderland. *United States Army in World War II China-Burma-India Theater: Stilwell's Mission to China*. Washington, DC: Office of the Chief of Military History, 1953.

Samson, Jack. *Chennault*. Garden City, NY: Doubleday, 1987.

Schultz, Duane. *The Maverick War: Chennault and the Flying Tigers*. New York: St. Martin's Press, 1987.

Scott, Col. Robert L. *God Is My Co-Pilot*. New York: Charles Scribner's Sons, 1944.

Scott, Robert Lee Jr. *The Day I Owned the Sky*. New York: Bantam Books, 1989.

———. *Flying Tiger: Chennault of China*. Garden City, NY: Doubleday, 1955.

Shilling, Erik. *Destiny: A Flying Tiger's Rendezvous with Fate*. Pomona, CA: Ben-Wal Printing, 1993.

Smith, Felix. *China Pilot: Flying for Chiang and Chennault*. New York: Brassey's, 1995.

Smith, Robert M. *With Chennault in China: A Flying Tiger's Diary*. Atglen, PA: Schiffer Publishing, 1997.

Smith, Robert T. *Tale of a Tiger*. Van Nuys, CA: Tiger Originals, 1986.

Stilwell, General Joseph W. *The Stilwell Papers*. New York: William Sloane Associates, 1948.

Tuchman, Barbara. *Stilwell and the American Experience in China, 1911–45*. New York: Macmillan, 1971.

US Strategic Bombing Survey. *Air Operations in China-Burma-India, World War II*. Washington, DC: US Government Printing Office, 1947.

USAAF. *Army Air Forces Statistical Digest, World War II*. Washington, DC: Director, Statistical Services, USAAF, 1945.

Walters, Maude Owens. *Combat in the Air*. New York: Appleton-Century, 1944.

Weaver, Herbert. "Commitments to China." In *Army Air Forces in World War II*, Vol. 1, *Plans & Early Operations, January 1939 to August 1942*. Washington, DC: Office of Air History, 1947.

Whelan, Russell. *The Flying Tigers: The Story of the American Volunteer Group*. New York: Viking Press, 1942.

Wilhelm, Richard, trans. *The I Ching or Book of Changes*. Princeton, NJ: Bollingen Foundation, 1950.

INDEX

INDEX

ABOUT THE AUTHOR

Bill Yenne is the author of more than three dozen nonfiction books, mainly on historical topics, as well as ten novels. General Wesley Clark called his biography of Alexander the Great the "best yet," while the *New Yorker* wrote of *Sitting Bull*, his biography of the great Lakota leader, that it "excels as a study in leadership." General Craig McKinley, president of the Air Force Association, wrote that in Mr. Yenne's *Hap Arnold: The General Who Invented the US Air Force*, he had done "a superior job helping the reader better understand General Arnold both as an individual and as a military leader."

His books on aviation and military history have included his *Area 51 Black Jets*, which T. D. Barnes, formerly with NASA High Range and Area 51 Special Projects, described as "not a book that the reader will lay down and not finish. It holds one's interest from front to back." His dual biography of Dick Bong and Tommy McGuire, *Aces High: The Heroic Story of the Two Top-Scoring American Aces of World War II*, was described by pilot and bestselling author Dan Roam as "the greatest flying story of all time."

Mr. Yenne has contributed to encyclopedias of both world wars, and has appeared in documentaries airing on the History Channel, the National Geographic Channel, the Smithsonian Channel, and ARD German Television. He is a graduate of the University of Montana and the Stanford University Professional Publishing Course. He lives in San Francisco, and on the Web at BillYenne.com.